MW01230893

MARK PETTIT

ANKRBOY

Cover Design: Getcovers

Printed in the United States of America

ISBN 978-0-98892-836-7

ALSO BY MARK PETTIT:

A Need to Kill

*A Need to Kill: The True-Crime Account of John Joubert,
Nebraska's Most Notorious Serial Child Killer*

A Need to Kill: The Death Row Drawings

ACKNOWLEDGEMENTS

I want to express my sincere gratitude to my writing partner, AJ Jones, with whom I worked closely to craft the screenplay from which this book is adapted. AJ is one of the most gifted screen-writers I've ever met and working with him was a joy, and the best therapy money could not buy.

Special thanks as well to my editor and collaborator, David Baclaski, who helped me tell this very personal story in the most compelling way possible. He told me on our very first planning call to "write from your heart and we'll rewrite from our heads." (He insists I mention he read that somewhere.)

Working with David was a master class in copywriting. As I told him when we first spoke, the way he writes (and thinks) makes doing laundry on a Sunday morning sound like a joyful jaunt through the English countryside where he resides. Just have a dictionary, a the-saurus and Google Translate handy if you decide to work with David. The man's vocabulary is unreal.

I also want to thank my former colleagues in TV news. It was a pleasure getting to work with you and an honor still getting to share my life with many of you.

To my family and close friends, thank you for your support and encouragement to live my authentic life. I only wish it hadn't taken me so long to do so.

What follows is a fictionalized account of my true-life story. Certain characters, conversations and situations have been created or recreated to protect the privacy of those involved and for dramatic effect.

The underlying story is true.

Believe me. I've lived it.

INTRODUCTION

After I finished my dinner, a homemade pepperoni and sausage pizza with fresh jalapeños, mushrooms and green peppers; I scrolled through Instagram and came across several posts that made me smile.

Almost as much as a homemade pizza.

ABC's Gio Benitez and his husband, Tommy DiDario, uploaded a video of themselves on a boat off the coast of Turks and Caicos. Dolly Parton and Kenny Rogers were singing

"Islands in The Stream" as they beamed.

Gio and Tommy were at the Shore Club on Long Bay with other members of their *Good Morning America* family, including Robin Roberts and her soon-to-be (and now) wife, Amber Laign. Popular weatherman Sam Champion and his artist husband, Rubem Robierb, were also part of the "TravelSquad."

"I remember the 'wall' I felt between me and the audience when I wasn't able to be fully myself," Gio told me. "I wasn't out to my colleagues. I wasn't out to the audience until I posted a photo proposing to Tommy in front of the Eiffel Tower."

Bonjour, America!

I've met both Sam and Rubem and they are wonderful human beings. Robin and I were competitors in Atlanta when she anchored weekend sports at WAGA-TV while I co-anchored the weekend news at WXIA-TV. She, too, is as genuine as she appears on *Good Morning America*.

I also enjoyed seeing photos of my friend and ABC News correspondent, Steve Osunsami, and his husband and artist, Joe Remillard.

Steve's smile could light up Times Square, and I love running into him from time to time in Atlanta. Most recently, I saw him at Pike's Nursery where we had a nice chat in the sunshine alongside the great selection of outdoor plants.

Thousands of miles away, ABC News war correspondent James Longman and his soon-to-be (and also-now) husband, Alex Brannan, posted photos from Paros, Greece, where they were on vacation. The couple glowed in the evening light as they sipped cocktails.

In another photo, James posed shirtless, his chiseled body a tribute to the Greek gods. I scrolled past CNN's Anderson Cooper in a *People Magazine* post where he had taken a selfie of himself, his two young children and his ex-boyfriend, Benjamin Maisani, with whom he co-parents. Their smiles conveyed happiness and contentment, bringing me joy.

Like Gio and Tommy, James approved of me mentioning him and Alex in this book. Same with Steve and Joe. It was Steve who connected me with Gio and Tommy.

I closed out the app and walked back to my bedroom closet in the Atlanta high-rise condo that I share with my French Bulldog, Kody. Retrieving a photo album from a drawer in the chest beneath a rack of clothes, I thumbed through it until I found the photo that I, too, would have happily posted on social media if there were such a thing in the late 1980s, and if it wouldn't have cost me my job in TV news.

This photo was of me and my very first real boyfriend. A man and a relationship I kept secret from all but the closest of friends. We squinted in the bright sun as my best friend, Mark Edge, snapped our photo along the white sandy beach of Panama City next to the beautiful blue ocean water.

In another photo we are shirtless (and me, nowhere near the specimen of James Longman) with another one of my best friends, Glenn Murer. Our faces sparkled in the bright afternoon light. So young. So innocent. So sweet. Before life changed and death and despair came calling. It is a photo and a moment that is seared into the safest section of my psyche. Seeing my boyfriend's Hollywood smile, and his beefy biceps, reminded me why I fell for him in

the first place. Thinking of his sweet spirit reminds me why I fell in love with him.

My boyfriend was a beautiful man inside and out, and a man I would have happily married.

If things had been different.

Like James and Alex, Gio and Tommy, Sam and Rubem and Steve and Joe, we were happy. Maybe the happiest I've ever been in my personal life. Yet, the contrasts in the time between the photos could not be starker. There was simply no way for me to be open and out thirty-plus years ago. There were no Anderson Coopers, no Don Lemons, no Shepard Smiths. Just a constant fear in the middle of the AIDS epidemic that I would die or, worse perhaps, be found out for who I really was: a gay man, at times who honestly hated himself and his life. A young man who would have paid any price he could afford to make it go away. To make him straight, to make him normal so that others would accept him.

What a tragedy. What a farce. What a shame.

Knowing what I know now, I would have walked into my news director's office and showed him the photo of me and my boyfriend at the beach. I would have told him I was happy and healthy and that I was no less of a journalist or a person because I was gay. I would have lived my life openly and honestly, and maybe things would have been different than they are today.

But I didn't have the courage then that I have now. The "fuck it all" freedom to tell you exactly who I am and what I've been through to get here. Candidly, I should be dead. I've done some crazy shit and came close to the edge a couple of times. I've dodged some serious health bullets that took the lives of several of my close friends.

Including the boyfriend that I hid from the world.

He died at 30 years old. I was 29.

To make matters worse, I had lost my job in TV news, despite having won three Emmy® Awards and writing what was to become a best-selling book. In an instant, it was all gone, and no one (it seemed at the time) wanted me on their news team. I was stunned. But deep in my heart I knew why. I knew they couldn't take the risk, or wouldn't, understanding they had viewers to keep and ratings to grow.

Back then, it wasn't cool to be gay on the evening news. I've joked with my friends that today it's a requirement.

This past August I turned sixty. Yes, sixty. What the hell happened? How did I get to this point? How did I get this old? How did I finally find true happiness?

You're about to find out.

I've done some things over the years that I'm not proud of and some things that I certainly regret. It hasn't been the fairy tale that I had hoped for, but that's what life is: a story that we don't get to write ourselves. It's something we experience. Something we handle the best we can with the strength we have at the time it's all unfolding.

David, my editor, asked me a very important question when we started this project: "Are there any scores you're trying to settle by writing this book?"

And I told him, "No. Just wounds to heal."

Writing this book as a fictionalized memoir has allowed me to make sense of a lot of things that happened to me over the years, including losing my career in TV news. It also helped me realize that maybe the news needed me more than I needed it, that the truth I should have been exposing was my own. And, simply put, writing this book has allowed me to add periods to chapters in my life that had been left unfinished. I've now completed the story that sets the record straight.

So to speak. There. A little levity to lighten the mood.

My hope is that once you finish reading this book, we understand each other a little better. And that going forward, we treat each other with a little more kindness and grace.

We've all lived through things that other people, even our family members and close friends, had no idea was going on at the time. In the end, I want you to be what I am today: happy, content, hopeful and finding the peace in your own life that I have finally found in mine.

Mark Pettit

PREFACE

Both my grandmother and my aunt kept a framed publicity photo of me in their homes until they passed away.

"To Aunt Evelyn: Thanks for believing! Love always, Mark," I wrote on my aunt's photo, my smiling, boyish face beaming under a mop of dark brown hair. I scribbled the same loving words on my grandmother's memento, which she proudly placed on a bookshelf next to her TV set.

Now, years later, I held my copy of the framed photo and stared at the young man's face. Behind the smile, I could see the hurt and fear in his eyes. And I hated myself for not doing more to save him. Without another thought, I lifted the frame above my head and smashed it against the granite countertop in my bathroom. The glass shattered into a dozen pieces. One of the shards pierced my left arm just above the wrist, causing a sharp pain. As blood began to leak from the wound, I pulled out the fragment and tossed the half-inch piece of glass into the garbage can next to the toilet. Then I licked the blood from my arm—eerily wanting to taste my own agony.

I picked up the electric clippers and brought the cold, metal device to my temple, like a revolver. Honestly, in the moment, if it had been a gun, I might have pulled the trigger.

I was a disgusting mess.

Looking in the mirror, I saw the remnants of the hair dye framing my face—making me look like Frankenstein or a young Rudy Giuliani. My eyes were deep and sunken. Empty. Devoid of the spark that once exuded from their sockets. The clippers buzzed to life, and I shifted my grip and shaved a swath from the middle of my head—top to back—revealing a silver streak. Then I carved a second line. Then a third.

How in the world did I wind up like this? How in God's name did this happen? For as long as I could remember, all I ever wanted to be was an anchorman. Like Dan Rather and Tom Brokaw. A real reporter. Not just some guy reading the news. I was on my way. Three Emmy Awards and a best-selling book. I had it all figured out. First stop: CBS News in New York and someday sitting in that famous chair on *60 Minutes*.

Then, *tick, tick, tick*. My time was up.

I stared at the reflection of my miserable, broken, defeated and dead self. It felt like going from starting quarterback on the high school football team to a sandlot and being the last little boy standing waiting to be picked.

So very sad. Pathetic. Yet, necessary. I had to be broken like a wild horse to find my new path in life. Everything I detested about myself was laid bare in stark relief. My demons now had to be chased. I had to get to them before they got to me.

He was right. They were paying me to tell the truth and I was living a lie, right down to the color of my hair. I raised the clippers once more and carved two more lines from my scalp. Fake brown locks fell around my feet.

When it all went down, my agent was blunt. She said, "There's nothing I can do for you now. They don't put guys like you on the evening news."

Three more laps with the clippers and it was all gone. I glared at myself in the mirror and at my silver scalp. I didn't recognize this person. I feared this person. But finally, he and I were free.

The pulsing sound of nineties music grew louder from my bedroom. My eyes narrowed, my doubt and fear shifting into a confident, internal rage. I was an animal who could no longer be caged. At this point—the lowest in my twenty-eight years—I had nothing else to be but myself. To live my truth.

And trust me. I didn't just come out of the closet.

I kicked the door off the fucking hinges.

DEAD MAN'S PARTY

Palm Springs, 1992

My entire body tingled as we made our way through the desert evening. I'm not sure if it was the crisp, cool night (and the fact that I was shirtless) or if I was just really, really excited. Either way, it felt like I had stuck my finger into the outlet while shaving, and the current was firing through my veins.

We each took a half-hit of Ecstasy before we left the hotel room. I was flying solo at a cool mid-century hotel where I hoped to have company for at least part of the weekend, and I began to feel the synthetic courage to make it happen. I peered into the distance as the night sky's lights danced like tiny stars among the hills beyond. Perhaps they were high, too.

If you haven't been to Palm Springs, go. Just not in the summer. It is hotter than a whore in church, as we rednecks like to say. But in February it's perfect. And I felt fantastic. It was a long way from small-town Georgia where I grew up, and I was no longer a naïve child in Sunday school. I was a grown-ass-man now with the body to prove it.

In high school, I had always been a little chunky. A little too much junk in the trunk, if you will. One July, before we headed back to school in August, my mother had to buy "Husky" jeans for me from the Sears store over in Rome, Georgia. Chunky didn't work for the guys I was now attracted to and whom I wanted to be attracted to me. I started running in the park and working out at the local gay gym. Slowly, my body began to transform. Hundreds of arm curls resulted in apple-like biceps. Rep after rep, bench pressing my body weight gave me a chiseled chest. Thousands of dips on the Roman chair helped tighten my flabby abs.

It was a necessary evil. I once read a quote from a guy who said, "If you can't look at yourself in the mirror and jack off, how can you expect someone else to?"

So, hi ho, hi ho, off to the gym I'd go.

In fact, things were going so well that I got a little cocky. I had T-shirts made for my gang of friends, with "Bar Stars" on the front and "Circuit Certified" on the back. The circuit referred to a series of all-night, and often all-weekend, gay dance parties. They were typically denoted by colors and, in most cases, fueled by drugs and sex (for example, the Black Party in New York—always dark and seedy). But what was to become the mack daddy of them all was the White Party in Palm Springs. It began in 1990 by a party promoter named Jeffrey Sanker. The first year, it attracted about 500 of his friends. This year there would be 5,000 people in attendance.

I adjusted my little angel wings as we approached the front entrance of the Marquis Villas Resort and flexed my biceps for a bit of a pre-party pump. My formerly dyed-brown coif was now a gleaming stream of silver hair that moved oh-so slightly in the cool breeze. I thought that younger guys, to whom I was always attracted, wouldn't like me with silver hair, but it was the opposite. Many younger guys love the daddies, and I now fit the proverbial bill. I was averaging three tricks a week and was on my way to a hundred for the year. ("Trick" is the word for a one-night stand or a hook-up in the gay world.)

As my late mother once said, "Don't pick the first watermelon you thump." And trust me, Mama knew what she was talking about. She was the Elizabeth Taylor of North Georgia. Married at least three times and had movie star looks when she was younger. I'm sure the cute boys were all chasing her.

My brother Don summed it up: "Mama loved men. She just didn't like 'em very much."

Amen, brother. I obviously got it from her. Born with a silver mattress on my back.

"I've heard this shit is crazy," my friend Diego said to no one as we joined the line to get into the party.

Out of my closest of four friends, Diego, twenty-nine years old, was the only one I was really attracted to—sexually. Standing right at six feet tall, he had sumptuous brown skin, dark hair and a billion-dollar smile. His dad was from Mexico but ended up marrying a beauty queen from Kansas (or Kentucky, I was drunk the night he told me) and, eight months later, Diego was born, a perfect combination of his parents. Diego radiated sex appeal and I was drawn to him from the first night we met at a neighborhood bar.

A few times, Diego and I got sweaty and handsy on the dance floor. We'd kiss like crazy and fondle each other a bit, but nothing much more than that. All the boys wanted Diego and I figured I'd lose him anyway if we ended up dating, so great friends we became. What made Diego even more attractive was his personality. He was always excited. About everything, with an almost childlike wonderment.

"Guys come from all over the world for this party and I hear they even fuck on the dance floor," he said in amazement. Again, not language we would have used in Sunday school, but we weren't in Kansas anymore.

"Is Dorothy here?" I asked my friend, Rick.

"Yeah, she just got here," he said with a chuckle as he reached into his famous fanny pack and handed me the small bullet-like bottle, which I quickly put to my right nostril. I sniffed deeply, taking a bump of the white powder.

Rick was our Julie McCoy (cruise director of *The Love Boat* fame) and the oldest of us at thirty. We'd all chip in cash ahead of our travels and good 'ol Rick took care of the rest. He planned out all the details behind what pills and powders we would be taking and at exactly what time during the weekend. Rick was perpetually shirtless to display his fantastic chest and always wore a fanny pack around his waist where kept our party favors color coded in small containers and baggies.

"Fuck!" I whispered. "Is that coke or K?"

With another laugh, Rick said, "Both."

I shifted the bullet to my left nostril and took another bump of the mystery mix. I then pulled the remaining half-hit of Ecstasy from my pocket, coughed up some spit and swallowed the tablet. As they say in Latin: *ludi incipiant.*

Let the games begin.

A security guard spied my bare chest, my crotch, and then cast his eyes upon my left wrist. Seeing the plastic armband that read "VIP," he waved us into the hotel. My heart was pounding. I was in for the time of my life, or a heart attack. Only time would tell.

We pranced through the hotel lobby and down the hallway like we owned the damn place. With abandon, we pushed the heavy metal doors of the ballroom open and were welcomed by a hypnotic blend of house music like I had never heard before. A beautiful haunting version of the Oingo Boingo classic "Dead Man's Party" played from huge speakers throughout the room. It spoke to me in a way I didn't quite understand at the time.

> I was struck by lightning, walking down the street.
> I was hit by something last night in my sleep.
> It's a dead man's party. Who could ask for more?
> Everybody's comin', leave your body at the door.

Thump, thump, thump, the music synched with my pulsating heart. I couldn't believe my eyes. It was an explosion of white. White jeans, white shorts, white clouds. Guys of every color and descent dancing, kissing and cavorting as far as the eye could see. A squad of drag queens sashayed by us, flogging us with their oversized feathers. I had to do a double-take as one of them looked exactly like Cher.

Hell, for all I knew it was her.

There was always the same rumor at every circuit party. "I heard Madonna's here," some random guy would say to us on the dance floor and our squad would spend the next hour of our high pursuing her.

I swear I saw her once at Warsaw in South Beach.

But Palm Springs was debauchery on a level I could not have imagined. And I couldn't wait to dive in. As I led our posse deeper into the party, I could feel the hungry eyes upon us.

"Take me to heaven, daddy!" some guy shouted. I shot him a "maybe later" glance and edged closer to the dance floor.

Not everyone was happy to see us. As we passed a bar, a ruggedly handsome queen flipped me the bird. "Fuckin' hillbillies," I heard him say as we walked by.

I turned around and looked him in the eye. I grabbed my crotch through my white jeans and mouthed "Suck it, faggot." I returned the bird and turned back toward the dance floor.

That's how we hillbillies roll.

An hour, two Jack & Cokes, and another half an Ecstasy later, I found my groove, grinding a hot Asian boy named Daniel up against the wall just off the dance floor. He was about five foot six, what some would call a "pocket gay." Daniel was a former gymnast turned business consultant from Chicago. For some reason, Asian American guys were at the top of my to-do list, especially when they were smaller than me and I could manhandle them. Like tossing a bale of hay up on the wagon at my uncle's farm when I was a teenager.

"God, you smell good," I said as I lifted him from the ballroom floor and up against the wall. I think the drugs heightened my sense of smell.

"Drakkar Noir," he whispered as he wrapped his thick athletic legs around my waist.

"Take me back to your room and fuck me," he said seductively. "Your friends can watch."

Hell no, they couldn't. This was my all-you-can-eat Asian buffet.

I leaned in for a deep kiss to seal the deal and felt a stranger's hand touch my chest, moving down my stomach to my belt. He pulled me away from Daniel and toward him.

"Get lost, he's mine!" the stranger barked at my would-be paramour, who took the hint and sheepishly scuttled away. No gold medal for him tonight. I turned my hungry eyes to the stranger, a gorgeous blond-haired, blue-eyed stud. He pulled me close and purred, "Cool your jets, country boy. Don't want you to boil over."

He slid his hand over my sweaty chest, exciting me. With his other hand, he pulled a cold bottle of water from his back pocket and offered it. I ripped off the cap and quaffed the entire bottle in three rapid gulps.

"Ahh. Thank you. My name is Mark. We're from Atlanta."

His tone changed. He was no longer in a flirtatious mood.

"I know who you are. Fuckin' hillbilly."

At first, I was confused, but then recognized him from the bar where the other asshole said those same words.

"Don't be a dick," I warned him.

"Take your country-ass back to Atlanta," he fired back. "Nobody wants you inbred faggots here."

I stepped up within inches of his face.

"Don't fuck with a country boy," I whispered. Sensing trouble, my friend Ace, the fourth member of our group, stepped in between us.

Ace, twenty-eight years old, was African American, six foot one and built like a brick shithouse, as they say. He always had a nose for trouble and staying out of it. He grew up in a housing project in Augusta, Georgia, and saw plenty of trouble while living there.

"Hey! Let's get out of here, Anchor Boy," Ace said as he pulled me away from our bubbling fracas. "That's enough dancing and dick for now."

I backed down and retreated from the blond-haired bully. His steely eyes followed me as we walked from the dance floor back into the throng.

I halted, feeling woozy and lightheaded. My stomach churned and, for a second, I thought I was going to puke.

It was a cardinal sin to mix alcohol with GHB, a so-called "date rape drug." I learned hard lessons before and always avoided G when out partying. I had felt this feeling before and knew it wasn't good.

"I need the restroom," I said to my friends.

"We'll meet you out on the veranda by the pool," Rick said.

I stumbled into the restroom and headed straight for the sink, where I turned on the water. My high had come to a crashing halt. I was dizzy and sweating, and not from the California heat. I tried washing my hands but could barely stay upright. My insides were churning, like my body was trying to repel poison. I almost shit my pants, which would have been a very bad thing at the White Party.

My brain felt like it was melting.

My hand hit the water. Water. The water! The blond-haired bully spiked my water. I knew I had to get out of there and find my friends. I made my way back out into the party area, all alone.

I staggered from the main room out onto the pool deck. Still no sign of my friends. I needed fresh air and kept moving. Another wave hit me. I thought I might pass out. I began to panic.

"Help me," I said to a guy standing nearby. "He spiked my water!" No response. The lights, the sounds and the party goers were turning into a nightmare. The music began to warp. The laughter turned into a haunting chorus. I was terrified and losing all sense of reality.

I slipped, then stumbled, and fell onto the concrete below, but not before hitting the back of my head on a brick column. I landed flat on my back, crushing my angel wings beneath me. Slowly, I felt a warm stream oozing down my neck and shoulders, onto my wings.

"Security! Security!" one of the go-go dancers screamed. "Get him out of here, he's ruining the fucking party!"

I realized I was losing consciousness. Then I felt a hand touch the side of my neck.

The last thing I remember was heaving and throwing up in my mouth. As I slowly slipped away, I turned my head and stared into the night sky, once again seeing the tiny stars dancing above the hills.

Then, nothing. Silence and darkness.

At the TV station, we used to joke that there were three ways to get on the news: do something great.

Do something stupid.

Or die.

HILLBILLY EUOLGY

Before I bid you adieu and some preacher speaks awkwardly over my body, I feel like I owe you an explanation, if not an apology. You see, I wasn't always a druggie. In fact, I had a deep disdain for drug use growing up. I hated the smell of pot and never touched coke or other hard drugs until my late twenties, just before I got the axe.

More about that later, but for now let's start at the beginning.

Before this gay angel flew too close to the sun, I was just a kid from Calhoun, Georgia, whose mother once took him to the doctor because he was asking so many questions.

"He must ask me a hundred questions a day," my mother said to the doctor. "Is there something wrong with him?" she asked with real concern.

"Did you confess to a bank robbery or tell him where the bones were buried?" the doctor responded, his attempt at humor flying straight over my sweet mom's head.

"No. He just asks me 'why' to everything," she said. "'Why did this happen? Why did you do that?' Just, why, why?"

The doctor put her fears at ease when he said, "He's just a curious little boy. There's nothing to be worried about."

Yep. I was born to be a reporter. Thanks, doc.

Before that, I was elected student council president at Calhoun High School and named "Most Likely to Succeed" by my classmates. Everything looked great on paper and in the yearbook, but the hometown hero had a little problem. He was homo and that was something we didn't talk about in Calhoun. Sure, there were rumors about a couple of teachers and there was that truant officer who convinced me and one of my best friends to strip down to our underwear and swim in his pond while he ogled us. And, of course, people gossiped about the truck stop down the road, but nobody I knew was gay, and Mr. Calhoun High wasn't going to be the first to come out of the country closet.

Not until I was forced out.

We'll get to that later, but first I had to get myself to Chattanooga, Tennessee, and a job in TV news. I tore my rotator cuff during my first year of college, where I played baseball. I lost my scholarship and left school to work for a local radio station. I did radio news at the local news leader. Writing and reporting the news every thirty minutes. It's where I learned to report, write, and repeat.

But I had my eye on a bigger prize. As I mentioned before, my dream was to be an anchorman, specifically in Atlanta, but knew I had to get my start somewhere, so a local fire captain used his home video camera to record me reading my radio news scripts. I cobbled together a poor man's demo reel and promptly mailed it off to Earl Lindenmeyer at the TV 6 Tri-State Report. Earl was a legend in radio news in Chattanooga, and I followed his move to TV 6 with great interest. If anyone was going to give a radio guy a shot in TV news, I thought it would be Earl.

I must have called Earl's office a dozen times, leaving the same message: "Would you please just take a look at my tape? All I need is a chance."

It finally happened! Earl called me back and invited me to come up to Chattanooga to meet with him. We hit it off immediately and he offered me a job on the spot. I was so excited I accepted the offer without even asking what my salary was going to be.

'Turned out it was $12,500 a year. That was decent money for a nineteen-year-old in 1982. It would be around $39,000 today, according to The Google.

Margie and Harold Crump, who owned a popular restaurant in Calhoun, loaned me their truck, and I moved everything I owned into a small basement apartment in a nice old lady's house not far from downtown Chattanooga. The entrance to the tiny apartment, which was about five hundred square feet, was off to the right side of the house and down a flight of about eight steps. I was allowed to park my car in the driveway, but I think my landlord, Mrs. Cantrell, did that so she could keep an eye on me coming and going.

And maybe to see who I might drag home at night.

Unfortunately, she didn't get to see much. I was either sleeping or at the station. I knew I had to put in the elbow grease (as my Grandpa Pettit used to call it) to get where I wanted to go. I was going to be a great reporter and someday an anchorman, so I had to put in the work.

I quickly made sources, many of them in law enforcement, who fed me story leads. One after another, I scored exclusives, breaking stories that other reporters didn't have. I was hungry for that lead spot on the six and eleven o'clock news and I worked my ass off to earn it.

I confessed to Earl over a hamburger that he had been an inspiration to me back in Calhoun, and I loved how he signed off from his radio broadcasts, making his name sound seven syllables long. "I'm EA-RL LIN-DEN-MEY-ER. More news at the top and bottom of EVERY hour, right here on East Tennessee's News Leader." He chuckled and said, "You gotta stand out from the crowd, son."

Not only was Earl a news legend, but he was also a patriot, having served in the U.S. Army, where he honed his broadcasting chops with American Forces Europe in Frankfurt, Germany. And Earl was smart. He had what the experts today would call exceptional "emotional intelligence." He could read a room, as they say, and he could tell a scoundrel when he saw one. Not long after I started breaking stories at the TV station in Chattanooga, we got sued by a weasel-like attorney who was upset that I exposed him for dipping into his unwitting clients' settlements.

We were in the deposition, and the opposing counsel got upset because he couldn't break me with his line of questioning. He broke down during the deposition and I sat across the table smiling at him.

"You little bastard," he said in a deep southern twang. "Sittin' there, grinnin' like the Cheshire Cat!"

Earl chimed in, "More like the cat that ate the canary."

Our attorney followed that with, "I guess we're done here?"

No further questions, your honor. The lawsuit was dismissed the next day.

But getting out of a lawsuit was just the beginning of the adventure. I almost got killed trying to bring home another story.

"Stop the car and let's get out here," I told my cameraman, David, as we pulled into the center of the small town. A group of African Americans were taking part in a peaceful protest. Homemade picket signs bobbed in the air. One of them read "JUSTICE FOR JAMES!" and another blared "I AM JAMES!" As they marched, the group sang the familiar spiritual, "We Shall Overcome."

"Where is everybody?" David asked as he pulled our TV 6 news car to the curb.

"We're it," I replied.

"Not even Channel 7?"

"Nope. Come on," I told him.

"What exactly are we doing? They've been protesting all week. It's old news."

I was emphatic. "I've got a source. They're coming."

Right on cue, a rumbling of voices could be heard from the other end of the town square. The black protestors stopped their singing.

"Oh, shit," David said as we grabbed our gear from the trunk of the car.

Rounding the corner was a group of skinheads. Most were wearing the Confederate Stainless Banner on their clothes. One carried a large Nazi flag. The counter-protestors were armed to the hip, with a couple of them proudly yielding hunting rifles. They noisily chanted, "White power!"

David and I rushed toward the commotion.

"This is the shot," I calmly told my colleague. "Roll on me and them."

Reluctantly, David said, "Okay, you're the boss."

I raised the microphone and looked straight into the camera.

"I'm Mark Pettit, reporting from Graysville, where protests continue over the death of a young black man a week ago. So far, the protests by African Americans have been peaceful. Now, it appears, that has all changed."

I motioned with my arm for David to follow me.

"TV 6 is bringing you these exclusive images of what seems to be an armed white militia heading directly toward the peaceful protestors. We can hear them chanting 'white power' as they get closer to our position."

That's when things got dicey.

The furious skinheads passed by us, way too close for comfort, just a few feet from David's camera. Out of the corner of my eye, I could see that a couple of the younger skinheads realized they were being filmed. At once, they rushed us. One of them grazed my arm and smashed into David, knocking his camera to the ground.

"What the fuck are you doing?" I screamed at the young man as I helped David back to his feet.

"This ain't none of your business!" the man yelled back. Then, out of the crowd, a large man who appeared to be in his thirties approached me. He leaned over and growled into my ear.

"Turn that camera off!"

As you already know, I'm not one to back down, and I stood my ground.

"We have every right to be here," I said.

Infuriated, the big skinhead looked over at David, who was holding the camera, capturing the entire encounter. With lightning speed, the big skinhead lunged forward, grabbing me by the shirt.

"Tell him to turn that goddamn camera off, you son of a bitch!"

"Hey, stop it!" David yelled.

Still in the big skinhead's clutches, I looked at my co-worker and said, "It's okay, David. It's okay. Turn it off."

I gave David a quick wink. He nodded and pretended to press a button on the side of the camera, placing it under his arm and stepped back. It was still recording.

Finally, the big skinhead released me.

"Now, you get the fuck outta here, pretty boy. And take that nigger cameraman with you."

Angry, I replied, "You can't talk to him like that."

The heated exchange continued.

"What y'all gonna do about it? They ain't never gonna find out what we did to that boy. He got what he deserved."

The big skinhead and I were now eye-to-eye.

Above the ruckus, police sirens blared. Whistles shrieked.

"Disperse! Now! Step away from the reporter!" a man's voice commanded.

In the nick of time, Tennessee state troopers blitzed onto the scene in full riot gear and face shields. The skinheads tried to make a run for it, but several were tackled and cuffed, while others managed to make it back to the group.

A friendly face approached me.

"You boys okay?" he asked. "You got here faster than I thought you would."

Thankful and relieved, I said, "Yes. And we appreciate the tip, Captain."

He politely nodded and headed back to do his job.

Our story led the six o'clock news with the secret camera footage rolling.

"They ain't ever gonna find out what we did to that boy. He got what he deserved…" we saw the big skinhead say again.

Now, on set, I calmly looked into the camera for my live tag.

"Tonight, thanks in part to that on-camera confession, four people are in custody, charged with the death of James Markel. On a personal note, my cameraman David and I would like to thank the Tennessee state troopers who came to our rescue. Despite the scare, we're hopeful our story helps bring justice for James Markel and his family."

I then looked to the main anchor sitting next to me.

"Fantastic reporting, Mark," he said. "We know you'll stay on it and keep us posted. Coming up, rain is in the forecast as the Lookouts get ready for a three-game home stand. Stay tuned."

And we were out. As the TV 6 Tri-State Report logo flew across the screen, I stepped down from the news desk to cheers and applause from my co-workers. I high-fived one of the cameramen as I left the studio.

Earl greeted me just inside the newsroom, extending his hand.

"You proved me right," he said.

"Thank you for taking a chance on me, Earl." I returned his handshake.

"You deserve it. Helluva job. You're going to impact a lot of people someday, son."

Then, offhandedly, he said, "You got a phone call. I left the message on your desk." I walked back and saw the bright pink piece of paper on my typewriter. I picked up the note, with the header: "While you were out" and read the message.

Call Carol. KN2-TV. Omaha, Nebraska.
402-555-2700.

I looked back at Earl, who had an awkward expression on his face.

Earl was like a father early in my career. He stuck his neck out and hired a country boy with nothing to show for but homemade tapes. His approval meant the world to me and fueled my desire to dominate the competition.

Later that night, in a cheap motel, I did just that. Wild, passionate sex with my crosstown rival and secret boyfriend, Luke Lawson. He was a year older than me, and I was crazy about him. He reminded me of John Boy Walton (from *The Waltons* TV series). Sandy blond hair, blue eyes and a great, square jaw. He even wore rimmed glasses like John Boy did, which drove me wild. I told Luke about this, and he fired back, "I pegged you as more of a Ben Walton kind of guy." His laugh always made me smile.

"He was fourteen on the show, you pervert," I replied with a laugh of my own. It was always like that when we were together. Lots of laughter, lots of joking around. And really, really, good sex.

There was just one problem. Luke was "straight."

Right.

As we went at it in the motel room, I grabbed Luke by the neck, forced him against a mirror on the wall, facing him toward it as I took him from behind.

"Oh my god, Mark!" he moaned as I rammed him. "I'm cumming! I'm cumming!" he warned before shooting on the mirror. I whipped him around, kissed him and tossed him on the bed.

"I'm not done with you yet," I said, with the fire of desire still raging.

"Whatever you want. Don't ever stop," he pleaded.

When it was over, I sat naked on the bed and watched him get dressed.

"You doing the eleven tonight?"

"Yeah. Should have been back an hour ago," he replied as he tossed his tie over his head, messing up his perfect blond hair.

I smiled as I approached him, reaching down and grabbing a comb from his Dopp kit. I gently brushed the back of his head as he continued to struggle with his tie. We shared a quiet intimate moment in the mirror.

"Why won't you say it?" I whispered in his ear. "You know how I feel."

He pushed me away. "Stop it. We've talked about this. Just please stop it, Mark."

Dejected, I walked back and sat on the bed.

"I love you, Luke Lawson," I confessed. "You don't have to say it, but I know you love me too."

We both finished getting dressed, a heavy tension between us. I followed him from the room out into the parking lot of the motor lodge, keeping a good distance between us. It was dark and quiet. The coast seemed clear, so I stepped closer to him.

"Friday night? Meet me back here and you won't regret it."

He stared at me, unable to say no. I smiled and pulled him to me, kissing him sweetly on the lips.

In the darkness, a car motor rumbled to life and a vehicle pulled out of the lot. I had an uneasy feeling but let it go.

"I'll see you on the news," I said to Luke as he walked away.

I watched him get into his car and drive away. I climbed into my used black Dodge Challenger and turned the ignition key. The small engine of the car struggled to life. I pulled out of the parking lot and headed back to my dingy basement apartment.

For another night alone.

GO WEST

t was like the television ads. I was lying in bed, arms splayed out, a pillow over my head. I'd turn one way and then flip to the other side. I looked at the clock. It was seven thirty. Screw it. I might as well get up.

I am not sure why I couldn't sleep. Maybe it was all the adrenaline from Graysville. Almost being killed by skinheads tends to distract one.

Or Luke. I should have kept my mouth shut. Unfortunately, when we tell someone we love them, what we really want is for them to tell us the same. To leave me hanging like he did was worse than being assaulted by a skinhead.

If I were being honest with myself, and who knows if anyone can do that, I knew why I couldn't sleep.

Her.

When Luke Lawson signed off at the eleven o'clock news, he'd go back to Her. She'd make sure her head was on his shoulder and his arm was around her as he drifted off to sleep. She'd watch to be sure. She'd be up early and put her face on and brush her teeth. Then she'd slip into bed, lying on her side so he saw her in the best light first thing in the morning. All the while, she'd be ticking off the days until they became Mr. and Mrs. Luke Lawson in front of five hundred of their closest family and friends.

Well, Luke and I never spent a night together. I wanted to fall asleep on his shoulder and wake up to his smiling face in the morning. I wanted to bring him coffee and take a shower with him and watch him shave in the master bathroom.

In *our* mirror.

I met Katie, his girlfriend, on a couple of occasions. Each time was at a local charity event where all the news people attended.

Luke and I were talking shop by the punchbowl. It was the usual nonsensical blather that industry folk discuss. Gossip, ratings, who's moving where. We do it unthinkingly. People came and went, joined in, moved out. We only go to these events for the free food. The joke that the more successful you are, the more free stuff you get is entirely true.

Luke lifted his little plastic cup of punch to his lips and felt a yank. He made an exaggerated move to avoid spilling onto himself. It was Katie, spartan in her reserve, with a pageant smile plastered onto her face.

"Luke, we got a whole room of people to say hello to," she said. "Don't be antisocial." She spoke just loudly enough for everyone to notice, with a big smile that said, *Can you believe this guy?* You heard a good-natured chuckle or two from folk nearby. "And why are you conversing with the enemy?" Again, the pageant laugh.

Luke excused himself politely, but Katie wasn't finished.

"Surely you need to be spending time with *your date*, don't you Mark?" she said. "Is she here?" Her head bobbed like a prairie dog's. "I'd really like to meet her."

My guts burned. I hated her. I hated her for having him. *He's mine, damn it.*

"I don't bring dates to work events," I said. "I'm here to get viewers, not parade a former beauty pageant contestant around."

"Now don't be that way," she said in a syrupy southern drawl.

"By the way, Katie," I continued. "Did you ever win? One of your pageants? Or is Luke your consolation prize?"

"Let's get out of here," she commanded.

Luke shot me a look. I knew that look.

"'Night John Boy," I said as they walked away.

Katie snaked her arm around his waist and turned back at me.

I will never forget that look, a mix of triumph and knowing. *He's with me!*

At nine o'clock the next morning, a little worse for the wear, I ambled into the newsroom. It was like in the old movies: crammed with desks, typewriters, TV monitors and a large TV 6 News logo on the wall. Phones rang. There was the constant clatter of typewriter keys hitting the platens. Occasional yelling across the room. Bad coffee, lousy food, full ashtrays.

I saw Earl off in a corner talking with one of the news crews before they headed off.

I weaved my way toward the back of the newsroom and my small desk, hidden beneath an avalanche of story folders. I picked up the small piece of pink paper and read the message again.

> Call Carol. KN2-TV. Omaha, Nebraska.
> 402-555-2700.

Omaha? Why the hell would Omaha be calling me? I'd never been to Omaha in my life and would have never heard of it had it not been for *Wild Kingdom*, brought to us weekly by Mutual of Omaha Insurance.

But for some reason that I didn't know yet, Omaha had heard of me.

I crossed the newsroom to a map of the United States hanging on the wall. I traced a path with my finger from Chattanooga over to Nashville, through Paducah, and up to St. Louis. I continued to move my finger across the map, up to Kansas City (both of them) and then landed on Omaha, home of the mysterious Carol.

A week later, I was on an Eastern Airlines flight to Omaha, Nebraska. I didn't know what to expect. And I know this sounds idiot, but I expected cows to be walking down the street.

I had no idea that I'd come to have a love affair with Omaha.

I landed at Eppley Airfield, deplaned, and waited for my bag to come around on the carousel. I went outside and hailed a cab.

"Woodmen Tower, please." My voice had a mixture of pride and curiosity. Home of the Omaha Press Club. I felt like I had made it.

Carol and I had agreed to meet for drinks and dinner at six forty-five.

The cab pulled up to the Woodmen Tower and I alighted.

Now this building is simply a pillar atop a box. The tower is striated with unbroken concrete lines from top to bottom and windows in between. Atop in big letters on all four sides is "Woodmen." Photos never capture the magnificence of the building, Nebraska's tallest until about twenty years ago.

I entered the marble lobby and waited for an elevator. Twenty-two floors later, I stepped off to view the most beautiful restaurant I have ever seen. The entire room was surrounded by windows, which provided a gorgeous panoramic view of downtown Omaha—a mix of the old and the new. You could see clear over the river to Iowa.

The room was filled with large, round tables and leather booths. On one side of the room, a jazz trio was playing softly.

The maître d' approached. He was tall, in his fifties, dressed in a tuxedo. This was an actual tuxedo, though, not a uniform.

"May I help you?" His voice was cool and devoid of accent. I believed he was genuinely curious if he could, indeed, help me. The man was a pro. I was at ease immediately.

"I am here to meet Carol Sanders."

He nodded once and opened a leather book resting upon a mahogany podium, lit by a little version of the old library reading lights with the green glass.

He smiled. "You're early. I cannot seat you for another twenty minutes. He extended his arm with his palm out. "Why don't you enjoy our bar and have a drink until your table is ready."

I did as I was told. I tried to look cool, but I couldn't help rubbernecking as I crossed the room.

I ponied up to the bar. I wanted a Jack & Coke, but I chose a more conservative club soda with a twist of lemon. The bartender was also an older gentleman, professionally and stereotypically attired, right down to the garters holding up his sleeves.

I took a sip of what was honestly the best club soda with a twist of lemon I'd ever had (I still don't know how he did it) and noticed the television above. It was KN2-TV, which I took to be an omen.

"Just a gorgeous night here in downtown Omaha," the helicopter pilot said, looking straight into the camera. "It's the perfect way to say goodbye to all of you as I move on to my new job in Dallas, Texas."

He saluted the camera.

"Skycam pilot and reporter, Theo Galdono," said the anchorman. "Thank you for your service to the people of Nebraska and KN2-TV. Omaha's loss is Dallas' gain. Fly safe, my friend."

I felt someone touch my shoulder.

"Mark?"

I started and turned around.

I did not expect to see a woman in a bright red dress in Omaha. Maybe it was from living down south. Red was the color a jezebel wore. This woman was serious. I could tell she meant business. Her brunette hair had a reddish tint to it and was pulled back behind her ears. Stylish, but corporate professional. Her wire-framed glasses were silver. She reminded me of a librarian who was "ready to move on" and got a makeover on *Donahue*.

She carried a clutch in her hand—the real McCoy, not that rich Corinthian leather Ricardo Montalban was hawking for Chrysler, and a blue folder. There was my name, "Mark Pettit," tucked into the file tab that someone made a label for and slid in.

"I'm Carol. Carol Sanders. KN2-TV. Welcome to Omaha."

I shook her hand and smiled.

"You're early," she said.

"Punctuality is the politeness of kings, Carol." I replied.

"Wow," she said. "French history and a face."

We both laughed as the maître d' interrupted.

"Your table is ready, Ms. Sanders. Right this way."

Carol had a confident gait, and you could see why. As she crossed the room, she passed out hellos to patrons close by and little waves to people in the distance. Everyone in the room knew who she was. For this, she was given the best seat in the house, a half-moon booth by a corner window. As I slid in, I looked out over Omaha and saw a bright red helicopter, with a large "2" emblazoned on its side, circle the building and fly off. I wonder if she wore a dress to match the helicopter.

"That's Theo," she said. "Tonight's his last night. New job in Dallas. He's a legend around here and his shoes are impossible to fill, so we're not even going to try," she said.

"That was very impressive," I told her. "Flying and reporting at the same time."

Carol smiled and said, "You see what I'm talking about. No way can we replace that. We're ditching the helicopter. From now on, KN2-TV's reporting will be on the ground."

"I prefer the front lines myself."

Carol smiled and said, "I had a feeling."

Another laugh between us helped break the ice. I was smitten with Carol. She was brilliant, with a hint of awkwardness, like the head of the National Honor Society back at Calhoun High.

"So, what got you interested in investigative reporting, Mark?"

Without hesitation, I said, "Wayne Williams."

"Oh, really," Carol replied. "Atlanta?"

"That's right. Twenty-eight murders."

"Not something most kids would choose to think about."

"I was obsessed," I confessed. "Did you know the cops came up empty on all but one of the murders?"

Intrigued, Carol asked, "What are they missing?"

"Someone like me."

"I'm guessing you have a theory?"

"I don't know yet. I do know that there must be more than fiber evidence to tie a guy to twenty-eight murders. You give me six months on that story, and I'll give you more than just a theory."

We were interrupted by the maître d'.

"Your waiter will be right with you," he apologized. "We had a group of eight, and he's finishing with them."

Carol smiled and nodded. It didn't matter. This was her place.

"How did you get to Chattanooga?" she asked me.

"Earl Lindenmeyer, TV 6," I replied.

She knitted her brow. "I don't think I know him."

"I grew up in Calhoun, Georgia. We could watch stations in two markets. Atlanta and Chattanooga. Earl was a radio legend up there before he switched to TV news."

Carol continued, "How'd he find you?"

"I found him. I mailed him a demo reel of me reading my radio scripts into a camera."

"Smart." I liked her smile; her eyes became kind.

I rolled my eyes, making fun of myself. "I must have called him a dozen times over two weeks. Asking him to just take a look at my tape. Then, one day, he called me back."

"Yep. That's how it happens."

"I was so excited I didn't even ask what my salary was when he offered me the job. I just took it. Turns out my salary was $12,500 a year."

Carol picked her clutch and the folder up from the table and put it on the seat next to her.

"It's what you gotta do in this business, right? If you want something, take it."

"Absolutely."

I was happy with the way this was going. Here I was, sitting in the best place in all of Omaha, up for a job at a television station in a bigger market. Here we were, and we were hitting it off.

"Good evening. My name is Paulo. May I start you off with a drink?"

I looked up and gasped slightly. Paulo was Brazilian and the best of what that country had to offer. He was handsome, his perfect black hair parted on the right. I became nervous and clasped my hands together under the table to keep myself from kvelling.

Carol looked up once to acknowledge him and moved her eyes back to me, smiling. "A split of your best champagne."

Paulo smiled. "Wonderful. Celebrating?"

Carol became effusive, spreading her hands out. "This is Mark Pettit, a great investigative reporter and, hopefully, a new member of the KN2-TV news team."

Paulo smiled. His perfect teeth were bright and lit up the area. I felt a spark pass between us. My stomach tightened.

He looked at me and asked, "So, you're going to be famous around here?"

My face turned beet red. I smiled at him, a bit overwhelmed.

"You'll be seeing plenty of his face," Carol said proudly.

"I hope so," Paulo said.

Carol looked up at Paulo and back at me. His countenance returned to business.

"I'll be back with your champagne."

Carol nodded and he walked away.

"So, do you have a girlfriend?" she asked, catching me off guard.

Fuck. I froze like a deer caught in the headlights. I looked down at my napkin and began unfolding it, placing it on my lap.

"I just ended something with someone."

She frowned, tilting her head.

"I am sorry. That's tough. The hours at this job make it difficult."

"It's okay. I found that relationships are too distracting from my real obsession."

"Which is?"

"The truth. Finding it."

Carol understood. She unfurled her napkin like a magician, laying it down on her lap, then pushed her silverware away from her.

25

She looked over her shoulder and pointed. I followed the line from her finger to the wall of framed photographs. I found it. I leaned forward and squinted. It was a young man in a suit, a hand to his ear, a large microphone in his other hand. I sat up, excited, and began smiling.

Under the photo was a caption that read, *Tom Brokaw.*

"He got his start right here at KN2-TV," Carol continued. "Everything he has, I see in you. There's no reason why you can't be the next Tom Brokaw."

I beamed at the compliment. She had said the magic words.

The spell was broken as our hot waiter returned with a small ice bucket and two glasses. He put on a little performance, presenting the bottle with a towel underneath. Carol barely looked at it but nodded. He flipped each glass, which was resting between his fingers, and placed each one at the tip of our knives.

I couldn't help but watch. He was confident as a professional and he was confident that he held me in his thrall.

He wrenched the wire cage off the cork and placed the towel over the top and twisted. There was a small pop, nothing like you heard in the movies, and he reached over Carol's glass and poured, filling the glass a quarter of the way up, letting the bubbles grow.

"For the lady," he said. She thanked him and opened her mouth to speak.

He did the same for me. "And for our handsome new star."

I felt the heat rise from my face. Thank God the tablecloth covered my trousers.

I tried to say *thank you*, but I ended up croaking something akin to *ahem.*

Carol's tone was stern. "Mark, I am going to be blunt."

I snapped back into reality.

"KN2-TV is struggling. And as much as I respect Theo and all he's done for the station, it's good that we're moving on. We need something fresh. Something new. We need you. You'll be our lead investigative reporter and our number two anchorman."

My eyes bugged out, like in old cartoons. I was startled, and, for once, I didn't know what to say.

"And, I have a story that just might pique your investigative interests. We have our own Wayne Williams, right here in Omaha."

She said this as I was taking a sip to mask my nervousness. The gas from the champagne wafted up my nose, causing it to itch. I scrunched my face.

"Omaha has a Wayne Williams?" I quizzed.

"Have you ever heard the name Jeremy Jonus?"

Twenty-four hours ago, if you had said *Omaha*, I would have replied with *Marlin Perkins*.

I shook my head.

She pulled out a folder and a pen.

"Open it," Carol instructed.

It was an offer letter. I did a double-take at the number written on it. Any hope I had of keeping it cool and being a pro disappeared the moment I set foot in this opulent dining room.

"Carol, this is incredibly generous." I thought about Earl and mentioned his plan to make me the lead anchor in a couple of years.

Carol's hand slid across the table and pulled the letter back. She reached into her purse and pulled out a gold Parker pen, twisting it theatrically. She slashed a single line on the paper, wrote something, folded the letter, and slid it back to me.

I unfolded the letter.

Jesus Christ on a cracker! She tripled my current salary. That was more money than my parents' combined income. The low rumble of conversations and the clink of silverware and glasses disappeared. I no longer heard the music.

My vision went tunnel and all I could see was that number.

I don't know how long I stared at it. It felt like an hour. I realized I was holding things up. I shook it off.

"When do I start?"

"Two weeks. I'll hire the movers in Chattanooga."

I snapped back. I knew what this meant.

"Don't bother. I just need my clothes."

Carol blinked a couple times and smiled at me. She was proud. "Sometimes what we all need is a fresh start."

I nodded.

She said nothing, letting me savor the moment. She watched me taking it all in. I met her eyes.

"Carol?"

"Mmm?"

"I do have one question. I'm all the way down in Chattanooga. How on earth did you see my work out here in Omaha?"

"Aah." She smiled.

"Dave Farrell. We're old friends. He's been sending me your tapes for a couple of months now."

My face dropped.

She laughed, a deep rhythmic laugh.

"Yeah. He really wants you gone."

That motherfucker. I never really liked him and now I realized why.

She lifted her glass. "To Dave!"

"To Dave." I tried to sound cheerful. Our glasses clinked.

"To Dave."

Luke was holding out on more than just affection with me. Our clandestine trysts and Dave's beneficent gesture were to have greater consequences down the road.

CHAPTER

4

EVERY MOVE YOU MAKE

L uke and the entire Channel 7 team were watching my skinhead
report in the newsroom as the segment ended.

"Fantastic reporting, Mark. We know you'll stay on it…"

"Shit!" one of his co-workers blurted out. "How the hell did he
get that story?"

A large glass door swung open. The employees snapped out of
their trances and quickly mimicked the appearance of work.

Dave Farrell, the station's hard-driving news director, stepped
into the bullpen. Furious.

"What the fuck was that?" he demanded. "Do we not have one
goddamn reporter at this station?"

The employees turned off the TV monitors. The newsroom
went silent as Dave whipped his attention to Luke.

"Lawson! My office. Now!"

Luke took a deep breath as Dave shuffled his way in, now pacing behind a large mahogany desk. After taking a moment to compose himself, Luke walked into the office.

"Pettit is kicking your ass on a regular basis."

Luke tried to explain.

"Dave. I'm so sorry. I have no idea how he got that tip…"

Not having it, Dave stopped him.

"Sit down."

Luke did as he was told as Dave sat down behind his desk with a dangerous look in his eyes.

"We've got a problem. You've got a problem," he said to Luke.

"I'll work harder, Dave. I'll get more sources."

A pause, and then.

"It's more than that, Luke."

Luke was perplexed. Dave stared him down for another beat. He reached for a drawer. A manilla envelope was set in front of Luke.

"What is this?" Luke asked.

"Open it."

Tentatively, he opened the envelope. To his horror, he pulled out a series of photographs. First, the exterior of a motel and its ratty neon sign. The second, the front door. Room 16. The third, Luke standing outside the door.

Luke could only stare. Mortified.

"Dave."

Disdainfully, Dave said, "Just be quiet."

Luke looked at the final photo. It's me, kissing him sweetly on the lips.

"You fucked me. You've fucked this whole station," Dave spoke with the fury of an evangelist.

Luke couldn't bring himself to say anything. Dave was more disappointed than angry.

"I signed you to a five-year contract and this is how you repay me? Do you understand what would happen if this got out? If people knew you were, this? You'd be ruined. This station would be ruined."

Luke nodded as Dave rubbed his forehead, thinking hard.

"Here's what's going to happen. You're never going to see him again. It'll be your choice. You're a family man now, Luke. You're going to marry your girlfriend, have a couple of kids, and we're going to follow it with our promo cameras. All the way to number one. You play your cards right and you're gonna be the next Bob Johnson."

Luke hung his head in desperation.

"Pettit is going to get a phone call. From a station in Omaha, Nebraska," Dave said as he leaned in. "When he tells you about it, you're going to advise him to take the job."

Luke looked up. Devastated.

"This is for your own good. Both of you."

Luke dropped his head, his eyes now red.

Later that night, Luke and I sat at a corner table at our favorite neighborhood post-news dive. Our ties were undone and our dress shirts were wrinkled.

I was still glowing from my exclusive report and was now a couple of beers deep. I wanted so bad to lean in and kiss Luke, to celebrate my victory.

He was unusually quiet.

"When he grabbed my shirt, I thought it was over," I gushed. "I thought, *This is it, I'm going to die for this story.*"

He didn't look up from the table, just replied, "It was some of the bravest reporting I've ever seen."

Even more animated, I said, "If those troopers hadn't shown up, they might never have found my body."

Luke remained quiet.

"Four arrests, though! Can you believe that? From our story!"

Luke deadpanned, "It's incredible."

Now it was time to rub it in.

"It's all about sources, Luke. Maybe if you got out from behind that desk and did some real reporting, you and Dave might take some of our viewers."

Luke looked up at Dave's name and I gave him a coy smile.

"Could your head get any bigger?" he asked.

"Why don't you make it?"

No response. He pulled away slightly. Another beat.

"Actually, there is something else," I told him as I pulled the small pink piece of paper from my pocket.

"Strangest thing. I got a call from a station in Omaha. The news director said she'd been following my work. From Omaha?"

Luke feigned surprise. "Wow," he said.

"Yeah. She wants me to fly out for an interview."

Luke interrupted. "You should do it."

A pause. I stared at him, taken aback, but I tried to laugh it off. "What are you saying?"

Now another pause. "You should take the job."

Again, I was caught off guard.

"What job? She hasn't offered me a job."

Luke became agitated.

"She will. Everyone loves you. She'll offer. You take it."

Now I was becoming agitated.

"Why would I move to Omaha? I've never even been there. I have no sources."

Undeterred, Luke said, "You'll make sources. The offer will be good. Just take the job."

What?

"I'm not leaving you, Luke."

"Stop it!" He spoke through his teeth. His jaw was set.

People around us sensed something was wrong.

He leaned in and whispered, "I can't see you anymore."

There it was. Like a bomb.

"I'm not like you," he said as a heartbreaking anger grew inside me.

"What the fuck does that mean?"

His face now a bright red, Luke looked at me and said, "You're dangerous! You don't care about consequences. Sometimes it feels like you want us to get caught. I can't. And..."

Then, almost hysterically, he continued, "If anyone finds out, if Katie finds out. I can't get caught."

I tried to reason with him.

"It's who we are," I say.

"No! I'm not like you. Not anymore."

I had no words.

"What do you want me to do? Anything, baby, just tell me."

He stared me in the eye and said, "For God's sake, Mark. For once, think about someone other than yourself. If you care about me at all you must go!"

After a silent moment, "What are you going to do?"

He paused, then said, "I'm going to propose to Katie."

A dagger to my heart.

"Why the hell would you do that?"

"Because I can't marry you."

Somber. Heartbreaking.

I surrendered. I stood, put on my suit jacket, and lingered for a moment before I turned to go.

"If I leave right now, you might never see me again," I warned him.

His eyes told me all I needed to know.

"I'll see you on the news."

A final, silent stare. Then, as I turned to walk away, I saw him bury his head into his arms on the table.

Back at the Omaha Press Club, in pain from the memory, I look up from the contract in front of me.

"Let's go become number one," I said to Carol.

She smiled brightly. She had her man.

With Luke out of my life, it was an easy decision. Then, out of the corner of my eye, I saw the young waiter as he finished his shift. I watched as he took off his apron and headed out the door. I could see the definition in his back, through his white cotton shirt.

My eyes followed him. Still hungry. Still hurt.

Two weeks later, I packed everything I had in my beat-up Challenger and headed for Omaha.

Permanently.

My friend Bruce Potts agreed to make the trip with me. We had grown up together in Calhoun. Played baseball together. Played tennis together. Shared so many good times together. His mom and dad, Lorene and Ronald (or "Pee Wee" as everyone called him), were like a second set of parents to me. During the holidays, I often spent as much time—if not more—with them as I did my blood relatives. That bond would not last and would be another crushing blow to my psyche and overall mental health.

I don't want to talk about it right now.

It was a long, exhausting drive from Chattanooga to Nebraska, especially across Missouri.

Good God, how can one state feel so small and be so wide?

We finally arrived in Omaha and took a tour around town. Past the Woodmen Tower, where I had met Carol, the Orpheum Theater—where I would later spend one of the happiest nights of my life—past the University of Nebraska, Omaha (where I would attend college while also working at the TV station). I was pleasantly surprised at how beautiful the city was. It was far from rural, and in fact, it was quite urban.

Yet, it was conservative, and I knew I'd have to be on my best behavior. Pour myself into my work. Forget about Luke and try to rebuild my life.

Bruce spent the next couple of days helping me look for apartments and then took a flight back home to Georgia. I was alone now. I didn't know a soul in the city, other than Carol, whom I had met for all of two hours.

After I got settled, Carol invited me to the station for a tour and to meet some of my new colleagues.

"Omaha is now in the top fifty news markets in the country," Carol told me as we walked through the newsroom's clacking typewriters. I heard voices squawking over the police scanners.

"You're going to get eyes here, Mark," she said. "I promise you that."

She led me from the newsroom, through a large metal door, and into the studio. It was much larger than our small, cramped studio in Chattanooga. The room was alive, and suddenly, the lights above the set illuminated, revealing the news desk and an empty anchor chair. The Omaha skyline was framed behind it.

"So, what do you think?" Carol quizzed.

I soaked it all up. This was the big leagues, or at least the bigger leagues, and I planned to swing for the fences. I naïvely walked behind the news desk and sat down in the empty anchor chair.

"Like I was born for it."

And then, a booming voice.

"Already planning to take my seat?" a silver-haired, heavy-set man asked me. I recognized him from the newscast the night I had met Carol at the Omaha Press Club.

"Mark, this is Bob Berry," Carol interjected. "Bob, meet Mark Pettit."

Stone-faced, Bob replied, "I saw your tapes from Chattanooga. You're a gunslinger on-air."

I extended my hand for his and replied, "The news should have some firepower, don't you think?"

Instant rivalry.

"We'll see what the people of Nebraska think," he replied curtly.

We stared at each other intensely. I had no intention of flinching. Then, a crack in the ice.

"My wife and I would love to have you and your wife over for dinner when you get settled," he offered.

"I don't have a wife."

"Fiancée, girlfriend, you know what I mean," he grumbled.

"I don't have either, but if you don't mind it just being me, I'd be delighted."

Bob looked at Carol with a puzzlement.

"Well, you still have time to fix that," he said with a stern glance.

A floor director called out, "Two minutes!"

Before heading off, Bob gave me one more parting shot.

"Now, if you'll excuse me, son. One of us has to do the news."

Touché.

"You'll get to know Bob," Carol apologized. "He can be territorial with fresh blood."

Tongue firmly in cheek, I replied, "I like him."

Smiling, Carol said, "I think you two will make a hell of a team."

I smiled and nodded. "I agree."

As the newscast began, Carol asked me to follow her to another area of the building. She led me down the hallway and into a compact, stuffed room filled with video tapes, files, and folders. It was like a jackpot of information and history. A researcher's wet dream. I was in heaven.

"This room is yours. Everything you could ever want to know about the Jeremy Jonus case is here," she said. "We have video from the searches for the bodies, police interviews, witness interviews. Anything you need on Jonus is in this room."

She then handed me a thick dossier with a mugshot on the cover.

"This will get you started," she told me.

I froze, seeing his mugshot for the first time. It was the first time I locked eyes with Jeremy Jonus.

I was shocked at how young he looked, around my age. He was attractive (my type, if I'm being honest) with a slight frame, chiseled jaw, and a tuft of black bangs.

"He's young," I said to her.

"Your age, actually. He was in the Air Force. Lived over at Offutt for two years. And, he was a Boy Scout leader, if you can believe that. Those poor boys. Thank God he's on death row."

What?

"Death row? I asked.

"Pleaded guilty. We have the trial tapes in here as well."

Confused, I asked, "So what do you need me for?"

She looked at me earnestly and said, "Everyone knows what he did. But no one knows why. Some people think he was abused as a child. Other people think it's because he's a homosexual."

I shifted uncomfortably at her words.

"But it's all speculation. More questions than answers as they say. There're even rumors that he killed another boy back in Vermont, but there's no evidence to prove it."

Carol gathered herself.

"I think what the people of Nebraska are looking for, Mark, is the same thing as you. The truth. I'll let you get settled."

She left, leaving me holding the heavy file folder. I looked at Jonus' photo again.

They say there are some people who come into our lives for a reason. At a moment you can only describe as destiny. They change us. So much so, that we can't even remember life before them.

I zeroed in on Jonus' unapologetic, shark-like eyes.

That person, for me, just happened to be a serial child killer.

CHAPTER

5

DON'T COME AROUND HERE NO MORE

y home, no longer a subterranean dwelling, was a brand-new two-bedroom apartment, a "unit" they called it. It had all the mod cons. My refrigerator was four times the size of my previous one (and was no longer stuffed behind a cupboard door). Plush wall-to-wall carpet throughout, and then an expansive view of downtown Omaha. I could see all the way to the Blatt, where the farm team for the Kansas City Royals played, and on to the Missouri River.

My bachelor altar was a 45-inch Magnavox rear-projection television in a wood grain cabinet. It must have weighed two hundred and fifty pounds. The guys from the rental store had it easy delivering it as the building had a freight elevator. They wheeled it right into my parlor. I handed them a sawbuck, and they were happy, even thanking me.

I now had a better view of Jack Lord, "Steve McGarrett," on *Hawaii Five-O.*

I confess. A better view of James MacArthur.

Book *me*, Danno.

On my new glass and brass dining room table were the contents of that heavy file Carol gave me. I poured myself a stiff Jack & Coke. Three ice cubes, cover the ice with Jack and top with Coke. I sat down and laid two photos down on the gray tinted glass.

Jeremy Jonus killed two teenage boys in an Omaha sub-urb. Two that the police knew about. Thirteen-year-old Jimmy Ray Easterly and twelve-year-old Robert Wilkins had been kid-napped in broad daylight, three months apart.

I spread open the top of the file and riffled through, pulling

out a photo of the rope used to tie up both boys. Next, a photo of the knife. It was found under the seat of Jeremy's car. It looked like an oversized kitchen knife. Steel blade, two rivets flush with the wooden handle.

He stabbed the boys repeat-edly. Brutal slaughter. Those murders have kept Sarpy County terror-ized for over a year now.

I held Jonus' mugshot and took a large swig of my drink.

If this were an ordinary photo of Jeremy, would I think he was capable of murder?

Why did this happen?

This was my Wayne Williams. I had to know.

I didn't realize it was getting late until I noticed the lights twin-kling over Omaha. I stood up and stretched, then carried my drink over to the window. Every city looks beautiful from a hundred feet up. The Jack Daniels was having its intended effect. It made me introspective.

I was hooked.

MARK PETTIT

Just shy of obsessed.

There was a branch of the Omaha Public Library over on Westwood, a short drive from the station. It was a new building and seemed inspired by Frank Lloyd Wright. I walked past the brick columns supporting red I-beams which jutted out and held the glass-enclosed second floor aloft.

The inside looked like a modern university library, with fluorescent lights and a drop ceiling. Wooden bookcases all around. Everything was being replaced with new buildings. The library in Chattanooga was new, having replaced the old one Carnegie built on 8th St. They looked the same inside.

I wandered over to the circulation desk. The librarian was a conservatively dressed woman. I suppose all librarians are. She wore a simple white blouse with a gray skirt. Her only jewelry, besides her wedding ring, was a gold chain from which hung her reading glasses.

She smiled at me and wished me a good morning. Her perfume smelled of roses. I envied the suave men in the movies who knew what a woman was wearing. Aside from Old Spice, I couldn't tell you what men were wearing either. I asked to see their newspaper archives.

She led me down aisles of bookcases to the farthest corner away from the entrance. A small wooden desk with two gray machines sat amongst a bank of wide gray metal cabinets with drawers about four inches high and six or eight feet long. The machines looked like voting booths from behind.

"This is our microfilm machine," she said. "It's where you'll find archived newspapers and public documents. Have you ever used one of these?" she asked.

"I'm sure I'll figure it out."

She walked over and flipped a switch. A large screen, which reminded me of the overhead projector the teacher would use at Calhoun, lit a yellowish white. There were two reels and a crank with a platter over which a metal plate hovered.

"I can get you started," she said with a smile. "What date are you searching for?"

I looked at my reporter's notepad to confirm.

"Monday, September 19th. Last year."

Her eyebrows knitted and then she looked stricken.

"You're looking for Jimmy Ray Easterly?"

"Yes, ma'am." I had no reason to lie.

Her demeanor went cold.

"Who do you work for again?"

"I hadn't said, ma'am. I am the new investigative reporter over at KN2-TV."

She tensed her jaw, trying to retain her composure. She turned and opened a drawer, grabbing an orange and brown box from amongst the dozens. She held her glasses up to her face and then let them drop back over her bosom.

"This is all we have," she said. "I'm sorry, I've got to get back to the front desk."

I smiled and said, "Thank you for your help."

I shook off her coldness, smelling her warm, faint aroma of rose.

The side of the box said OMAHA WORLD HERALD and stamped underneath it was 9/17/83–9/23/83. I pulled out the reel of film and examined the machine. Indeed, it was easy enough to figure out. I pressed it onto a mount and led the film across the platter to the other empty reel, where I fed some film into it and turned the crank until it caught. Pressed the clamp down. The image was the reverse of a newspaper. The photos were negative, and the type was white against a dark background. I turned the crank until I found the nineteenth. I noticed a sign next to the machine saying that copies of images could be made for a quarter.

I found what I was looking for.

LOCAL PAPERBOY GONE MISSING

I got out my pad and began taking notes.

My stomach started to gurgle. I looked at my watch; two hours had passed. I figured lunch was in order. I left the library and drove over to Big Fred's Pizza. I thought food was big in the South, but nothing prepared me for the Goodie Roonie. It was a huge slice of double-crust pizza with hamburger, cheese and tomato inside. I was ready for a nap, but I had more to do.

I pulled out a map from my glove compartment and checked my notes. It looked like about a ten-minute drive. I wasn't dug in yet. I knew how to get from my apartment to work and a few other places. If it was afternoon on a weekday, I figured traffic wouldn't be too bad.

I arrived in a typical middle-class neighborhood. It was all built in the forties or fifties, with a renovation or an addition here and there. I drove the Dodge Challenger slowly, not realizing I probably looked like I was casing the street. I counted the numbers and found the house I was looking for. A classic midwestern ranch-style house, stained blue-gray paint with white trim and a red door. There were two cars parked in the driveway, both over ten years old. Rust was working its way around the wheel wells. The lawn was overgrown, and the concrete was cracking. Time was not being kind to this homestead.

Next door, I saw a middle-aged woman carrying the groceries into her house. Once inside, I exited the car and walked to the front stoop. I knocked on the screen door. It made a hollow metallic noise and sounded like trouble, though I wasn't any. I waited and she answered.

In my shirt, tie and khakis, I must have looked like I wanted to share the Good News. She smiled and said hello.

"Are you Mrs. McFarlane?"

Her smile disappeared. She moved her head back and squinted at me. She was a smoker. I could tell by the lines around her lips.

"Who's asking?"

"My name is Mark Pettit. I'm with KN2-TV, I was wondering if I could ask you a few questions?"

She eyeballed me. I could see the wheels turning.

"Regarding?" It wasn't a question though she used a rising inflection. She was leading me. She knew the answer.

I turned my head ever so slightly toward her neighbor's house. She pulled the screen door shut. I heard the lock click.

"Stop it! Are you serious?" she fumed. "After everything this community has gone through? Still going through? How many times are you all going to dig up those poor boys' bones?"

I motioned like a pedestrian trying to slow a car down.

"Ma'am, I'm new to town. I'm just trying to learn as much as I can…"

She rolled her eyes and looked heavenward, taking a deep breath like one does when they are in total disbelief.

"Unbelievable. Absolutely unbelievable. Young man, have you no sense of decency?" Her voice cracked from anger to sadness.

I took a step back. I didn't like being this close as I wounded her by merely telling her my job.

"Ma'am, please, I didn't mean to upset you," I pleaded.

She took my courtesy as weakness and shot back, her voice filled with righteousness.

"Where'd you say you work again? KN2-TV?"

I nodded. "I'm sorry, I don't have cards yet."

"That's Bob Berry's channel. He would never do this to us. He would never violate us like this!"

I stood there chastised. I didn't know what to do. For once, I didn't know what to say.

"And God help you if you bother the Easterly family. Those people don't deserve anymore."

She shook her head once for "good day" and slammed the door. She pitched a fit as she walked off.

I turned around, trying to see if anyone saw this altercation. It didn't seem so. I took a step on the grass and then thought that would be seen as rude. Well, ruder. I walked down the sidewalk and turned toward the Easterly house.

I approached the front door and took a moment to compose myself.

I rapped the metal door twice. It sounded menacing, especially after the way my previous visit went. Don't these people have doorbells?

There was no answer. I tried again.

I heard footsteps approaching. The deadbolt turned and the door creaked as it was slowly opened.

I saw Frances Easterly, a mother aged from having her soul ripped out of her. The shadows added texture to her pain.

"May I help you?" She wasn't whispering, but her voice was weak and tired.

"Mrs. Easterly, my name is Mark Pettit. I'm the new investigative reporter at KN2-TV."

She closed her eyes and shook her head.

"I'm sorry. We don't speak to reporters anymore," she said softly.

"This is entirely off the record, ma'am," I implored. "I just wanted to introduce myself."

"I would appreciate it if you left."

She closed the door quietly. I heard the deadbolt set.

Couldn't she tell I was here to help her? I stepped back and tried to see through the bay window, but the sheers made it impossible. I did a little box step on the concrete path, unsure of where to walk next. I decided to go for it. I knew I could convince her.

"You don't know me, but I promise you that I will not stop until every question is answered about what happened to your son and your family. I swear to you."

I am not sure what I expected. I supposed she'd invite me into the kitchen, maybe even offer me some coffee, and we'd talk. Looking back, I don't know where I got that idea. Perhaps I had been watching too many police procedurals. The mothers always said they'd told the police everything, but then they asked you in.

I waited.

From behind the closed door, I heard her say, "If you return, I'll call the sheriff." She didn't yell. It was just resignation.

I walked to my car. As I was unlocking it, I peered over the roof. Mrs. MacFarlane stood in her window. She saw the whole spectacle. She lifted her arm and pulled down. The venetian blinds tilted shut.

I returned to the station and walked into my bunker, where a mountain of tapes and files awaited.

I was deep in concentration. The door slammed and I sat up, startled.

It was Carol. She was pissed.

"If you're trying to get fired before you cash your first paycheck, you are well on your way."

My shoulders slumped. I felt like I was in the principal's office. I wanted to crawl under the table.

"Sit up and look at me, Mark. I am going to tell you this one time and one time only."

She stood with her arms behind her back, eyes burning with fury. I thought she might hit me.

She registered my befuddlement. It made her angrier. She closed her eyes and took a breath, starting over.

"Mark," she said, moving her arms from behind her back and clasping her hands in front of her as if we were in communion. "You need to understand, this is Omaha. You may believe you are a very important young man with a flashy job. Nebraska is not like that. This is a conservative, God-fearing place with good, hardworking people who are kind and respectful." Her eyes were kind and begging. Her voice became quiet. "Do you understand?"

"Yes, ma'am."

Carol became Drill Sergeant Carol again.

"The Easterlys want you fired. What in the name of Christ were you thinking, going to their house? And harassing neighbors?"

"You told me to dive in."

My blame-shifting did not go over like I had planned. She gritted her teeth, shook her head and rolled her eyes. I expected the ol' heave-ho, right then and there.

"You need to remember where you are. You did some good stuff back in Chattanooga. That's why we took a chance on you. But you still have a lot to learn. First and foremost is how to be Nebraskan."

"I remember why I was hired." I said it. It came out. I sounded like a seven-year-old.

Carol turned a shade of red reserved for ragtop Corvettes or ladies of the night. She was so red, the glitter elements of her rouge and eye shadow twinkled in contrast.

She lifted a finger like a stiletto.

"I got a call from Sheriff Pete Timmons. Play your cards right and you'll make a friend."

I went from petulant child to eager puppy as she slid a piece of paper over. Her script was neat but loopy, very feminine. It was an address. Back to my AAA map of Omaha.

"He's expecting you."

Carol turned and exited, closing the door extra softly in that way angry people sometimes do when they are finished. I had broken the rules but she still handed me a big break.

Thirty minutes later, I was at the Sarpy County Sheriff's Office. It was a two-story rectangle of brick, which resembled your average middle school.

I walked down the hallways of the sheriff's office with Pete Timmons, a big, burly yet likable lawman. He reminded me of "Buford Pusser," the six-foot-six Tennessee sheriff from the 1973 movie *Walking Tall*. Pusser made a name for himself as a baseball bat–toting warrior against moonshining, gambling and prostitution. Joe Don Baker played Pusser in the first movie but decided not to reprise the role in the second film. Pusser was cast to play himself. He never made it to the silver screen. He was killed in a car crash before filming began. Bo Svenson ended up playing Pusser in *Walking Tall Part 2*.

They should have cast Pete Timmons.

The big sheriff lumbered in front of me, dressed in a brown suit, white shirt and a brown paisley tie. *Miami Vice*, a new police drama where the cops dressed in Day-Glo blazers with white linen slacks, had yet to influence midwestern law enforcement's sartorial habits. His large keyring jingled as we walked down the hall. About halfway, he stopped and opened a door, leading me in. There were desks, tables and chairs situated neatly in the open room. It was eerily quiet.

"This was the HQ for the entire operation," he said. "We had FBI and lawmen from across the state in here." It wasn't the first time he'd told the story.

"We had guys and gals working the phones twenty-four-seven. I think they took in more than 1,000 leads in the first forty-eight hours after Jimmy Ray went missing. Twice that when Jonus snatched Robbie."

Timmons paused, his eyes vacant.

"Worst days and nights of my life."

I watched him as he was lost in thought. I scanned the room, the painted concrete, the cork board riddled with pinholes. I imagined the empty coffee cups and overflowing ashtrays that once littered the room. I began to think of myself there, studying the maps and photographs on the wall, trying to make sense of the horrors we were forced to participate in.

The sheriff clapped his hands together, smacking himself out of the past.

"Okay. Getcha to the good stuff." He led me out of the room and closed the door behind us.

An officer passed by, nodding in acknowledgement of his superior.

"Down here," he said, leading the way.

We reached the end of the hallway. An engraved sign in faux wood indicated this was the evidence room. Timmons thumbed through his big ring of keys until he found the magic one. He slid it into the lock and opened the door.

"After you," he said in a courtly manner.

The room had floor-to-ceiling metal shelving filled with stacks of cardboard boxes. They had fold-over edges secured with twine wound around a metal clasp. This room was colder than the previous room. It felt sad here.

"Everything we have on the Jonus case is in here," he said. "If you're serious about getting to the bottom of what happened, take whatever you need."

I gave the sheriff a puzzled look.

"Any of it?" I asked.

"If it helps you find out why that bastard did what he did, by all means. Might bring peace around here."

I walked down the row. Boxes were numbered from one to maybe one hundred or more. I heard one of the shelves rattle. Timmons was leaning against it, his arm up on one shelf in a relaxed pose.

"Son, you riled up the Easterlys and their neighbors." His voice was warm and avuncular, but firm. "Two more minutes, we'd've brought you out on a stretcher." He smiled. "These people have been through hell. We all have."

I felt my throat burn. Today was exhausting. I should have been tipped off by the librarian that I was jumping into the deep end. I felt like a fool, but I also knew I was right.

"Nebraskans value hard work. I promise you'll get that from me."

The big sheriff smiled. He had a toothy grin. "When you get tired of television, call me. Maybe you'll make a helluva detective."

He walked over to the shelf closest to the door and pulled down a box labeled JONUS #1. He held it out to me like a Christmas present.

I am not sure why, but I became nervous. Perhaps it was the sense that I was closing one door and opening another, knowing nothing would be the same. I took the box. It was heavier than I expected, and I placed it on the floor. I turned the box and unwound the twine.

I took a deep breath and undid the flap. There was a butcher's knife in a plastic bag. I gasped.

It was the knife that Jonus had used to slaughter Jimmy Ray and Robbie.

"Take what you need and sign it out. Find one of the men, they'll get you sorted. Bring it back when you're done. And make sure it is returned the way you found it."

I looked up at him with wide eyes and nodded.

"You know, son, you're the only reporter we've let in here," he said. He knelt down on one knee in front of me. "You make sure your heart is in the right place and you're sincere about wanting to find the truth. We don't need some hotshot trying to make his bones off the graves of those two boys."

"I won't let you down."

I meant it too.

I pulled down seven more boxes and stacked them neatly by the door. I peeked down the hall to find someone to help me sign them out. One of the officers finally came over. He said he'd send someone by in a couple minutes.

A young officer with a thick navy binder came in. He jotted down some numbers and had me sign for the boxes. I thanked him and was left to carry all eight by myself through the corridors, out to the parking lot and into my car.

Later that night, I laid out the crime scene photos across my dining room table. I had to be careful, for they were meticulously inventoried, and I couldn't mix them up.

The first images were from Jimmy Ray's murder. You think you are prepared. I'd seen a couple fatal car crashes and a little bit of blood, but nothing prepared me for this.

It was horrific. The boy's hands were tied behind his back with what appeared to be half-inch round, white rope. It was unusual, frayed at the ends, revealing colorful strands.

I picked up another photo of the rope, similar to the one I had seen inside the KN2-TV file Carol had given me. This one gave me a closer perspective of the fibers. There were flecks of dried blood around. I held the photo up and peered through a magnifying glass, looking for clues, anything.

It was like *Kojak*. Except it wasn't.

Jimmy Ray's feet had been bound with the same rope, and his body was found face down in a ditch surrounded by high grass. In the corner, I could see a little of his dark blue underwear, the kind a boy would wear, like the Batman ones they sell with a matching T-shirt.

The next photos were worse. Stab wounds in Jimmy's bloodied chest and back. I looked down at his leg. It looked like a puncture wound. Later, I found out that Jeremy bit him. He stabbed the boy and then tore into his flesh with his teeth. The back of his neck was sliced.

I was sickened. I'm not a coroner or a detective. How do they push this down and get on with life? I mixed myself a Jack & Coke and waited for the booze to kick in. And there it was. The slight numbing in the stomach, spreading out warmly through my torso. My shoulders uncoiled.

I next sifted through the autopsy photos.

Young Jimmy Ray now lay nude on a cold steel table inside the morgue. My eyes welled up. I envisioned the Easterlys being led into the room, a sheet over Jimmy's body. Mr. Easterly tenderly insisting to his wife that he'll take care of this, for her to go outside. She, shaking her head, demanding to see her boy. The attendant tenderly lowering the sheet so only Jimmy's face was visible. The cry. That awful wail. Until that moment, it could have been someone else's boy. But it wasn't. It was Jimmy Ray.

I reached into the box and pulled out the plastic bag holding the knife.

I opened the bag slowly and pulled out the weapon from between the plastic sheets of the container. I was holding a murder weapon. This knife killed two boys.

I thought about Sheriff Timmons. He knew exactly what he was doing.

You're the only reporter we've let in here.

He gave me the knife. He wanted me to become Jeremy Jonus. The adrenaline. The power.

I couldn't anymore. I set the knife down and walked into the kitchen. A couple dozen photos rested on the counter. I picked up Jeremy's mugshot. I felt myself becoming him.

I looked at another photo. A body. Measuring tape. Numbers. My vision was unfocused, blurry.

I was there.

The trunk of a '79 Nova opened. Inside, tied up with the colorful rope, was Jimmy Ray Easterly. Terrified.

Jimmy Ray was lifted from the car and carried to a grassy ditch.

In the distance, the stacks of the Allied Chemical plant billowed smoke. The plant's exterior lighting cast an orange glow over the morning sky.

Jeremy Jonus knelt before Jimmy Ray, yanking the rope from around the boy's hands. Boy Scout. Experienced with knots. The rope left red rings around Jimmy's wrists.

"Take off your shirt."

Jimmy Ray's chest pounded. Tears ran down his cheeks, his eyes wide with fear. He did what he was told. It was chilly. Jimmy Ray's flesh pimpled and turned pink. His face showed modesty and embarrassment. He covered his chest with his arms.

Ragged breath. Untying his feet. Tugging the boy's jeans off.

Jimmy Ray was turned face down. His wrists held behind his back. A rope, folded in half, slid under his wrists. The bight held in place, coiling the ends of the rope around his wrists. Jimmy Ray whimpered. The coils wrapped a third time and pulled tightly. Jimmy Ray cried out in pain.

The loose ends of the rope wrapped around, forming a double-column tie. Working quickly. Bending the rope in half and forming a coil around the ankles, crossing the bight, pulling the ends tightly, securing the wrists and ankles with a square knot.

Jimmy Ray wondered maybe he wouldn't die. Maybe he just wanted to do things to him. Maybe there was hope he'd get out alive.

He looked up, looked into the eyes of the man hovering over him. Seeing him lift his shirt up. A knife. No.

"Please! Please don't kill me!" Jimmy Ray screamed, tears flowing.

Silence. Regarding each other. Jimmy Ray's breath catching, uneven.

A hand grabbing the rope, turning him. The knife plunging into his back. Jimmy Ray gasping, then screaming in pain.

"Please don't kill me!" he pleaded. "Just take me to the hospital. I won't tell!"

Silence, save the boy's desperate crying.

The knife plunged into the boy's back four more times. Blood pooling in the grass. The rope being pulled, exposing his bare chest, a hand caressing the smooth flesh. The knife pressing through his undeveloped pectoral muscles.

Again. Again.

Again.

No more screams, a phlegmy gurgling.

Jimmy Ray, silent.

A hand reaching under his blond hair, lifting the head up, the knife slicing across the back of the boy's neck. The head falling onto the dirty grass.

Caressing his now pale thigh with two hands. All goes black and then the feel of flesh on the lips, between the teeth, biting down, through, the sweetness of the skin and a ferric aftertaste. Biting harder. Biting the back, the shoulder. A electrifying frisson through the body, excitement, arousal.

From behind, footsteps crunching the grass. Looking up and seeing me.

I pause, seeing Jimmy Ray on the ground and then Jeremy is gone.

I begin examining the crime scene. There is only a ditch, dirt and grass.

The body of Jimmy Ray Easterly is gone.

I held a glossy photo in my hand, my Jack & Coke in the other. Jimmy Ray lying in the weeds bound by that colorful rope.

I felt his terror, his helplessness. The rumble of a chemical plant drowning out his screams.

Isolation over the prairie.

Now I stood outside the Kwik Shop. It was earlier that same morning.

Across the street, at the local Dairy Queen, Jimmy Ray is on his knees folding newspapers.

He's clean, healthy. A normal kid. Just trying to get his work done and rush home for some breakfast.

A bottle slams into a trash can, startling me. I look over.

It's Jonus.

He's staring at Jimmy Ray with dead, shark-like eyes. A shark in landlocked Nebraska. He turns and sees me, staring. We are face to face.

A pickup races into the Kwik Shop, bass thumping. I look back across the street.

Jimmy Ray is gone.

I turn.

Jonus is no longer next to me.

Four men in their twenties pop out of the cab and head into the store. They left the truck running. The one with a beard, gruff, wearing a red plaid flannel sees me staring. Our eyes meet.

A familiar feeling passes through us.

I dropped my eyes. Is he "family" or a threat? He lingered behind his friends, just for a moment. Then he entered the store without a word.

I shivered from the intense moment and headed back to my car. As I opened the door, the guys rushed back out, clutching energy drinks, hopping back into the truck.

"To the Max!" one yelled as the truck began peeling out. They cheered.

I watched the truck disappear around the corner. I was left with the sound of my heartbeat pounding in my ears.

I clicked my seatbelt into place and started the ignition. I thought for a moment and then shrugged.

I followed them onto 80 and then to 480 into downtown Omaha. The truck parked in a lot next to a windowless building clad in corrugated metal. I pulled over farther down from them.

I heard the thump of a deep bass coming from the building. I looked over and saw a bright neon sign above the door. THE MAX

There were lights in a rainbow of colors and a line waiting to get inside.

It was almost exclusively men.

What was this place? Like a moth to a flame, I got out and took a few steps forward. Men were holding hands. Their outfits revealing, seductive.

I could only stare.

CHAPTER

6

LIKE A ROCK

The next morning, there I was in my bunker of an editing room, sitting in front of the typewriter. I flicked the paper bail up and inserted a sheet of letterhead behind the platen, turning the knob to feed it in.

I stared at the concrete wall, painted white. There was a hint of blue from the fluorescent lights. They can't be good for you.

I pushed the carriage return a couple times and began.

October 2, 1985

Here goes nothing.

Dear Jeremy,

The door opened. I looked up. Carol rushed in, a little breathless. I could hear the clickety-clack of typewriters and the dull murmur of conversation. The telexes were dinging. UPI, AP, Reuters. The dings represented the importance of the report coming in. Something was up. They were all printing reports at once.

"Stop what you're doing. You're going on." Her face was hard, tense.

My heart hit my stomach, like when you get a phone call while you are sleeping. It's never good news.

"Sure." I stood up slowly from my chair, fixing my tie and pushing my shirt down into my slacks. "What's going on?"

"AP reports Rock Hudson has died. Experts are saying it's 'gay cancer.'"

My face fell, which Carol read but did not comment on.

"Bob isn't in until after lunch. You're going on the air."

My face brightened.

"This is it. Prove me right in hiring you." She smiled, but it didn't mitigate the stress she was experiencing.

"You got it!" I dashed out of the room. I could feel the adrenaline.

I stood in front of the make-up mirror in the men's dressing room, combing my unwieldy hair. I grabbed some Max Factor Tan Pancake #2 and patted it on my face. It evens out the skin tone and takes away shine. I looked in the mirror. This was going to have to do. No one was going to wait around for me.

I got up, grabbed my jacket and headed into the studio. As I walked to the set, I began doing Lamaze breathing. I took the step up, sat down, and inserted my earpiece.

This was happening.

From above, it must have looked like a stampede. Cameras dancing around, careful to avoid each other's cables, settling into place. Crew checking clipboards, speaking hurriedly into headsets. Everyone jockeying for their positions.

But I couldn't see much of that. The studio lights form a blinding proscenium. You learn to look through it. It is hard to explain.

Through the luminous haze, Carol approached.

"How are you feeling?" Her mien was warm and maternal, aided by a glowing halo that surrounded her from being backlit. She was my angel.

"Like I was born for it."

She nodded once and stepped back, disappearing into the light.

"Thirty seconds!" the floor director said. Carol was to the left, watching a monitor.

I checked my notes, held them up and tapped them. The teleprompter in front of me showed my first lines: GOOD MORNING, I'M MARK PETTIT…

The thunder of the news theme and then the announcer's voice in my ear.

"This is a special news bulletin from KN2-TV!"

The teleprompter blinked and went dark. I squinted, trying to find my lines.

The floor director began to shout.

"Hold on the title! We just lost Camera One and the prompter! Hold on the title!"

All eyes turn toward Carol, who was still watching the monitor.

"Abort?" the floor director asked. He'd seen it all before. Not a hint of panic.

"No!"

And the eyes turned toward me.

"Give me air to the prompter on Camera Two. I've got it."

Eyes back to Carol, including the floor director's.

Carol nodded. Everyone went back to work. In movies, this scene would be stretched out for dramatic effect; but I assure you, this all happened in like half a second. Most of the crew has been in television for over a quarter of a century. A teleprompter failure is nothing. All in a day's work.

The floor director counted us down.

Three.

Two.

One.

I am live, a television Wallenda.

"Good morning, I'm Mark Pettit. We interrupt regular programming here in Omaha to bring you breaking news from Los Angeles. The legendary actor Rock Hudson has died at his home in Beverly Hills. The Associated Press is reporting that the cause of

Hudson's death is believed to be related to the mystery disease known as AIDS."

I got through the headlines and was still on the air while I interviewed a doctor whom Carol had called in to provide analysis. He was a serious man, professorial in his thick glasses with heavy black frames.

"We still don't know much about the disease," he said. "Only that once diagnosed, it's nearly 100% fatal."

I kept my composure. "Let's hope a cure is found soon. Thank you, Dr. Virley, for joining us here on KN2-TV."

I turned to the camera, still ad libbing.

"That's the latest on Rock Hudson's death for now. I'm Mark Pettit, KN2-TV News. Stay with us for the latest tonight at six with Bob Berry and for breaking news as it happens from the national network news team."

I heard the sign-off tag in my ear and then, "We're out!" from the floor director.

It was over. I was high. I took a deep breath to contain myself. Rock Hudson. Jesus Christ. I lowered my head, thinking how his fate awaited all of us.

I heard noise from the floor. I looked up. The crew was applauding. Nothing crazy, no whistles or cheers, a simple acknowledgement that I did a good job when we were all in a spot.

"Great work, Mark," Carol said, clapping along. One thumbs up.

I stood and gave a "thank you nod" to everyone. I double-timed it off the set. I made it to the editing room and closed the door behind me. The adrenaline was waning and it left me shattered.

I sat down in front of the typewriter. I folded my hands in my lap. I closed my eyes.

"You're a man now, mazel tov." Her quiet tone gave me a start. I opened my eyes.

Carol stood behind me. I turned the chair enough to face her. She was examining me.

"How are you feeling?"

"Great," I lied.

"You should be proud. Exceptional work under pressure."

"Thank you."

She returned to Work Carol. "Take the rest of the day off." She peered over my shoulder, seeing the letterhead and my salutation.

"Who are you writing?"

"Has anyone talked to Jonus?"

She pursed her lips and shook her head. "No, not since he's been in prison."

I opened my hand toward the boxes around the room.

"All these tapes. Dozens of witnesses. Evidence. It just tells us what he did. It doesn't tell us why."

I paused and turned to the typewriter.

"I have to talk to him face-to-face."

Carol chuckled. "His lawyers will not permit that."

"I am not asking his lawyers."

The corner of her mouth turned up as if to say, *You little son of a bitch.*

"I can't describe it. I feel something about him, a connection. I don't know what it is. But he'll talk to me if I ask him."

She was lost in her thoughts.

"Brokaw would have done it."

She turned to leave. As she was closing the door, she stopped.

"Hey, you got a phone call after you aired. No name, but he said he's a fan. Give him a call back to say thanks. Nebraskans appreciate the little courtesies."

She handed me a slip of paper and left, closing the door quietly.

I laid the paper down, folded my hands again and closed my eyes, coming down.

Wait. What? A fan?

I picked up the slip and took a look. Just a phone number written in a rushed hand. I set it back down and stared at the typewriter. I finished the letter and pulled it out, hearing the familiar zip of the platen turning quickly. I patted myself for a pen but couldn't find one.

I looked over at the message again. There was a wall-mounted phone by the door.

Later, I walked over to a sports bar a few blocks away from my apartment. I'd been there a few times with friends, not enough to be a regular. Televisions hung in a horseshoe pattern around the bar. With the baseball postseason coming up in a few days, the Cards and the Royals were divvying up the locals for the pennant race. Omaha doesn't have any pro teams. We were only a month into football season.

So it was a slow Wednesday night when I found myself there. A couple of hockey teams were playing. I distinctly remember it was the St. Louis Blues taking on the Detroit Red Wings. I had no skin in the game, but I rooted for Detroit as I sipped my Jack & Coke. Carol is from Detroit. Why not? Other monitors had the Washington Capitals skating it out against the New York Islanders in the Big Apple. Behind the bartender, a lone screen played ABC's *World News Tonight*.

There were about fifty guys and gals milling about, drinking, laughing. Some were watching a game intently, others eating wings or pizza and having a Hump Day night out.

But across from me in a corner booth was a handsome young man, maybe a couple years older than me, taking a sip from a large rocks glass packed with ice and limes, my self-described fan.

"Is that a daiquiri?" I asked.

"No, it's a Caipirinha. Well, it almost is. You can't find a bar within 500 miles that carries cachaça."

My eyes widened and my head shook a little. It would have been easier to just say, "Huh?" He picked up on my confusion.

"Fermented sugarcane juice. Most drinks in Brazil are made with it."

I indicated I'd like a taste. Paulo, that's right, Paulo, my waiter from the Omaha Press Club, slid his drink over to me. I shook the glass a little and took a sip. It was good, thanks to a lot of sugar killing the rum's vaporous undertones.

He was still in his hospital scrubs. I peered down the vee of his neckline, down to that amazing chest only hinted at. He was gorgeous. He stood out amongst the ordinary Omahans with his skin of brown, yellow and green creating a luminous bronze deeper than a tan. You've heard beauties described as looking good in a burlap sack. Paulo's scrubs made no difference. If anything, the lack of definition in his clothing made his physical features starker.

Paulo looked the part of a doctor on a soap opera. His square jaw was darkened by a shift's worth of growth, which led up to his hair, black and luxurious, framing his face and falling slightly over his ears. He was about two weeks overdue for a haircut.

He lifted his drink. His bicep flexed. It was rock solid, with a prominent vein running down the length of his forearm. He had lovely thin hands.

All these years later, with every thought of Paulo I have, and I have them daily, he was never more handsome than this first time we met.

I sat across from Perfection.

My synapses blasted like the fireworks over the National Mall. I was completely present and totally distracted. I wanted to taste and touch every inch of him.

"I haven't stopped thinking about you since that night at the restaurant. We had the TV on at the clinic this morning, and when I saw you do that special report, you were so good. I had to call."

I could feel my nerves tightening me up. I made a "slow down" gesture with my right hand. I leaned toward Paulo, who followed.

"I need to make sure you understand something," I told him, his bright eyes showing concern. "You can never do that again. My boss can't ever know about this. If she finds out, I won't just get fired, I'll never work in TV news again," I warned him.

I leaned back in the booth, perhaps too aggressively, giving him a curt nod.

He looked down at his drink with an expression of defeat. He thought for a moment and sat up straight with honest reserve.

"I understand. I would never want to hurt you or your career."

"Thank you. I think we've cleared the air."

He relaxed and began to laugh. What the hell is it with Brazilians and perfect teeth?

"I'm not crazy." He tugged at the loose fabric covering his shoulder. "I'm in med school. I'll do my residency in ID."

He registered my being impressed.

"You thought I was just a waiter, didn't you?"

He egged me on, and we both started laughing.

I shrugged. "Waiter, actor, doctor. You know what they say."

He asked where I was from, and I gave him the bullet points.

"I was born in São Paulo." He said "São Paulo" with an extra hit of Brazilian which knocked out the flatness of his midwestern diction. The three syllables almost became four.

He kept it brief, telling me a little about his parents and his childhood in Brazil, how he got to Nebraska and what it's like here.

I stared at him like a fawning teenager hearing Elvis sing a ballad. I even rested my chin on my fist.

"I understand if you can't have a boyfriend."

Wait, what? Whoa!

My head swung back and forth across the bar seeking the merest indication of anyone having heard that. My jaw tensed as I squinted at him.

"Shh. Keep your voice down." I continued scanning the crowd. "Absolutely not," I whispered in a hoarse growl.

He leaned toward me and said, "I feel a connection, Mark. I want to get to know you, spend time with you."

"Here it is! Here it is!" the bartender whooped. He wielded a remote control like Zorro and, one by one, all the televisions were on ABC.

"Listen up! Listen up!" he hooted as a familiar face appeared around the bar.

The crowd belched a confused murmur. What was going on?

"Good evening, I'm Peter Jennings in New York," he said in his soothing baritone. "We are getting more information from California following the death of famed Hollywood actor, Rock Hudson. The

L. A. County Coroner's office now confirms that Hudson died from complications related to AIDS. Again, we can now confirm that the cause of Rock Hudson's death is AIDS."

The bar erupted into applause. Dudes cheered and howled, high-fiving each other while downing beers. Some of the girls rolled their eyes and playfully slapped their boyfriends as if to say, *These guys, really.*

I was twenty-two years old and mortified. I thought that if these people hate Rock Hudson, they're never going to like me.

I stood up, straightened my clothing, and walked out of the bar. With each step, I felt like a mule was kicking me in the back. The air became heavy, constricting. It was harder to breathe. I marched faster and faster, but the door was farther and farther away. I tried not to touch anyone. I had to weave through the herd of happy frat boys.

I made it to the door and was slapped in the face by the bracing autumn air. I was out of there. I could breathe, but I still couldn't. My throat burned and my eyes were blurry. My face tightened, along with my stomach.

I leaned up against the cold concrete of a building about a block away. The cold Nebraska night cut right through me. I shivered and my shivers became sobs. I slid down to the pavement.

I put my head down and felt my shoulders heaving.

"Mark! Mark!"

I looked up and rubbed the tears from my eyes.

It was Paulo. He ran toward me holding my leather jacket in the air. He knelt and wrapped me in it. Then his arms embraced me, his hand caressing my back and arm.

"Stop it," I demanded.

Paulo looked at me. He was sad and his eyes began to well.

"Mark, Mark! Look at me. You are freezing. Let me hold you." He was clinical and pleading.

"No."

"Take me somewhere I can."

We walked to my apartment in silence and rode the elevator in silence too.

Back at my apartment, life became a movie. We kissed passionately in front of my door as I clumsily dug in my pocket for the key.

"Damn it," I said, taking my lips off his to breathe.

"Kick it down."

I finally got it together and opened the door. We pushed our way in, closing the door and picking up where we left off, a tangled mess of arms, hands, legs and lips.

Paulo stopped.

I opened my eyes to find him just standing, arms at his side, his head moving from the left to the right, viewing my empty apartment, save the bookcase-sized television. He took his breath in and walked over to the living room.

"Wow. That's a wonderful view," he said, looking at the Omaha skyline.

"Wait till you see the one from the bed," I said to him as I took him by the hand and led him to my room. Just inside the door, he pushed me up against the wall.

He reached my neck.

"Easy there, Pelé. Don't mark me. Lower your aim."

"Pelé?"

I shrugged. "He's the only Brazilian I know of."

Paulo grabbed at my shirt, ripping the collar as he yanked it over my head. His mouth went to my chest and stomach. He licked what felt like every inch of me and grabbed at the belt of my jeans.

I could tow a wagonload of bricks without using my hands.

I grabbed at his scrub top and worked it over his head.

"You smell great," I tell him.

"Brazilian soap," he said between heavy breaths. "My grandmother makes it and sends it to me."

I pulled him close and kissed him deeply, like I wanted to when I first saw him. His mouth tasted like sweet tea from back home. My tongue danced with his. He was the best kisser I'd ever been with, girl or boy.

He pushed me toward the bed and gave a heavy push to make me fall on it. He slid on top of me.

"No. No, wait." I said, nudging him from me.

"What? We're in private now."

I stood up and pointed.

"My grandmother made me a quilt before I moved here," I told him. "Let's try not to destroy it."

I watched him remove it from the lower third of my bed.

My grandmother Rebecca lovingly sewed it together for me. It was a patchwork of colorful fabrics, like Dolly Parton's mom did for her when she made the "Coat of Many Colors." That's what country folk do when there's no money for store-bought gifts.

I was in Ellijay visiting my grandmother to say goodbye before my big move. She handed me a bundle covered in leftover gift wrap.

"Open it," she said. I tore the paper with the fervor of a child at Christmas. I unfurled the blanket and smiled.

"I've never been to Nebraska, but I heard it's cold. I hope this will help keep you warm."

She walked over to her little cabinet just off the kitchen and retrieved two small bottles of Blair ointments, which she peddled on the side. She handed the small containers to me and said, "If you do catch a cold, rub this on your chest before you go to sleep. Just don't get it on the quilt."

I opened one of the containers and caught a whiff of what smelled like peppermint and camphor.

"Thank you, Grandma," I said as I hugged her. "I love it all."

I watched in the shadows of the city as Paulo gently folded the quilt and then placed it neatly on the dresser in my room.

"There," he said. "Your grandmother's gift is safe."

I smiled, grabbed him and pushed him down on the bed, tugging at the bottoms of his scrubs. This was my favorite part: getting to see a guy's underwear for the first time. Drum roll, please.

Tight white bikini briefs. They glowed against his skin.

His body was incredible. His bronze chest and back were hairless, as smooth as silk.

I began stripping down, soldiering through a burgeoning inferiority complex. But, hell, this wasn't the first time I went for something out of my league.

Like a duck on a June bug, I pounced on him. For a while.

After, we lay at the head of my bed in each other's arms, looking out the windows at the expanse of Omaha. We could see the moon's reflection in the Missouri River as it flowed into Iowa.

I held Paulo from behind, our heads on top of the two pillows, so we could enjoy the perspective together. I ran my hands up from his waist to his chest and squeezed him tightly. Once more I could smell the Brazilian soap, a mesmerizing mix of clay, oil and berries. Açai, he would later tell me. I could have laid there for hours just smelling him and listening to our hearts beat together.

"I told you the view was great from here," I whispered in his ear.

"*É lindo. Assim como você,*" he replied in Portuguese, in a sweet, raspy tone that drove me wild.

"Remember, you're dealing with a country boy here," I joked. "I barely know English."

He laughed a kind, boyish chuckle.

"I said, 'It's beautiful, just like you.'"

"*Você é o homem dos meus sonhos,*" he said as he turned to kiss me.

"One more time, Romeo?"

"*Você é o homem dos meus sonhos.*"

"You are the man of my dreams," he said.

His English was perfect, as was he.

It might have been the sweetest moment of my entire life.

Then, it was over. He sat up and swung his legs over the side of the bed with that little groan guys do for no reason. The mood shifted.

"It's getting late," he said, "I've got to be back at the clinic at six." He began collecting his clothing.

I rolled over onto my stomach, trying to look alluring.

"Or we could just stay up all night."

"Next time," he said. "If you want there to be a next time." The words were recited in a flat deadpan.

I didn't know what to say, so I said nothing. I rifled through my dresser drawers in the moonlight and found a pair of underwear and a T-shirt. I followed him into the kitchen and flicked on the light.

Aw, shit.

The one area of my apartment that was furnished was a mess. Boxes of evidence were strewn about. Every surface of my kitchen and dining table were covered in grisly photos, bags of bloodied clothing, binders of notes.

Lying on the center of the table was my Dear Jeremy letter. I planned to mail it tomorrow, which might have been today.

"What is all this?" he asked.

"It's the case file from a double-murder. His name is Jeremy Jonus. He's a serial child killer."

Paulo's face was a mix of confusion and revulsion.

"Mark, is it healthy to keep all this stuff out like this? Your home is empty." He picked up Jonus' mugshot and held it close to his face. "You've been in Omaha for months."

I began stomping around the table, grabbing notes and photos, making neat little piles. "I'm very busy, Paulo, trying to crack this story," I lectured in my most important tone. "I need to get to the bottom of this. I need to know why he did what he did."

"Okay, you're the investigative reporter." He didn't believe it.

"And you're not my boyfriend."

I saw the words come out like a little balloon in the comics. I immediately tried to stuff it back into my mouth and swallow it down so I could shit out that idiot jumble of letters.

He sat the photo back down on the counter and grabbed his jacket as he headed for the door.

"I'm not sure I could compete with this guy anyway," he said, as he walked out into the hallway, toward the elevator. The door closed with a heavy thud behind him.

To be honest, at that moment, he couldn't compete with Jeremy Jonus. Nothing could. Rock Hudson's death had petrified me. And as much as I wanted a hot hookup, there was no avoiding the fear that came with it with the growing AIDS epidemic.

I needed Jonus.

If for no other reason than to take my mind away from the real world.

CHAPTER

7

MOVIN' ON UP

Once again, I found myself in the editing room at the crack of dawn. The Jonus case had burrowed into my thoughts. My quest to deliver a semblance of peace to the shattered families continued.

My fingers twisted the knob on the panel back and forth, fast-forwarding through the endless hours of recorded interviews. I was searching for a specific moment at around one minute and fifteen seconds. There it was—Sheriff Timmons. His face was etched with exhaustion and determination as he stared directly into the camera lens.

Offscreen, a question: "If the killer is out there watching, Sheriff, what would you say to him?"

The reporter's question hung in the air, a gauntlet dropped. Timmons, a man of few words, took a deep breath.

"I'd tell him he's a coward," he growled, his voice resonating with a raw anger that sent shivers down my spine. "It's easy to prey on little kids. It's easy to kill little kids. He should be a man and pick on someone his own size. Or better yet, turn himself in. To a church, a priest, or to me."

A sense of awe washed over me. He knew the killer was out there, watching his every move and he was determined to provoke him, to flush him out into the open. It was a daring gambit.

A knock on the door jolted me back to reality. I paused the videotape and emerged from the dimly lit editing room into the hallway. Carol stood waiting with a look of concern etched on her face.

"Hey, sorry to interrupt," she said. "But I need to talk to you. It's important."

I braced myself for the worst, my mind racing through a list of all the possible transgressions I might have committed. I had spoken to a few more witnesses who might have seen something suspicious on the days both boys disappeared. The possibilities were endless, and each one sent a wave of anxiety coursing through my veins.

As we entered Carol's office, her expression softened, the tension in her shoulders easing. She closed the door behind us. She removed her glasses and rubbed her eyes. Then Carol dropped the bombshell.

"Bob is leaving the station," she announced, her voice rising from a whisper. "He's going into advertising and PR. We haven't announced anything yet, but we've known it was coming for a while." She smiled, but I could tell this had weighed on her.

My stomach did a flip. Bob, the veteran anchor, was leaving. It would be a blow to the morale of the newsroom.

"I'm sorry to hear that. Bob's a good anchor."

Carol nodded sympathetically. "He's a *very* good anchor," she acknowledged, "But this is the nature of the business. An anchor goes and I have to fill those shoes before the viewers change the channel."

"Do you have any candidates in mind?"

Carol was ahead of me. "Three: two really strong anchors. One is from Atlanta, one from Cleveland, and you."

My jaw dropped, my mind struggling to process the information. This was too good to be true.

"Me? For main anchor?" I tried to play it cool. It wasn't working.

Carol's expression softened. "The logical play is to bring in someone with experience," she explained. "Get you more reps on the set and then have this discussion again in the future."

I smiled.

"Whatever you think is best, Carol, I fully support." I meant it too.

Carol paused, well aware she buried the lede.

"Then we held some focus groups. They want you."

I was baffled.

"Your field reporting has been outstanding. People are connecting with you, they believe you care about the community, and more importantly, they like you," she said, opening the file and looking down at what appeared to be statistics. "Your Q rating is through the roof."

"My Q rating?"

"It's a measurement of perceived familiarity and appeal to the viewer," she said in a professorial manner. "The higher the Q score, the more they hold you in high regard."

I knew there were Nielsen ratings, which was the percentage of households watching a particular show, but I had no idea individuals were ranked.

"Is this common?" I asked her. "I've never heard of it."

"We don't make any serious decisions without research," she said. "We've done the research and, well, *vox populi*. They want you to be our next main anchorman."

I sat in silence, taking it all in.

"What got you over the finish line was the special report on Rock Hudson," she said, again looking down at her stats. "We played it in each of the focus groups, and the respondents were blown away."

I wanted to sit on my hands. I had no clue how to behave. I managed a strange grin.

"Even though you are only twenty-two, Omaha wants you. You're doing me no good toiling back there." She waved a hand out to indicate my bunker. "I need you front and center."

I beamed while being completely in shock.

"Do you want it?" She sat up like an anchorman and riffled through her pages, finding the one she needed. She slid it across the blotter of her desk.

It was an offer letter, like the one she presented at the Omaha Press Club.

"Of course. It's all I ever wanted."

"Great." She was smiling. Her posture was lightening.

"Do I have to drop the Jonus story? I have been working pretty hard on it."

"No. Just deliver."

She opened a folder and began poring over the details.

"Three-year deal," she said. "Double your current salary, increases each year, clothing allowance, bonuses contingent upon the ratings."

I was nonplussed.

"Thank you," I said. "This is truly an honor, Carol."

She handed me the folder. I looked over the legalese.

"Just one request, Carol. If I get an offer for an anchor job in Atlanta, you'll agree to let me out of the contract to take it. There's only one other place I'd rather be than here, and that's Atlanta. It's where my family is."

She put out her hand and I gave her the folder. Just like at the Omaha Press Club, she made an addendum: *Atlanta only out*, she wrote in block letters.

"Done," she said. "At some point, we all want to go home."

She stood and extended her hand. We shook. It was done.

Her expression became businesslike again. She opened her calendar and spoke in a monotone.

"Okay. I'll set up the promo shoot for this Friday," she said. "The promotions department will get with you on wardrobe." She was like the director of a feature film. "I'm thinking you on a tractor in a hay field. It'll make you look and feel more Nebraskan."

"I used to haul hay back home," I bragged.

"Great, she said. "Authenticity is important in promotions."

That made my stomach flutter, but I was too excited for it to matter.

"And speaking of promotions, the station is switching affiliations. NBC has effectively dropped us, but we're being picked up by CBS," she told me. "And they are taking it seriously. They're paying to fly you to New York to do promos with Dan Rather."

My jaw hit the floor.

"Dan Rather? Are you kidding me?" I sounded like a kid who was told to pick out all the toys he wanted.

"Yes. I want you to go up to New York next week and bring home a behind-the-scenes series on CBS. We'll play it all up as you take the main anchor chair."

She had one more bomb to drop.

"And, we're also going to take a chance on a new talk show. Have you ever heard of Oprah Winfrey?"

It was clear I hadn't.

"There's talk that she could be the next Phil Donahue. Or bigger. She'll be coming to Omaha next month," she said. "I want you to introduce her at the Orpheum Theater."

The good news washed over me like a tidal wave.

"This is a dream come true."

She smiled in a motherly way.

"Just one more thing," she said. "Can you tell the *World Herald* you're twenty-three?"

I started laughing. She joined in, but I could tell she was serious. She was sticking her neck out for me. At twenty-two, an anchorman, the youngest in the city's history. Maybe any city's history.

"Daryl Strawberry was hitting home runs in the majors at twenty-one. I think the *Omaha World Herald* can deal with me hitting them here at twenty-two."

A couple nights later, my living room now furnished thanks to a couple phone calls to area furniture stores, I had Paulo over to celebrate.

We sat on my new couch enjoying a glass of wine as we looked out the windows. He was tired from a long day at the hospital but kept his game face as I talked on and on about what happened.

I winked at him. "You're stuck with me for another three years," I purred.

"Three more years in the shadows," he sighed. He broke into a smile. "I can't wait!"

Brazilians are incapable of sarcasm. They are emotional and honest, their hearts always on their sleeves.

I bounded up from the sofa. I grabbed his hand, but he wasn't getting up.

"I'll make it worth your while."

He set his glass down on the coffee table and followed behind me, hand in hand.

"The only shadow I want to see is from you naked in the moonlight."

I sat on the bed and pulled him toward me, leading him to join me. As he laid down, he saw the copy of the *Omaha World Herald* on my nightstand. I had made it above the fold: "22-Year-Old Anchorman to Lead KN2-TV."

We celebrated together until the middle of the night, eventually falling asleep.

A few days later, I was atop a tractor dressed in an "Omaha tuxedo," a red and blue flannel shirt, in the middle of a hayfield they rented for the promo shoot.

There was a small crew running around, listening to the promotions manager give orders from a clipboard held by an assistant. They were efficient and organized, having done this many times a year.

She yelled up to me in a monotone, "Okay, this is looking good. Just unbutton the top button of your shirt."

It struck me as odd. She knows what's best, so I did what she asked.

"Unbutton the next one too. It's still a little tight at the top of your chest."

"How's that?" I asked. She was looking at me intently, thinking.

"Maybe the camera will register a little sweat." She looked around at the goings on. "Does anyone have a spray bottle?" She waited for a response, which never came.

I unbuttoned the next one down and wriggled my shoulders to loosen my new shirt.

Coming from a small town and a Southern Baptist upbringing, flaunting one's skin and body was frowned upon. But when we were out in the Georgia hayfield, shirts only added to the pain of picking up and slinging the hay bales up on the tractor bed.

I remembered back home and those sweltering summers in the field with my best friend. He was developing into full manhood. I'd watch his pecs expand and contract, the sweat like glitter over his tan body. I ached to touch him. I wanted to taste his sweat.

I tried my best to suppress these sinful thoughts. Desires of the flesh were a one-way ticket to Hell.

What if my reaction was normal? We're all sexual beings. It doesn't make you evil. Hiding them made you miserable, I was learning.

"Hey, you up there!" she yelled, waking me from my reverie.

The shoot went smoothly from then on.

A few weeks later, Paulo and I were hunkered down in front of a Big Fred's pizza. It had every meat you could think of. It's still my favorite pizza joint. I scarfed my two pieces down and mumbled something about an extra hour at the gym. I patted my stomach and got up, moving over to the couch in front of my television. I looked to find Paulo. He was shirtless in the kitchen, washing dishes. Credit to Big Fred, but Paulo was tastier and a lot more satisfying.

Suddenly, some quiet horns played a languorous America-themed fanfare.

"Through the years we've been like special friends, making memories that never end…" began the jingle, sung in a choral fashion of mostly female voices.

I grabbed the paperback-sized remote control.

"Here it is, baby! My new promo. Come watch it!"

Paulo turned the water off and ran over, wiping his hands on a dishcloth as he stood nearby. He whipped it over his shoulder, creating a domestic aiguillette. His hands were on his hips.

There I was, behind the wheel of a tractor in the golden Nebraska sunshine in my red and blue flannel shirt.

"Through the years you've turned and found us there…" it continued.

"Two thanks you, for the good times, together!"

Then, a booming voice.

"Watch your friend Mark Pettit, weeknights at six and ten, on KN2-TV."

I watched with a beatific look on my face, throughout all the corn.

"What do you think?" I asked.

He sat down next to me, eyeing me like I was a poker cheat.

"Did you like it?" My eyes were wide and my smile was broad, my mouth slightly open in anticipation as I nodded.

Paulo burst out laughing. It was a full-body convulsion. Howling and kicking his muscular legs out, he laughed and laughed as my balloon slowly deflated.

"That's the gayest thing I've ever seen, Mark! That's supposed to make you look straight?"

"No," I whimpered. "It's supposed to be Nebraskan."

That made him laugh harder. He was wiping a tear from his eye as he tried to catch his breath. He quieted down then let out a guttural grunt of suppressed laughter. He caught himself.

"It was Carol's idea, not mine." I clicked the television off with a sharp flick and tossed the remote aside.

He put his arm around me. His voice was soothing.

"It's all for show and ratings. I get it. I'm really proud of you. This is a very big deal and I understand it."

"Thank you," I said.

He gently kissed my lips. He began speaking between kisses.

"You'll have a voice now, right? You'll get a say on what gets on the news?"

Still full of myself despite Paulo's reaction, I bragged, "Yeah! I'll be right there in the editorial meetings with Carol."

Paulo grabbed my shoulders and shook me once. His face was alight.

"That's incredible, baby," he said. "Just think about all the good you can do. You can stop doing these pointless crime stories and actually report on real news. Like the AIDS crisis."

I stiffened and pulled back from him.

"It's never on the news. Anywhere. You've been given such an amazing opportunity," he said.

I started to backtrack from my earlier bravado. "I don't have editorial control. The broadcast is broken down into a summary of the national and local news. There's sports, weather. There're other reporters too. Stories like that have to be signed off on by Carol."

His speech became more rapid, he started gesticulating.

"That's perfect! She'll listen to you. I mean look at what you've already done for that station. They were in dead last and now people are buzzing."

My head was buzzing as I hung it down.

"Sure."

"Someone has to report about it. It's the biggest thing happening in this country," he said, his Brazilian rising. "But because it's happening to us, the mainstream is allowed to ignore it. Well, now one of us is in the mainstream."

One of us. I just became an anchorman. Now I am supposed to carry The Cause on my shoulders? They began to knot.

Paulo got up and marched over to the dining room table. He picked up Jeremy Jonus' mugshot.

"At the very least, you're done with this," he said.

"Why do you keep bringing him up?"

"It doesn't matter." He set the photo down, nervously wringing the dish towel. "I'm not your boyfriend anyway." He turned and went back into the kitchen where he puttered aimlessly.

I watched him. His body was beautiful. He was a gorgeous, caring man who always spoke his mind.

"Do you want to be?"

He stopped and stood up straight, his back to me. He didn't turn immediately. I supposed he was wondering if he heard right.

He turned with a hopeful smile on his face.

"What?" His eyes glistened.

"Do you want to be my boyfriend? I've never had one before, and honestly, I don't know what it means," I said, still high from all the excitement. "I just know I love being with you."

"Of course, I do," he said, running over to me.

We embraced, his arms rocking me back and forth.

This time, I held us apart.

"We just can't tell anyone," I warned him again. My eyes were serious.

"Understood."

I looked into his big brown eyes. From behind them, I could see the synapses flaring. He was thinking, *Half a loaf is better than none.*

But not by much.

BE A MAN, LIKE DAN

Reporters are expected to maintain a dispassionate demeanor and simply report the news. Edward R. Murrow standing on a rooftop during the London Blitz, entrancing radio listeners in a placid, cigarette-tinged baritone, is still considered the gold standard. That's our job. It is expected. Walter Cronkite swallowing hard while telling the nation JFK died, or, most famously, Herbert Morrison wailing, "Oh, the humanity!" as the Hindenburg burned are deeply etched into our collective memory. They are the exceptions which prove the rule.

January 28, 1986, is a date I will never forget. It was my first day as the main anchorman at KN2-TV.

Coincidentally, I was in a journalism class when my pager went off. 911. It was code for CALL THE STATION IMMEDIATELY. I knew something terrible had happened.

Carol answered on the second ring. "The space shuttle just blew up. Get here as fast as you can."

Shit.

I bolted out of my seat, jamming my notebook and other stuff into my bag. The distraction stopped my professor, who looked at me.

"I have to leave," I said. "To report the news."

"Knock 'em dead." Like stage actors, we're a superstitious lot, always avoiding good wishes.

The station is only about a fifteen-minute drive from UNO. I think I made it in ten. I rushed through the lobby into the newsroom. Carol leaned out from her door and called me in. Her face was hard from stress. It was barely lunchtime and it was going to be a long day for us.

"This is a moment in history that people will never forget. They're going to remember where they were when they got the news. And tonight, people are going to watch you on the news, and you need to know what you're talking about. Follow me," she said.

I followed her to one of our small editing rooms, where Dan Rather was doing a live feed to CBS stations across the country.

"Sit down and watch him," Carol instructed. "Learn everything you can about what happened this morning. About NASA, about space. You are our Dan Rather now."

An hour later, someone from the university delivered a model of the space shuttle that we placed on set as we reported the news and talked to local experts. Things went better than I expected, thanks to Carol and thanks to Dan Rather.

After we signed off, I taped a couple of promos for the ten o'clock show and then walked back into the newsroom. One of the camera guys, a smart ass with a wicked sense of humor said, "Hey, Pettit, do you know where Christa McAuliffe is spending her vacation?"

I looked at him with a blank stare.

"All over the coast of Florida," he said with a laugh.

Other members of the news team laughed awkwardly.

I didn't think it was funny, but I understood that's how news people deal with death and destruction. They try to make light of it, or distance themselves from it. It can be easy for any of us to find ourselves in a dark place otherwise.

Maybe I was still stinging from the Rock Hudson incident.

I remember back, about four months ago, Paulo and I were sitting in bed. I brought up the bar from that evening.

"Mark, I see this all the time at the hospital. Tell a man he has stage 4 cancer, and the family all starts laughing. They don't know what else to do. Doctors are the same way. Gallows humor. That's what happened at the bar. People were confused. The bartender gave them a direction. It wasn't personal. It is just a herd mentality. Left to their own thoughts, they don't think that way."

I'm not sure I bought it, my nerves were still raw, but Paulo's bedside manner relaxed me.

I've learned from experience that covering horrific events takes a unique combination of empathy and disassociation.

Look at the way reporters and anchors cover modern-day atrocities like the recent massacres in Israel. Seeing that level of depravity up close cuts to the soul of any human being, even jaded journalists. It was difficult to watch Anderson Cooper report on babies being beheaded, knowing he has two little boys of his own. More than once, Cooper's voice cracked and he choked back tears as he spoke to relatives of those slaughtered. It was like I could feel the pain through the TV screen as I watched Dana Bash anchoring the coverage.

"As a mother and a member of the community, this is horrific," she said. "We haven't seen atrocities like this perpetrated on Jewish people since the Holocaust."

I broke while covering difficult stories. In Omaha, Mayor Bernie Simon died on Friday, April 15, 1988, after a year-long battle with cancer. We had been covering the story non-stop and I hadn't gotten much sleep. I was co-hosting our Sunday morning news magazine show and was interviewing the mayor's priest.

"Ask him about the dream," my producer, Carrie Schultz Murphy, whispered through my earpiece—the IFB, Interruptible Fold Back, in case you were wondering—as the priest was finishing a sentence.

"Father, can you tell us about the dream?" I asked him on command.

"Oh, dear God!" he exclaimed. "I dreamed that I saw Bernie walking in Heaven! And, as soon as I awoke, I looked at the clock and it was four thirty a.m. Exactly the time Bernie passed."

I burst into tears.

I'm not sure what caused it. Maybe exhaustion. Maybe it was because I liked Bernie. And I didn't let a few wet drops fall, these were heaving sobs that I couldn't control. My co-anchor realized I couldn't continue and tossed to commercial break. I apologized to the crew and left the studio. I simply couldn't go on.

A year earlier, March 6, 1987, Nebraska senator Ed Zorinsky died of a heart attack while performing a song and dance number at the annual Omaha Press Club Ball. Senator Zorinsky was making fun of himself during the routine, playfully threatening to once again switch parties as he had done in 1976, when he bolted from the Republican to the Democratic party.

My co-anchor and I were at the black-tie event when Zorinsky collapsed. As paramedics rushed to his aid, I ran over to try and get a closer look at the senator to see what was wrong. They quickly placed him on a gurney and, as he was wheeled by me, I looked over at him. I can still see his face, a deep ashen color. I knew something was wrong and a few minutes later, another high-profile politician walked up to me and said, "He's gone."

We did the newscast live from the venue that night, still dressed in our formal attire. Initially, we couldn't report what we knew, that the senator was dead. We had to wait for official confirmation from the hospital, which happened an hour and a half after our newscast began.

When the newscast was over, I went home and cried.

Just not on camera this time.

So much for the tough guy, huh?

9

START SPREADING THE NEWS

hadn't mentioned it to Carol, but I'd never been to New York City. Hell, my only air miles were round-trip from Chattanooga to Omaha for my interview. I boarded the flight from Omaha, excited to see what all the fuss was about in this place they called the Big Apple.

As the plane circled LaGuardia, I looked out my window at all the skyscrapers and shook my head in disbelief. Like they say, *It is just like the movies.* That small island, crammed with skyscrapers. I can't believe it hasn't sunk.

This was all happening to me, an as-of-yet high school graduate from Calhoun.

Calhoun taught me that a college degree didn't matter. Hard work did. Keep your promises, tell the truth. I tried to practice all three.

In my teens, I often accompanied my mother to her job, a poor man's "Take Your Child to Work" day, if you will. It was a big, noisy factory whose machinery looked like something out of Rube Goldberg, with its giant spools of colored yarns and rolls of carpeting being pulled.

She was a mender in the carpet mill. It was her job to find any flaws as the unfinished rolls were fed toward a machine that applied the border. As the rugs came off the huge machine, she'd look for rips or tears. Finding one, she'd lift this machine, which looked like the unholy union of a jackhammer and a crochet hook. I can still hear the cacophonous rat-a-tat-tat of the mending gun. It was difficult work, requiring both physical strength and a surgeon's dexterity.

I felt sorry for her. She'd watch with intense concentration then, she'd turn and lift the gun with her sinewy arms, ropy from the constant exertion. Sometimes, she'd hand the gun over to me. I'd shake and wobble as I tried to maintain control.

Come Christmas, she gathered us around the kitchen table and presented a little gift guide from the plant. The mill rewarded its employees with their choice of one of the items showcased in their colorful brochure. They were all utilitarian: an iron, a crockpot, things of that ilk. Every year, she brought the guide home for me and my little brother, Jeff.

"Pick whatever you boys want," she said. She smiled a tired smile. In Calhoun, everyone's parents were tired.

We'd rush over like pigs to the trough, yelling, *Oh, boy!* and flipping through the pages, arguing like Clarence Darrow as to why our pick was the correct one.

My mother's eye caught something, a lime green Hoover Dial-A-Matic vacuum cleaner, which she pointed to.

"It's pretty," she said.

Nope. We always went for something like a four-band transistor radio (it picked up television stations!) or an Eveready camping flashlight. Anything which could be used in our ramshackle leftover plywood fort.

I am still racked with guilt.

Mama taught me the value of hard work. Watching her toil her life away at the mill stoked a fire in my belly. I had to get out of town.

And television was my escape. Anyone who grew up in the sixties and seventies would tell you the same. There was a whole wide world available through that little box.

I was an odd duck. I didn't want to be Napoleon Solo or Steve Austin. Every night at six thirty, I'd stare rapt as Chancellor, Cronkite and Brinkley sat in their reserved suits and ties and reported the news.

I had to get an education. I was going to become an anchorman.

My stomach hit my throat as we glided over the green water of Flushing Bay and did a bump-de-bump on the runway. The inertia from the wing flaps braking the plane pushed me into the back of my seat.

"Welcome to New York City LaGuardia Airport. It is ten fifty-five local time. Please…" I relaxed as the flight attendant relayed her information. "We're now on Eastern Time, so please adjust your watches accordingly. We hope you've enjoyed your flight today and wish you a great stay here in New York or wherever your final destination might be."

Thirty years later, it's the same old spiel.

Despite everyone being told to remain in their seats until taxiing was completed, I joined the others in unbuckling and grabbing my belongings. Avoiding elbows and rear ends, I reached below and retrieved my trusty Samsonite attaché. Television didn't just provide me with a profession, it also taught me how to look professional. I bought that sucker when I was still begging Earl for a job in Chattanooga, and I carried it like it was cast in gold.

The airline, in a loving tribute to Nebraska, herded us like cattle and led us up the runway to the gate. It didn't matter, I could feel the excitement building. New York City!

And soon, I'd be meeting Dan Rather.

Or so I thought.

I stood in the middle of the airport chaos, looking for my baggage claim. There were signs for everything but where I needed to go. LaGuardia is too small an airport and it is built like a maze. I stood at the gate as people behind me bumped me with their carry-on bags.

Throughout the tumult, I heard a young boy's voice.

"Mark Pettit! Mark Pettit! KN2-TV!"

It is an odd feeling to be minding your own business in an airport and hear your name, let alone hear it shouted. I was shocked anyone in New York would recognize me.

I turned toward the voice and saw a towheaded boy, about eleven or twelve, pulling his mother's hand my way. I stopped as they approached.

"I'm so sorry to bother you, Mr. Pettit," she said. "But Scott just had to meet you."

The boy's face was lit up like Rockefeller Center at Christmas as he reached to shake my hand.

"I watch you on the news all the time," he said. "Someday, I'm going to be a reporter, just like you."

He was sweet. What a pleasant surprise. And, just like me, he found his dream on the television.

He handed me his boarding pass and asked, "Could I please have your autograph?"

I stumbled forward as another passenger hit me. I figured it would be best to move away from the gate.

"Come over here," I told them. "Let me grab a pen out of my briefcase."

The boy beamed.

I popped open my trusty Samsonite and grabbed a pen from a pocket inside the case. I then took the boy's boarding pass. Not quite sure what to say.

I wrote: *To Scott, Good News Always*, and signed my name.

It's how I sign books today.

"Thank you, Mr. Pettit," the boy said.

"Please, just call me Mark," I told him. "And thank you for watching KN2-TV. I'll be seeing a lot more of you soon. I take over the main anchor job next week."

His mother smiled.

"Then you need to become an anchorman someday, Scotty," she said. "Just like Mr. Mark."

I thanked them both, turned and made my way to the escalator, down the stairs to the baggage claim where I retrieved my overnight bag.

I've seen New York in a million movies, but nothing prepares you for how slowly you move in a taxi. I forgot about editing. After what seemed like an hour, the taxi pulled up outside the famous building I had only seen on TV and in photos.

The CBS Broadcast Center.

The famous eye greeted me. And, just like in the movies, I exited the cab and looked up to the top of the skyscraper.

This was the Holy Grail of TV News, and I was about to enter its kingdom. I shook off my nerves and headed into the building and toward the security station.

"Mark Pettit. KN2-TV News in Omaha," I told the guard. "I'm here to meet with Dan Rather," I said proudly.

Nothing impresses a New Yorker. Without looking up, he said, "I'll need to check on that," as he tapped three numbers on his phone.

"Ms. Holiman will be right down to get you," he said. "Wait over there by the elevator."

I sat with my Samsonite on my lap, looking around. Five minutes passed and then my energetic escort bounded over from the elevator.

"Hi, Liz Holiman," she said, "Welcome to CBS. I'm in the PR department here at the network."

I shook her hand and said, "Thank you. It's an honor to be here and to meet Mr. Rather," I said.

I barely finished my sentence when she started. "Yeah. About that," she said. "This is really going to be an in-and-out thing. He's really busy. We're going to pull him aside for a grip and grin."

Since I hadn't begun my reply around the word "grip," she picked up the slack as we hightailed it to the elevators.

"You know, photos of you two like you've known each other for years," she said, rolling her eyes. "Or in your case, since you were born."

I brushed off her New York charms.

"My news director is expecting me to come back with a behind the scenes look at CBS News," I told her.

As the elevator doors closed, she said, "Yeah, that's not going to happen, sweetheart."

I watched the light above the doors *blink, blink, blink*, as we ascended into the rarified air of CBS News.

The doors opened and we stepped into the whirlwind of the newsroom. It was like KN2, but on a higher level (literally). Typewriters clacking, people racing about, newsfeeds coming in from around the world.

And then, there he was, in the flesh: Dan Rather. He was taller than I imagined. Television gives no sense of scale. He was elegant and far better looking than he appeared when made up for broadcast. He huddled among what I guessed to be the broadcast producers.

"We're going to try to get him over here by the CBS eye," she said. "Our staff photographer will come over and get a couple of shots of you two together."

She made a beeline for the group and placed her hand gently on Rather's elbow. He turned and faced her.

"Sorry to bother you, Mr. Rather," she said, "It's a guy from our new affiliate in Omaha. We just need a couple of photos of you with him to promote their local news and our show."

The meeting stopped. Rather walked from the glass room.

"What's his name?" I heard him say. There was less diaphragm in his ordinary voice.

"Mark. Petite, I believe it is," she answered.

He approached me with a broad smile and an extended hand.

"Hello. It's Mark, right? Petite?" he asked.

"Actually, it's Pettit," I replied with my best southern manners. "Mark Pettit, KN2-TV News in Omaha. Nice to meet you, Mr. Rather. It's a true honor."

He held a hand up. "Please, call me Dan." I wondered if he said that to everyone. "I hear you're up from Omaha. That's a very important market to us."

You never get used to meeting famous people. You see them in magazines or on TV and they are real but unreal. Suddenly, they are in front of you, speaking to you. I idolized Dan Rather. I remember him at an event in Houston, his home turf. President Nixon was fielding questions.

"Mr. President, Dan Rather, CBS News."

Nixon loathed the press. It was evident then and later proven when the tapes were released. A couple of jeers rose from the crowd. Nixon plastered on an ingratiating smile.

"Are you running for something?"

"No, sir, Mr. President. Are you?"

Here I was, toe-to-toe with the man. I tried to maintain my composure.

"So, how's it going so far? Your visit to CBS News?"

Remember the part about my mother teaching me to tell the truth?

"Actually, I have a problem," I said.

A perplexed look crossed his face.

"I get paid to fix problems, son," he said. "Tell me what's wrong."

He opened the door and I ran through it before he closed it.

"My news director sent me here to do promos with you and come back with a behind-the-scenes series of reports on CBS News," I told him. "Ms. Holiman said something about gripping and grinning and that would be it."

He scowled.

"Give me a minute, Mark," he said. "Liz, come with me," he said to her. She gave me a "threw me under the bus" look.

Back in the glass room, I heard their raised voices through the din of the newsroom. He returned, determined, with Liz in tow.

"I've cleared an hour on my schedule for a sit-down interview with you," he began. "You can ask me anything you want. I've called Ed Bradley up at *60 Minutes*, and he can make a half hour for you to interview him."

He turned to Liz.

"Assign two camera crews to Mark and have them light and shoot everything like it was going to air on the *CBS Evening News*."

I couldn't believe my ears.

"Follow me, Mark." Before I could react, he was already on his way to the newsroom. I grabbed my attaché and hightailed it over to him. We went down the hallway through two oversized metal doors.

And there it was.

It was a news set the likes of which I had never seen. It was two stories high and brightly lit. I looked at the anchor desk with its bas relief Mercator projection.

"This is the new home of CBS News," Dan said. "You're one of the only people outside the network to see it. We'll set up in here for our one-on-one interview. Then we'll shoot promos to air back on your station."

He was proud. You forget he was once a rookie too. He didn't forget.

Jackpot! It was like hitting the trifecta at Ak-Sar-Ben back in Omaha.

It was an incredible experience interviewing him. He made it easy. It was like talking with a buddy. We covered Vietnam, Nixon, his being attacked at the Democratic National Convention in '68 and Mayor Daley. I was in fucking news heaven!

The interview ended. The lights went down and the crew went about their job.

"I want you to go back to Omaha and do great work. Tell good stories. That's what it's all about. And who knows, someday you might be back up here working with me."

Jesus could have called me home at that very moment and I would have died a happy boy.

An hour later, I was sitting across from Ed Bradley in his elegantly decorated office. He had photos of himself with world leaders and pieces of beautiful African art. He was a kind, gentle man, who spoke softly and sincerely.

"Who has been your favorite person ever to interview on *60 Minutes*?" I asked, interviewing him like a reporter from the *New York Times* or *Rolling Stone*.

"Oh, no question, Lena Horne," he said without a pause. "One of the sweetest, toughest ladies I've ever met. I'd put her right up there with Margaret Thatcher."

Mind you, I was twenty-two. I am on my second interview of the day with two old pros who put serious numbers on the board. And I am being spoken to like an old friend and a real reporter.

Like an anchorman.

I landed in Omaha with enough footage for a three-part series on our evening news. KN2 promoted the hell out of it, especially as we needed to impress upon Omaha that we were CBS now.

That series was the highlight of my burgeoning career. I had been to the Promised Land and returned with angel wings.

Carol was as proud as the NBC peacock that had kicked our little station to the curb for our crosstown rival, whom I'm sure thought would dominate the ratings.

"Excellent work," she said after the third report aired.

"How did you get them to give you that kind of access?" she asked. "We didn't even know they were switching to that new fancy studio. And, one-on-one with Ed Bradley? You understand what a big deal that was?"

I shook my head in agreement.

I recounted the day's events. Carol was amazed.

"Forget what I said about Tom Brokaw," she said with a proud smile. "You're going to be the next Dan Rather."

From her lips to God's ears.

10

GONNA BE A BIG STAR

Oprah Winfrey.

I had never heard her name until Carol said it.

Her story is old hat now. Back in 1984, Oprah got her big break in Chicago. WLS-TV hired her for its show in dead last called *A.M. Chicago*. Within a month, it was number one in its slot. The station execs renamed the program *The Oprah Winfrey Show*.

Starting in September of 1986, everyone would know her name. She was already an Oscar®-nominated actress.

Paulo and I walked around Standing Bear Lake on the outskirts of Omaha.

"She's amazing," I gushed.

It was early September, a magical time in Nebraska. The sky was bright blue and there was a hint of chill in the air. Soon, there would be snow around the lake, but for now it was picture perfect.

Just like Paulo.

I danced around and began walking backwards to face Paulo as I became Oprah's official biographer.

"She grew up dirt poor. Then she was molested and had a baby at fourteen. By nineteen, she was anchoring the news in Tennessee. She moved to Chicago and now she's going national. Carol said she's going to be a big star."

Paulo watched me, bemused, as we rounded a bend behind a blanket of trees. He grasped my hands.

"You're going to be a big star, too, baby."

I could feel the old paranoia rise up inside me. I wanted to let go, but I couldn't. I pulled him close to me, trying not to be caught looking around. I kissed him. I kissed him slowly and deeply. His lips were succulent and I loved gently biting them. He had told me before that no one had kissed him like I did and how it excited him when I nibbled at his lips.

I ran my hand up his shirt and felt his firm chest. His sigh made me crave more. I pushed him against a tree and began mouthing his taut stomach. I lingered on his chest. I smelled wood and berries.

The smell rose from the lake or was it a reminder of our morning shower where I lathered him with his grandmother's soap. I worked more of his chest, savoring it. My hand slid down his jeans and stopped on his belt buckle.

I came to my senses. We couldn't have been alone at the lake. I tugged the waistband of my jeans to adjust myself and released him from my grip.

"You're going to get it later."

"Big talker, Betty Stocker." A bit of the Brazilian tripped him up.

"Big talker, Betty Crocker," I said. "Get it right, boy." We laughed. Our happiness echoed over the lake.

He hit me with that paralyzing stare. It was my Kryptonite. I'd have signed over everything I owned at that moment. My heart zoomed up and down my chest, getting caught in a net of conflicted feelings. I was in love. I wanted us to be together forever.

After Luke, I was damaged.

I wasn't going to make that mistake again.

I kissed Paulo and said nothing.

At home, it was bliss. Paulo was the best. He was intelligent and I'd lose myself listening to him discuss his work.

"We are trying to isolate the virus. We want to attack it, before it attacks the CD4 cells," he told me.

"CD what?" I asked.

"CD4. They're the white blood cells that protect our bodies from infection," he said, explaining things to me with the precision of a college professor. "If HIV gets to the CD4s first, it's like a multiplying effect, spreading the virus throughout your body. Once that happens, it most often leads to full-blown AIDS."

Full-blown AIDS. You heard that a lot now and it scared the shit out of me. I thought about Rock Hudson, barely dead a year.

Paulo was so passionate. It was one of the reasons I loved him so. Brazilians ooze passion.

And it was a relief to listen to him. After twelve hours in the newsroom, asking me to carry on a conversation was like asking a cab driver to go for a ride.

Paulo. There he was, stretched out on the couch, his feet in my lap. He'd tell me about the hospital, his life in Brazil. It was magical.

Maybe we were getting a little careless, but we started exploring Omaha together.

Thus, our trip to the lake that early September morning.

"Carol wants me to introduce Oprah next week when she comes to the Orpheum Theater," I told him as we headed through the batch of trees back into the open trail around the lake. "She's doing a tour across the country to launch her show."

He listened to me with that smile on his face. It was amusing to him, watching me go crazy over this.

I stopped.

"I want you to go with me. Well, not with me." He tilted his head and squinted. "I want you to be there. Carol says I can bring a guest," I told him. "I want you to be my guest." I smiled.

"You're inviting me to something so public?" he said with a quizzical look on his face. "That theater holds a couple of thousand people."

"It'll be a memory, the two of us. And Oprah. I'd love you to experience it with me."

Paulo smiled, his teeth sparkling in the autumn sunshine. "Sure. I'd love it."

I had another trick up my sleeve.

"I'm going to rent us tuxedos. We'll go today and try some on." My hand reached for his.

No, I thought. Someone might see us.

Later, we were at Omaha's famous men's store, Halsted's. It was downtown's best haberdashery. It looked like something out of the Roaring Twenties, with green baize and rich wooden shelves and glass counters. I watched Paulo, I loved watching him, as he caressed the fabrics. That caress meant so much to me. He pushed a few hangers to the side and stopped on a plastic divider that read "40R."

"That's my size too," I said.

We held up the first two options against our chests.

"I love navy blue. What do you think?" he asked.

I scrunched my face.

"Navy is nice, but I think we should go more formal. Black, like we're hitting the theater in New York."

Paulo smiled. "I can't wait to go to a Broadway show with you."

Our spell was broken by an *ahem*. A salesman stood behind us with a look of suspicion on his face. His attire was bespoken with all the little details filled in. I found his cufflinks, lapis lazuli and silver, to be ostentatious, but no one asked me. His cologne was an eye-watering sandalwood, oily, like his demeanor.

"And which one of you is the groom?" "Groom" had six ohs in it, each oh inflected higher than the last. He finished with an "mmm," like a soup ad.

Paulo and I became an Abbott & Costello routine.

We pointed at each other.

"He is." We began to laugh. Paulo said, "I am." At the same time, I said it was me.

"Brothers or lovers?" he replied, lifting his nose in the air to further look down it.

"It's for a work function." I held up two fingers. "Two suits, forty regular, black," I commanded. "And the butler thing that goes over the stomach."

Pity I didn't have a piece of wheat sticking out of my mouth.

"It's called a cummerbund," he said with forced unctuousness. "I'll also show you some vests. You can mix and match, if you prefer."

He inhaled deeply and made a show of looking at our shoes and then working back up to our faces before he turned and left.

Paulo dug his chin into his neck and smirked. It made me giggle.

"It's clear he prefers you," he said.

Minutes passed. We smelled the salesman. He was arranging his choices on a felt-topped table with real Bananas Foster fanfare. We walked over. There were four options from which to choose.

I pointed at Paulo. "Start with him. He's our guinea pig."

"Oink, oink," Paulo snorted.

Paulo removed his T-shirt with a lack of self-consciousness which I always admired. His jeans hung just right at the hips. I wanted to devour him like a plate of biscuits and gravy.

Our salesman regarded Paulo like he was judging horseflesh. He placed his hand underneath his chin, I assume to show us he was thinking. The lightbulb popped above his head. He turned and handed Paulo a ventless black jacket in silk with shiny lapels.

"Let's try this without the shirt first so I can get a look at how it's going to fit around your chest and waist." Just at the end, very quietly, he murmured a *hmm*. Whether it was a question or a statement, I've no idea.

Paulo followed directions. The jacket fit him perfectly. He walked over to the trifold mirror, salesman in tow. Now I was looking at four Paulos, if only, while the salesman fussed over him, tugging at the back and pulling on the sleeves. He stroked both shoulders and patted the lapels.

The salesman turned Paulo to face him and took one step back. Again, the nose rose up and down.

"You must wear a vest," he bellowed like Caesar at the Globe. "It will accentuate your chest and hips."

I laughed to myself. Paulo could wear the proverbial Hefty bag and grace the cover of *GQ*.

"Are you Spanish?" he asked. "You bear the sepia palette of the Iberian."

I coughed once to hide my guffaw. Paulo had the advantage of understanding English literally.

"I'm Latin. From Brazil," trilling the ar with his uvula to mess with him. "São Paulo."

"*Delicioso*," he said, reaching over for a pair of slacks. "Do you want to try on the trousers out here or take them back to the dressing room?"

Paulo replied without hesitating, "The dressing room." He snatched the pants and walked away.

It was my turn. His attention was solely on me now.

"Let's get you out of that shirt and see what's what," he said, adding that little *hmm*.

Suddenly I was back at the pond in Calhoun, being told to strip down by an authority figure. I lifted my shirt off, lacking Paulo's grace. My shoulders turned inward, sinking my chest.

"Stand up straight," he admonished. He jostled me into the center of the trifold mirror.

"I think you might be a thirty-eight regular," he said. "Your friend's chest is a little more defined than yours." He went to the aisle to procure a jacket for me.

As the salesman returned with the coat, my mind drifted back to my days working for Jerry Mulkey at the Haberdasher, a men's clothing store in downtown Calhoun. Jerry was like a second father to me and had hired me as a part-time salesman my junior year in high school. Jerry taught me how to tie a tie and how to dress for success. His secret weapon in the store was Sansabelt slacks, which, as the name suggests, were dress slacks without a belt. They came in navy, black and even bright green. I think I had a pair in every color and am almost certain I was wearing a pair of Sansabelts the day Earl hired me in Chattanooga.

More than anything, Jerry taught me to be a better man. I loved Jerry's wife, Judy, too. Judy worked across the street at the Calhoun First National Bank and would stop off to see us on her lunch break or after work. Jerry would see her coming and tell whatever customer he was with at the time, "Come here and look at this beautiful girl coming across the street!" and, of course, it would be Judy.

Judy's mother, Jean Goble, taught me how to gift wrap presents and I loved working at the store during the holidays. I can still see us all huddled at the counter in the backroom of the store, listening to Christmas carols and competing for who could wrap the best present. Jean often won as she had a magical touch with corners, ribbons and bows.

Jerry was an incredible salesman. Often guys would come into the Haberdasher looking for one pair of pants and, because of Jerry, they'd leave with three. Mainly he made people feel good about themselves. Many times, I would stand near the front desk and watch him work his magic as clients came into the store.

"Well, hello there, Charlie!" Jerry said with genuine enthusiasm as a heavy-set gentleman walked in the door. "I haven't seen you in a month of Sundays. You're looking good my friend, have you lost some weight? I think you might be down to a forty slim," he'd say with a chuckle.

"It's *Henry*, Jerry," the man said, with a scowl. "How long have you known me now?"

Jerry had a knack for calling people by the wrong name, but often played it off as he was just aggravating them.

"Of course, *Henry*," Jerry would say. "I was just trying to get your goat."

Both men laughed it off as Jerry led the man to the latest

arrivals in the store. My sweet daydream of Jerry and the Haberdasher was interrupted by the snooty salesman.

"Uhh hmm," he said as if I were keeping him away from something more important.

Again with the tugging and pulling. His nails were buffed to a sheen equal to his cufflinks.

"Looks pretty good," he said. "I'm thinking thirty-two waist, maybe thirty-one," he said as he handed me the pants to try on. I stepped from in front of the mirror as Paulo returned.

The salesman fell to his knees like a nun at Lourdes, mumbling with pins in his mouth.

"It's formal, so no cuffs," he instructed. "Two pins here and that should do it," he said, finishing the fitting.

Paulo stepped from in front of the mirror as I walked into the stall around the corner to try on my pants. They fit well at the waist, causing me to breathe a sigh of relief. No more Husky jeans for me, I thought.

I walked back out and stepped in front of the mirror. The salesman repeated the same process on my pants.

"No cuffs. Two pins here, and we're done," he said.

"What about underwear?" he said, looking at Paulo. "Boxers or briefs?" he said, making me cringe.

"We've got plenty of underwear at home," I said. Then catching myself, "I mean, we don't need any underwear. Why don't you grab us some shirts and cufflinks?" giving him the brushoff. "Fifteen, maybe fifteen and a half."

"Spread or pinpoint? Silver or gold?"

"All of it," I said, catching Paulo's eyes in the three-perspective mirror as the salesman walked away.

"I love it!" he said. "You're jealous of him," he laughed.

"I am not." I said like I was in the schoolyard. "He's just weird. Let's get this over with and get home."

"*Relaxe querido*," he whispered. "*Eu sou todo seu.*"

I had no clue what he said.

"I said, *Relax baby. I'm all yours.*"

Portuguese, it got me every time.

And honestly, I don't think I was jealous of the snooty salesman. I think I was scared of him. I could tell he knew that Paulo and I were much more than friends. As guys used to respond back in Calhoun when someone called them "queer"—"It takes one to know one." I knew that the salesman knew about me, and it frightened me. I didn't want anyone knowing my secret. He had gotten too close for comfort.

"Here you go, gentlemen," he said from an aisle over as he returned with the shirts and cufflinks. I think fifteen and a half should do for both of you,'" he said. "And I think you should wear these matching silver cufflinks."

His lips pursed and stretched into a thin smile.

"You know, they say couples start to look like each other the longer they're together. They can often wear the same clothes," he continued. "Cuts the wardrobe expenses down by half." Oh, did he slay himself. I was shocked he didn't slap his knee.

I held up my credit card between two fingers in keeping with the ostentation.

"We're ready to go now."

"Of course, sir." He paused, inhaling as he lifted his nose up. "You look really familiar." He read the name on my card to help himself along.

Paulo, that sweet puppy, said, "He's on the news. He's going to be a really big star."

"He'll need to be, to keep up with you," the salesman said as he walked away with my credit card.

"You didn't have to tell him that," I whispered to Paulo.

He hit me in the chest playfully with the back of his hand.

"Your face is going to be on billboards all over the city in a few weeks. You better get used to people recognizing you."

A feeling of dread came over me. Fame. People. Recognition. Everything I wanted in this profession. Each success in TV news was another bar in my personal prison. I ignored my thoughts. I still needed to get out of this sartorial slammer.

"Enjoy your wedding," the salesman interrupted. "These will be due back next Saturday," he said, handing us the flimsy plastic garment bags with the Halsted's logo holding our rentals.

It was Wednesday, the big night. Paulo and I dressed in the bathroom, helping each other out.

"Every man is handsome in a tuxedo," Paulo said to himself in a singsong voice. He stepped behind me to fasten my clip-on bow tie. He pecked my cheek. "Especially my man."

I reddened as I watched him lift my collar. He clicked the tie in place.

His hands worked their way down my neck and shoulders, landing on my ass. He clenched it tightly and growled, "And I love that ass in these pants."

"*Eu quero te comer*," he whispered in my ear.

"English, please!" I replied with a hint of frustration.

"I want to eat you up," he said. "Like Big Fred's Pizza."

We both laughed.

"We gotta get out of here," I told him. "Miss Oprah Winfrey's plane should be landing any minute," I said. "She's coming straight to the theater."

Paulo finger combed his already perfect hair, and we were ready.

I looked at us in the mirror and wished we were headed to our wedding.

We sat in my BMW waiting in a line of cars for the valet. All of Omaha seemed to turn out for this. There were lines down the block with people eager to get in. We opened our doors. The valet handed me a ticket.

It was electric outside. Every station in Omaha had a reporter outside. As I led Paulo to the box office, I waved to the KN2 crew in the distance. I approached the will call.

"Mark Pettit, KN2-TV," I told the clerk. "I'm introducing Oprah." I couldn't help myself. "And, you should have a ticket for my uh, my friend, Paulo."

She shuffled through a box of tickets, quickly reaching a section labeled N-O-P.

"Mark Pettit. There it is. Here's your guest's ticket. Front row, Orchestra. One of the best seats in the house," she said with a smile, admiring our matching tuxedos and silver cufflinks. "You must be a really special friend."

I grabbed the tickets and put my hand behind Paulo's back, guiding him toward the entrance. An usher led us to the front of the line and inside the theater.

"Okay. It's showtime," I told Paulo as I handed him his ticket. "I'll look for you from the stage. Enjoy the show."

"You're going to do great," he said. "Oprah better not steal you from me."

I winked as I headed for the back of the stage. I pulled some notecards from my jacket pocket and gathered my thoughts.

> WELCOME TO OMAHA
> NEW NATIONAL TALK SHOW STARTS
> NEXT WEEK
> LEAD IN TO OUR FIVE O'CLOCK NEWS
> MISS OPRAH WINFREY

The stage manager startled me.

"Mr. Pettit. Are you ready?" she asked. "I'm told Miss Winfrey is about two minutes from arriving at the theater."

"Yes, I'm ready," I said, shaking off my nerves. "Let's welcome Oprah to Omaha."

I could hear music pumping throughout the theater. Quincy Jones and Rod Temperton's theme song was about to become the most recognizable theme song in television talk show history.

Do, do, dah, do. Da, do, dah, do.

Amidst the audience's roar, the announcer's voice.

"Ladies and gentlemen, welcome to the world-famous Orpheum Theater in downtown Omaha!"

The crowd cheered, a few whistles rounding out the applause.

"Fifteen seconds," the stage manager told me as she handed me the mic. "Just flip the little button on the side, up, and you're live."

It was that moment where terror became nervousness and then total excitement as my instincts kicked in.

Showtime!

Lights, camera, action!

Once again, the thundering voice of the announcer.

"And now, ladies and gentlemen, please welcome to the stage, Mark Pettit from KN2-TV! Soon to be Omaha's News Leader!"

The station's promotions department had clearly worked around the clock.

Oprah's theme song played louder.

I took a deep breath, flipped on the mic and headed for center stage to another wave of applause.

The spotlight hit my face and I couldn't quite make out the crowd. Holding the mic with my right hand, I raised my left hand just high enough above my eyes to block the light. Then I saw the landscape before me.

The theater was jammed, floor to ceiling. It was mostly women, screaming like bridesmaids at Chippendale's.

Do, do, dah, do. Da, do, dah, do.

I soaked it in. Then, I raised my mic.

"Welcome, ladies and gentlemen! Well, mostly ladies!" I knew the demos.

Another round of loud applause and squealing voices.

"I'm Mark Pettit, the brand-new anchorman at KN2-TV!" I said to another round of light applause.

To my right, I could see the stage manager, giving me the thumbs up. She mouthed, "She's here!"

"It is my great honor to introduce a woman whose new national talk show will start airing at four p.m. next Monday, leading into our new five o'clock news. Please welcome to the great stage of the Orpheum Theater, MISS OPRAH WINFREY!"

The crowd erupted, and then, in a burst of energy, Oprah came bounding on stage in a beautiful bright purple dress.

Without warning (and no prep beforehand!) she embraced me. Instinctively, I kissed her sweetly on the cheek. She stepped back, glowing in the spotlight, soaking up the love from the capacity crowd.

"I just got sugar from Oprah Winfrey!" I screamed into the microphone, before handing it to Oprah.

The crowd went wild.

Like a pro, she declared, "Hello, Omaha! Give it up for my new friend, Mark Pettit! Together, we're going to take KN2-TV all the way to number one!"

Another round of wild applause.

As I tried to take it all in, my eyes fell to the front row of the theater. Center, Orchestra. And there, Paulo stood, as glamorous as Oprah, in his sparkling rented tuxedo. I tear up now even thinking about it.

He applauded enthusiastically, just like the rest of the crowd. "Woo hoo!" he yelled. I recognized his voice instantly.

For a couple of seconds, time froze as I looked at him, our eyes meeting from the stage. He looked so happy for me. His face beamed as he applauded.

I wish now I could have acknowledged him from the stage.

"And Oprah, please give it up, for my man, the one, my only. Paulo!"

My heart almost full, I broke my glance with Paulo, turned and hugged Oprah once more and then headed for stage left and my exit.

It was her show now.

Do, do, dah, do. Da, do, dah, do.

CHAPTER

11

PUSH IT REAL GOOD

O prah was the first of a parade of celebrities who would make their way to Omaha and whose acquaintance I would make.

Brent Musburger, Geraldo Rivera, Alexander Haig, and two of my all-time favorite interviews: Ann Landers and Dr. Henry Kissinger.

Secretary Haig decided to seek the Republican nomination for president in 1988 and was one of about a dozen candidates, from both parties, that I was fortunate enough to interview at KN2-TV.

I was alone in the men's dressing room, trying to tame my mane, when Mr. Haig walked in. Alone. No security, no PR people, just him and a lost look on his face.

"I'm sorry to bother you," he said, "Is this the men's room?" Recognizing him immediately, I told him yes and to come on in.

"I'm here for the interview," he said.

"Well, I'm the guy doing the interview, so you've come to the right place."

104

We shared a slight laugh, and I began patting the Pancake #2 on my face.

"Oh, great," he said. "You're going to look like Jack Kennedy under the lights and I'm going to look like Dick Nixon."

He was referring to the very first televised presidential debate back in 1960. Kennedy was telegenic, poised and confident in front of the camera, while Nixon looked uneasy at best, often breaking into a sweat on camera.

The secretary and I shared a hearty laugh.

"We can't let that happen," I said, motioning Mr. Haig over to the lighted mirror. I handed him my small compact that contained the Tan #2 makeup.

"Flip the pad over," I told him, pointing to the little circular pad beneath the make-up itself. "The other side is clean. You can use that side of the pad."

I watched with a smile on my face as Mr. Haig dabbed the make-up on his face.

"Smooth it out on your forehead and across each cheek," I told him. "Just enough to keep you from shining like a northern star on camera."

"More Jack Kennedy, less Dick Nixon," he said with another deep laugh.

It often amazed me to be in the presence of legendary personalities like Secretary Haig. They had seemed so big, larger than life on camera, but what I found was that many of them were shy in person.

Later on the set, I asked Secretary Haig a question that I worried might offend him: "On the day president Reagan was shot, do you regret saying "As of now, I am in control here, in the White House, pending return of the vice president?" I queried as the cameras rolled.

"You have to understand the context," the secretary began. "We were all in a state of shock. For all we knew, the president could die. Vice president Bush was on a plane back from Texas. I just wanted people to understand we, the team, were in place and *the situation* was under control," he said, trying to clarify his words.

He would later tell *60 Minutes*, "I wasn't talking about transition. I was talking about the executive branch, who is running the government. That was the question asked. It was not, *Who is in line should the president die?*"

We finished the interview, and I thanked Mr. Haig for his candor.

"Thank you for the make-up," he said, "At least I didn't break into a full sweat when you asked me the question."

Yes, Mr. Haig was shy. Ann Landers, on the other hand, was not.

We were in our early afternoon editorial meeting as one of the assignment editors went down the list of story ideas. An arraignment for a murder suspect, the woes of Nebraska farmers, and a visit by the famous advice columnist, Ann Landers. Born Esther Pauline "Eppie" Lederer, she took over the wildly popular column in 1955.

My mother read her columns religiously, along with her other favorites, *The National Enquirer* and *Reader's Digest*. So, by osmosis, I was a fan of *Ask Ann Landers* too and I was jazzed about the opportunity to interview her.

"She's got a twenty-minute window at two fifteen," the assignment editor said.

"I'd love to interview her," I piped up from a chair in Carol's office. "My mother adores her."

"He knows Ann Landers but didn't know Joan Baez," one of the surly nightside assignment editors chimed in. It was true. She had happily announced during a previous editorial meeting that Ms. Baez was in town to perform.

"Who is Joan Baez?" I said as eyes rolled around the room.

"She'd be one of the most prolific songwriters of our time," the editor retorted. "And this is the guy we have fronting our news?" She looked at Carol with disdain.

Years later, I would understand the feeling when guys half my age didn't know who Roy Orbison was.

My photographer and I arrived at a hangar not far from the main runway at Eppley Airfield right at two o'clock. Ann Landers didn't fly commercial. She would be arriving by private jet. We were setting up the lights and chairs as her plane landed. She bounded from the airplane in a full-length mink coat.

She came in like a nor'easter, flashing her million-dollar smile as a small group of fans applauded. A photographer from the *Omaha World Herald* snapped her photo.

"Right this way, Miss Landers," an aide said as he pointed her in my direction. I saw him whisper in her ear as they approached us.

"You must be Mark," she said, dragging her tongue over the ess in "must." I couldn't believe it. Ann Landers had a distinctive lisp. It only made her more intriguing.

"It's an honor to meet you, ma'am," I said, reaching to shake her hand. "My mother is a huge fan."

"Well, that's delightful," she said, once again her tongue hanging on the ess for dear life.

"Gerald," she said to her aide, "be a dear and grab me a publicity photo for Mark's mother. I'll sign it before we leave." Game over. I was blown away.

We finished the interview right on time, and, as instructed, her aide came over with the photo and handed her a felt-tipped marker.

"What's your sweet mother's name?" she asked, removing the cap from the marker. "Her name is Dorothy. Everyone calls her 'Dot,'" I said.

She took the pen and wrote to the left of her face on the photo, *To Dot, My fondest wishes*. She signed her name with dramatic flair and blew on the ink to make sure it was dry.

Her aide handed me her fur coat. I froze, as in a Nebraska blizzard with no clothes.

"Put it on my shoulders, silly." she said, her lisp now louder than ever.

"Oh, okay," I said. "We don't see many fur coats where I'm from." Ann Landers flashed her famous smile, and she was gone.

Before my interview with Dr. Kissinger, I spent a day in the library reading anything I could find about him. The nice lady at the front desk, friendlier than before, helped pull up stories on him from the *New York Times* and the *Washington Post*. It was clear that around the time I was born in the early 1960s he was in his glory, dealing with multiple crises at once.

We met him at the Omaha Press Club. As it happened, Paulo arrived to start his dinner shift just as I was being introduced to Dr. Kissinger. We came within inches of bumping into each other as Paulo wrapped his apron around his waist.

"Excuse me," I said to him, pretending like I didn't know him.

What the fuck was wrong with me?

Why didn't I stop to introduce Paulo to him? Hell, Paulo was smarter than me and probably should have been doing the interview.

"Dr. Kissinger, this is my boyfriend, Paulo," I should have said. "He's originally from Brazil and is in medical school here in Omaha. Someday, he's going to help find a cure for AIDS."

Instead, I walked right by him like an ordinary stranger.

I felt a twinge of guilt as I sat down in the chair across from Kissinger while reaching for my notecard of prepared questions from the inside pocket of my suit coat. In the distance, I could see Paulo walking up to greet his guests with a smile, just like he did for Carol and me the first night I met him.

Regaining my composure, I did my best Dan Rather and asked him a wide range of questions, trying my best to honor him and history by not making a fool of myself. What would he think of me if he realized I didn't know who Joan Baez was, much less the president of Türkiye.

After we finished the interview, Kissinger greeted a select number of guests who had been invited to meet with him privately. Then, we were politely told to wrap it up, that Dr. Kissinger had a lecture to get to at the University of Omaha, where I was now a student.

Yep. College student by day. Celebrity interviewer by night.

As we were all hustled onto the elevator, I found myself standing right next to the man himself.

He leaned over and, in his thick German accent, said, "You were very well prepared for our interview. You asked very intelligent questions." I was thrilled by his compliment.

Then, he handed me a pearl of wisdom: "The battle is often won by the general most prepared for war."

The doors of the elevator opened, and his aides escorted him out.

It was yet another highlight of my still-young career.

But I must admit, not all my stories were network-worthy. I knew I had to get eyes on our newscasts, and sometimes I took chances to appeal to a wider audience.

Like the night Carol almost blew a gasket.

As was often the case, I skipped dinner to work on a story. This evening, it was about a homeowner who had shot two intruders trying to break into his home the night before.

On the ten o'clock news, viewers watched a reenactment from the intruders' point of view as they made their way to the back door of the home.

And then my voice, as an intruder's hand reached for the sliding glass door.

"The Andresek family was sound asleep last night when the masked gunman entered their home," I narrated, as the sliding glass door slid open. "But the gunmen got more than they bargained for as they entered the premises."

Out of the dark I appeared, holding a 9mm pistol. I lifted it and pointed it straight at the camera.

"Homeowner Gary Andresek confronted the two men with his 9mm pistol. He fired four times, killing one of the intruders and seriously injuring the other."

Just as I finished the sentence, the camera fell out of frame, as if having been shot.

Back on the set now, I looked directly into the camera.

"Police say no charges will be filed in the incident as Mr. Andresek clearly feared for his family's safety."

I turned to my co-anchor Linda and said proudly, "We'll continue to follow this story as it develops."

She looked at me strangely.

"Really disturbing report, Mark," she said, as she tossed to commercial.

The next morning, I got a phone call from Carol asking me to come into the station early. I opened the door and walked in. It was like walking into a buzz saw.

"What the hell was that last night, Mark? she fumed. "My anchorman pointing a gun at the camera? You could have killed Gary."

Gary was my cameraman.

I tried to calm her down.

"Relax, Carol," I said softly. "The gun wasn't loaded. It was for effect. I wanted the viewers to see and feel what those intruders saw and felt."

Carol shook her head.

"Unbelievably dangerous," she said.

"This is TV news," I said, trying to defend myself. "It's about the visuals."

Now, she was angry.

"No, Mark!" she said, so loud I thought the entire newsroom might hear it. "It's about the optics. I've told you several times now. The people of Omaha want stability. They want an anchorman they can trust. Not some guy pointing a gun at them at ten o'clock."

"And that's why Bob Berry is selling used cars!" I fired back at her. "He bored people to death, Carol. So what if I gave viewers a little scare with a pistol? You hired me to get this station to the top. I'm trying to do that."

She seemed defeated.

"I want to win, Mark," she confessed. "But not at the price of sensationalism. This is the news, and we have an obligation to our audience."

I snapped.

"Okay. Then let's talk about that obligation, Carol. We're not fulfilling it."

With a puzzled look on her face, she replied, "What do you mean?"

In a hushed voice, I said, "We're not reporting on everything we should be."

"For example?" she asked.

There was no going back now.

"We need to talk about how we're covering the AIDS situation."

"The AIDS situation? What do you mean?"

"One of my best friends is a doctor, or about to become a doctor. He says we're not covering the story properly. Not telling people what's really causing it," I said.

"It's gay cancer," she replied. "We say it every time we mention it on the news."

"It's not, Carol," I replied. It's not 'gay cancer.' Guys are getting it from unprotected anal sex. We should be saying that on the news."

It looked like her head was going to blow off her shoulders.

"Have you lost your mind? This is Omaha," she fired back. "We can't say *unprotected anal sex* on the six o'clock news!"

"That's what it is Carol! You're paying me to tell the truth, right? Then let me report it. We have the eyes of Omaha," I said. "You said it yourself: we have an obligation to our viewers."

She hesitated for a moment.

"This means that much to you?" she asked.

"Carol, a thousand guys are dying every day. We have to stop it. We have to start reporting the truth. It might as well start in Omaha. This is a medical town."

Quietly, she said, "This could cost me my job."

I didn't hesitate.

"If it does, I'll walk out the door right behind you," I said. "We're a team. And if we're going to be number one, it's time we lead like number one."

She paused. Collecting her thoughts.

"The next time we have a story on AIDS in the rundown, write it into the script," she said. "The producers will bring it to me and I'll approve it."

"Thank you," I said.

Then, she looked at me.

"Are those gray hairs up there? This job is starting to age you already."

The following week, it happened. I was reading copy from the AP wire when I saw the headline: FDA APPROVES NEW AIDS TREATMENT.

I read the story and walked back to my desk.

"Let's add in a thirty-second reader on a new drug approved to fight AIDS," I told my producer.

"Okay, I'll work it into the top of the B-block if you'll bang out the copy."

"Blocks" were the different sections of our newscast. A-block was the top stories of the day before the first commercial break. B-block was the top of the second segment of news coming out of the first commercial break. The first story in each block is the most important in that section.

"On it," I replied as my fingers went to work on the keys of my typewriter. Within a minute, I had knocked out the copy. I pulled the multi-layered sheet of paper—which provided multiple copies of the story (to the producer, to the talent, to the teleprompter, etc.)—and handed it across the desk to my producer.

She snatched it from my hand and tossed it to the side of her own typewriter.

"I'll get to it in a minute," she said, hurriedly preparing for our newscast.

"You might want to look at it now," I told her.

She paused what she was doing and reached over for the single-paged, thirty-second reader I had prepared for her. In news jargon, a "reader" is a story without video or other images read by the anchor straight into the camera with a single graphic over the anchor's shoulder. As my producer's eyes made their way down the page, I could see her reaction.

"Mark, what are you thinking?" she asked. "I can't approve this copy. This will have to go to Carol."

"I had a feeling," I said as she rose from her desk and headed to Carol's office.

After a few minutes of discussion with Carol, my producer returned to her desk. Without looking up, she said, "Top of the B-block. You, on Camera One. God be with us."

As we headed into the commercial break after the first block, I saw Carol enter the news studio. She quietly took her place next to one of the monitors, just to the left of the teleprompter on Camera One.

Our eyes met as she settled into place. She gave me a slight nod and my eyes returned to the text in front of me.

"We're back in thirty seconds!" the floor director announced. I heard the show director's voice in my ear.

"Camera One, Mark, the graphic is over your right shoulder," he told me.

"Got it," I said.

"Ten seconds," said the floor director," then, "Five, four, three, two, one…"

And I was on.

I paused for a second, causing a brief panic from the control booth.

"Mark! You're on! Camera One!"

I regained my composure and looked directly into the camera. I didn't need the teleprompter for this one. I had the story memorized by now.

"The FDA today approved a new drug in the fight against HIV/AIDS. It's called AZT," I said with authority.

Paulo told me it was coming. He said it was a drug originally used to treat cancer in the 1960s and that researchers had rediscovered the drug, finding that it might be an effective agent against HIV.

"It's a class of drugs known as nucleoside reverse transcriptase or NRTIs," I continued. I had written out nucleoside reverse transcriptase phonetically on a notepad by my desk to make sure I got the pronunciation right.

"Health officials stress the drug is not a cure for AIDS." I looked dead into the camera. I knew what this moment meant. And I knew

Paulo would be watching. I had called and left a voicemail message at his desk at the lab.

"They say prevention of HIV transmission is key. Officials at the CDC say unprotected anal sex among gay men is the reason infection rates are spreading so quickly and urge those with multiple sex partners to wear condoms," I finished.

I heard a gasp in the studio. Several crew members looked over at Carol, still standing by the TV monitor. She remained as calm as ever.

"In other news…" my co-anchor said, bringing things back to reality and normal.

After the newscast ended, I walked from the desk without speaking to any of the crew members. I didn't want to have to explain myself. I wanted it to be normal, just like any other news, delivered with sincerity and honesty.

But I wasn't stupid.

I walked through the double-panel doors from the studio back through the newsroom and straight to the front desk. The receptionist kept a large book where she documented every call that came in.

I saw the switchboard was lit up. I watched her listening and writing down the comments in the large book.

"Thank you for calling KN2-TV," she said. "I'll relay your message."

"KN2-TV, can you please hold? KN2-TV, can you please hold?"

Seeing me enter the lobby, she paused and gave me a strange look.

My heart sank.

"How bad is it?" I was ready to take the heat.

"Bad?" she said as she broke into a smile. "It's ten to one, positive!"

"Positive?"

"Yes! The response has been overwhelming. Most people are saying how much they appreciate us reporting on the true cause of AIDS. It's crazy."

She went back to the phones.

I took a step back to collect myself before returning to the newsroom.

Had I been wrong this whole time? About my life? About myself? Maybe viewers could cope with the truth. Maybe even about me.

I looked over at the receptionist again. The lights kept blinking on the panel before her.

YOU'VE GOT MAIL

I t snowed seven inches one of the first weekends after I moved to Omaha. In the south, panic would have ensued. If we get an inch of snow in Georgia, there will be dozens of cars scattered off the interstate and city side streets. Instead, in Omaha, they adapt. I remember seeing ladies who weighed around a buck and a quarter carrying fifty-pound bags of salt over their shoulders and out of the hardware store.

"What am I supposed to do?" I asked the assistant news director when I called into the station. "The snow is like seven inches deep," I mewled.

"Get in your car and drive to work."

So that's what I did.

And snow was for openers. I had never felt the chill brought on by a stiff wind across the prairies. It was not uncommon to see the temperature drop down below zero. As a matter of fact, on the day of Ronald Reagan's second inauguration (January 20, 1985), Omaha firemen battled a blaze threatening to destroy a historic part of the city's Old Market. At the time, it was eighteen below zero. With the windchill, it was twenty-seven below. (It was so cold in Washington that Reagan's swearing-in was held at the White House. The official ceremonies were moved to the Capitol Rotunda the next day.)

That was another reason it was so nice to have Paulo in my life, if only secretly. He radiated heat and good energy as we lay together in bed. I loved sleeping next to him on the nights we could steal time away together. I apologized several times for the comments I had made on the first night we made love, and he forgave me.

We had been secretly seeing each other for over a year now as I continued to do my day job, and on nights and weekends, I continued to investigate the Jonus case.

It was a balmy forty degrees as I made my way to the station on February 4, 1987. I parked my slightly used, but new to me, BMW 325i in the parking lot and headed into the building, my briefcase in one hand and my coat in the other.

It had been almost two weeks since I mailed my letter to Jeremy Jonus, and, frankly, I was beginning to think I had it all wrong. I thought that by reaching out to him, he would happily respond. Oh, the naïve nature of a young journalist. An idealist who thinks his mere words can change the world.

I had worked for more than two years to piece together the why behind Jonus' crimes. I had examined every piece of evidence from the boxes that were loaned out to me by Sheriff Timmons, talked to dozens of people involved in the case, but unless I could get to him, I realized that I was never going to get to the bottom of things.

I had started the letter multiple times: *D-E-A-R J-E-R-E-M-Y,* but never had the courage to finish and mail it. Until I did.

Like every day, when I arrived at the station on that February morning, my first stop was at the newsroom mailbox. It was made of small wooden slots that formed a box with about thirty mini-mailboxes. Below my designated slot, my name was spelled out in bold letters: PETTIT.

I peeked into the box, and, seeing nothing, I walked back to my desk in the newsroom. Then something pulled me back to the box. I peered deeper inside and noticed that an envelope had been placed so close to the left that it was barely visible. I reached in and pulled the envelope away from the far wall.

And there it was: the self-addressed stamped envelope that I had included with my letter to Jonus from two weeks before.

It worked!

For some reason, I clutched the letter like I was hiding something I had stolen and shuffled into one of the editing booths, not far from the assignment desk. As I sat down, I took a deep breath. I looked closer at the envelope. In the upper left-hand corner, I noticed the writer had crossed out the station logo and return address, replacing it with his name: Jeremy Jonus, his prison number and the address for the state penitentiary.

The handwriting caught my immediate attention. The penmanship was excellent, and the lettering so small that it drew me in. I gently ripped down the ride side of the envelope, taking care not to damage the message inside. Whatever it was seemed to be written on thin printer paper. I slowly removed the document, unfolded it and was amazed to find an almost full-page, handwritten letter, once again featuring the perfect cursive, so small it could barely be read without a magnifying glass.

As I read the first paragraph of the letter, my heart dropped. Jonus started his response politely, referring to me as Mr. Pettit and stating that while he appreciated me reaching out to him, he felt there was no way his court-appointed attorney would approve an interview.

And then, in the second paragraph, he wrote:

> I'm not sure that I know just what story you feel I could tell, however, I would not be opposed to your coming out here to present your questions if, and only if, this could be done with the

understanding that would be under no obligation to participate in an interview.

My heart began to race as I continued to read the letter.

> In the event that you choose not to come to
> Lincoln, I have two questions for you. There is
> no need to respond. Do you see any need to air
> a piece which will only serve to amplify the hurt
> of the victims' families? Do you really believe that
> people could watch such a piece and come away
> with an understanding of "who Jeremy Jonus
> really is"? Would they not say, rather, "It is only
> an act to gain our sympathy?"

> Sincerely,
> Jeremy Jonus

Interestingly, Jonus signed his name in cursive lettering and printed out his name below it like he was signing a business document.

Just to make sure I had it right, I read the letter again. Then again. Yes, he had invited me to visit him in prison and to make my case for an interview in person. I walked out of the editing room toward Carol's office. She was in the middle of a meeting, but this couldn't wait. I rapped at her door three times with my knuckle and opened it.

"I'm sorry to interrupt, Carol, but this is important."

She could tell by my face and tone that it was.

"Give us five minutes, gang," she told the small group of people who grabbed at their papers and made a quick exit. I watched them leave and then turned my attention to Carol.

"It worked!" I whispered. "Jonus wrote me back!"

Like a proud child with his report card, I handed the letter to Carol. Like me, she examined the outside of the envelope first.

"This is our letterhead," she said. "How did he get this?"

"I sent it to him, with my letter. I figured he might not have money to buy a stamp to write me back. So I asked the office manager to run an envelope through the postage machine so I could send it to him," I said with a smile.

"As I've said before, a face and a brain," she laughed as she set her glasses on her nose. She read the letter. Once, then twice like I had done.

"You did it!" she said. "The door is open now. Time to kick it in."

"If I can arrange it, I'd like to take Friday off to go down and meet with him. No camera, just me and him."

Carol pondered for a moment and said, "Do it. No one has even come this close to talking with him. I'll tell the assignment desk to take you off the roster for the day."

I walked back to my desk in the newsroom and grabbed the Lincoln phone book. I found the number for the Nebraska State Penitentiary and punched in the number. The front desk receptionist answered in a friendly, but no-nonsense manner.

"I'm calling to get on a prisoner's visitation list. For this Friday, if possible," I said.

"What is the inmate's name and number?"

"Jeremy Jonus, 3598," I said.

There was silence on the phone.

"Are you his lawyer," she quizzed. "No one has ever come to see him besides his lawyer."

"I'm not a lawyer, ma'am," I said. "I'm a reporter. Mark Pettit from KN2-TV."

"Very well. I have you on the visitation list for eleven a.m. You can stay for up to two hours," she instructed.

And then, *click*, she was gone.

I shook my head in somewhat disbelief. I was finally going to meet him. Face-to-face. Jeremy Jonus and me.

After I got home from work, I called Paulo to celebrate. He had seemed to come to terms with my obsession with the Jonus case.

"He responded!" I said. "Jonus responded to my letter. I'm going down to Lincoln to meet with him on Friday. Can you believe it?"

"You sound like a schoolboy who just landed his first date," he said. "Are you going to bring him flowers?"

The jealousy in his voice. It had been like this since the night he first picked up Jonus' mugshot.

"Don't be jealous," I said jokingly. "I don't even buy flowers for you."

Another lead balloon.

"I have to get back to the lab," he said. "I guess you'll be busy the rest of the week?"

"I'm never too busy for you," I cooed. "How about dinner at my place on Saturday night? I can tell you how the meeting went and cook us hamburgers on the grill, if it's not ten below zero." I laughed to try and make up for it.

"Okay. You know I can't say no to you. I'll bring my bag if you want me to stay over," he said sweetly.

"I'd love that," I whispered, almost slipping to say, *I love you.*

It was another one of those times when I wished I had.

Friday morning came and I found myself in a quandary. What do you wear to meet with a serial child killer face-to-face? I looked through the closet in my bedroom and picked one of the three dark suits I owned, a white shirt and a dark burgundy tie.

This was serious business and I felt like I should dress for it. Dark suit, blue or white shirt, that was my standard uniform.

"Why do you always wear blue and white shirts?" one of my co-workers once asked me. "I think you would look great in a pink shirt. Why don't you try pink?"

I cringed at her words. Pink meant "gay" to me, and, in my perceived situation, I couldn't even risk wearing that color. Looking back, it was silly, but at the time, everything I did had to project "man"—a "man's man."

An anchorman.

Before I left, I looked around my place at all the Jonus case photos still strewn about. I thought about taking a couple of the crime scene photos and pulling them out of my briefcase to show Jonus and prove to him that I knew exactly what he had done to those boys. To convey that he couldn't lie to me about what happened.

I decided against it. I was going to do my best to be what I was paid to be—a journalist who neither condemns nor condones—a seeker of the truth. I placed my notepad and a small tape recorder into my Samsonite attaché and headed out to my car.

The weather had improved dramatically from the previous week. So much so that I didn't need to wear my anchorman khaki trench coat. I tossed the coat and the briefcase onto the passenger seat of my car. As I walked around the back, I looked down from the trunk and saw the license plate.

ANKRMN.

Yes, I was that cocky. I thought it would be cool to have a vanity license plate so people could better recognize me as they passed me on the highway or as I buzzed past them. So I ordered the plate and proudly placed it on my car.

Lincoln is an hour's drive from Omaha but it feels like three. Between the two cities, there isn't much besides farmland. I always enjoyed looking out my window at the intricate irrigation systems that arched across the fertile fields. Center pivots, I think they're called. The state was blessed with an intricate network of aquifers, water beneath the surface that farmers were able to tap to water their crops. The huge web of piping helped spread the much-needed water across the crops.

I also enjoyed seeing the huge grain silos on some of the farms. It reminded me of my Uncle's Turk's farm back in North Georgia. He had an old barn and a room loaded with ears of corn that he would store to feed his cattle and horses in the winter. Next to the corn, he kept a steady supply of potatoes. I honed my pitching skills by tossing them through an open window. Several times, Uncle Turk questioned me about the diminishing supply of potatoes.

"Brother Mark…" He always called me "Brother Mark." "… something's happening to the 'taters. I keep loading them into the barn and they keep winding back out on the ground outside the window. Do you know anything about that?" He had a puzzled look on his face.

"I sure do, Uncle Turk. I've been practicing my pitching by throwing the 'taters through the window in the barn."

I think he appreciated my honesty.

"That's fine, son," he said, the mystery solved. "Just pick 'em up and put 'em back in the barn after you strike out Hank Aaron."

I would go on to be a good baseball player, specifically a pitcher. I credit Uncle Turk and that never-ending supply of 'taters. After a successful high school career, I wound up getting a partial baseball scholarship of eight hundred dollars to attend Shorter College in Rome, Georgia, about twenty miles from my hometown of Calhoun. In addition to the scholarship, I was given a job with the team after my classes.

My job? To wash and dry our team uniforms. We played around fifty games during the season, so it was a lot of work. I think my pay was around $2.10 an hour. But I needed the money. I took the job and washed and dried those uniforms like my social life depended on it.

My high school guidance counselor, Vivian Smith, had personally taken me to visit several colleges, including the University of Georgia over in Athens. Honestly, I was intimidated by the massive campus and was too scared to attend UGA. Getting the scholarship at the small Baptist college made my decision much easier, and I would get to continue pursuing my passion for playing baseball.

Not that I got to do a lot of playing.

In fact, what I mostly did for Coach Robert Hampton "Hamp" Alexander and the Shorter Hawks was throw a lot of live batting practice. Live batting practice is like playing a real game but intrasquad. Like a ceremonial sacrifice (for the team of course), Coach Alexander, a gruff, no nonsense baseball genius, started me regularly in these practice games. He knew I could throw strikes and occasional "junk" as they call it, like curve balls, sliders and even a knuckleball, which would be great practice for my teammates who actually got to play in the real games.

I was a great fungo hitter. For the uneducated baseball fan, a fungo bat is a small, lightweight wooden bat used by coaches (and sometimes players like me) during practice and pre-games to hit grounders to infielders and fly balls to the outfielders.

Whack, whack, whack, I smashed the baseballs at my teammates.

"Go to one," I'd say to the third baseman, before hitting a shot right at him. "Now, turn two," I would say to him, meaning to turn a double-play. "Reverse it and go the other way!" I shouted to the second baseman, before hitting a hard line drive at his feet, commanding him to also turn a double-play.

It was great fun and I enjoyed it. It was like being both a player and a junior coach on the team.

One day, after a good round of practice, Coach Alexander approached me near the dugout. In his deep, southern drawl, he said, "Pettit. You might be the best fungo hitter I've ever seen, son," he said, looking out into the distance like he was gazing at some far-off dream.

Getting a compliment from Coach Alexander was rare. He didn't suffer bullshitters lightly and coached us like Joe Torre coached the Atlanta Braves. Dead seriously.

As I soaked in the afternoon sunshine and Coach Alexander's compliment, I smiled. Then I was brought back to reality as he continued in his matter-of-fact cadence.

"Yes, son, you're definitely the best fungo hitter that I've ever seen play the game. But, unfortunately, there ain't much room in the major leagues for fungo hitters."

And there it was. In the kindest of ways, Coach Alexander told me the hard truth. That as good as I thought I was, I wasn't good enough to move on to the next level, which several of my teammates did. They went on to play Major League Baseball.

As fate would have it, near the end of the season, I was pitching in one of our live practice games, when I heard a little pop in my right shoulder as I delivered a fastball over the left corner of the plate.

"Strike!" one of my teammates yelled from behind the plate where he was playing the part of umpire, the next worst thing to being the practice pitcher. As the catcher returned the ball to me, I caught it in my gloved left hand. But as I reached to retrieve the ball and to prepare for the next pitch, I realized something was wrong.

I couldn't lift my right arm above my elbow.

"Time!" Coach Alexander shouted from the dugout as he jogged out to the pitcher's mound.

"What's wrong, Pettit?" he asked as he approached.

"I don't know, coach. It just snapped."

Coach Alexander wasn't good at hiding his feelings. "Oh God," he said. After all, it was a Baptist college. "Get in the dugout and let's ice down your shoulder."

It didn't sound good, and it certainly didn't feel good. I walked from the field to the dugout with my right arm hanging like it belonged to a rag doll.

And that was that.

Coach Alexander took me to a shoulder specialist, who after doing tests and x-rays declared, "Torn rotator cuff, coach. He's going to need surgery. And even after that, he might never play again."

Coach Alexander looked at me and I looked at him. We both knew it was over.

Breaking the tension, I said, "Don't worry, coach. As you said, there ain't much room in the major leagues for fungo hitters." He smiled an awkward smile. For a moment, we connected.

"It's been nice having you on the team, son," he said. "You're a good kid." He might as well have handed me a golden glove.

"Thanks, Coach," I told him. "God definitely broke the mold when he made you."

A suitably Baptist complement.

And that was the end of my baseball career. I finished my first year at Shorter, which would be my last. I figured I no longer needed college. I had my sights set on a different major league now: Television News.

As I approached downtown Lincoln, I pulled my car over in a parking lot and reached over for my briefcase. I checked my notepad and looked at the address: 4201 South 14th Street.

I found my location on the map. (There was no such thing as Google Maps back then.) I traced my finger across the map to make sure I knew where I was going.

A few minutes later, I was pulling into the drive of the prison. It was a massive complex, built just a few years before to house Nebraska's burgeoning prison population. It housed a combination of inmates, from low-to-mid-level criminals up to the most dangerous of them all.

Inmates like Jeremy Jonus.

My heart began to thump in my chest as I neared the guard shack just outside the prison walls. I pulled my car up to the crossing gate and watched as the corrections officer exited the small building where he guarded the front entrance.

He carefully eyed my car, walked completely around the vehicle and then approached the passenger side. I stumbled for the power button to lower the window and as it neared completely open, I addressed the officer.

"Good morning, sir," I said. "I'm here to visit an inmate."

He returned to the guard shack and retrieved a clipboard.

"What's your name," he asked.

"Mark Pettit, sir," I said politely. "I'm with KN2-TV in Omaha."

He looked at me briefly and replied, "Yeah. I've seen you on TV. You were covering that Rock Hudson thing. Pretty sad how he ended up." He shook his head.

Again, the shame hit me.

"Who are you here to see," he said, thinking nothing of his assessment of the dead actor.

"Jeremy Jonus."

"You've got to be kidding me," the guard said. "Who would want to talk with that son-of-a-bitch?"

"Me, sir," I said. "I'm trying to figure out why he did what he did."

The guard eyeballed me suspiciously and said, "You're on the list. You're good to go. Park your car and go to the front desk to check in."

I looked at the guard and said, "Thank you, sir. It was very nice to meet you."

Growing up, I was taught to respect law enforcement, to follow the rules and not stick out from the crowd. It was a lesson I learned to use in different parts of my life. Especially the part about not sticking out from the crowd.

I continued through the entrance to the prison and paused to take in the size and enormity of the complex. I wondered which building housed Jonus and what made death row different from the cells that held the general population.

Off in the distance, I could see inmates walking around an outdoor area of the prison. I wondered if Jonus got to walk those grounds, and if so, alone or did they allow him out with other inmates? They no doubt knew why he was incarcerated, and I could imagine the taunts and jeers he would hear if he was allowed to mingle with other prisoners.

Finding a visitor spot not far from the entrance to the prison, I parked my car and turned off the engine. I took a deep breath to compose myself. This was a moment I had worked on for more than two years. I didn't know quite what to do or say, but I knew this might be my only chance and I couldn't blow it.

As I entered the front door of the prison, I was struck by the oversized words written on the wall.

OUR MISSION IS TO REHABILITATE
AND RETURN PEOPLE TO SOCIETY.

This clearly wasn't meant for certain inmates. Like Jeremy Jonus. The only way he was leaving prison was in a pine box driven by a hearse. He pleaded guilty to the two murders in Omaha and had been sentenced to death by a three-judge panel.

There would be no chance for rehabilitation for Jeremy Jonus.

I approached the front desk where another uniformed guard, this time a female who appeared to be in her late thirties or early forties, was manning the station.

"Good morning," she said, barely looking up from the stack of papers on her desk. "How can I help you?"

I repeated my story. "I'm here to visit an inmate. Jeremy Jonus."

This time I had her full attention.

"I need your name and your driver's license," she said firmly. The mood lightened a bit when she took my license and saw my name.

"You're that cute guy from KN2-TV," she said with a smile and a flirtatious tone. "I've seen you on TV. Did they hire you to replace Bob Berry?"

"Yes, ma'am," I said with a grin. "Anchor and investigative reporter."

She put two and two together.

"So that's why you're here to see Jonus, right? You're trying to get to the bottom of things, aren't you. As far as I'm concerned, they can execute him tomorrow. He's a despicable human being. The electric chair is too good for him."

"I'm not a judge or the jury, ma'am," I told her. "I'm just a reporter, looking for the truth."

She nodded.

"Walk through that door and to the metal detector," she instructed. "One of the guards will take you in."

I thanked her and held my Samsonite briefcase to my waist like a plastic blanket. I couldn't believe this was finally happening. In a matter of moments, I would be coming face-to-face with one of the most hated men in Nebraska's history and now one of the most infamous serial killers in America.

As I approached the metal detector, I heard voices in the distance. Banging and clanging, like pots and pans in a kitchen. Doors opening and closing. I never visited a prison before and certainly never interviewed a serial killer. My senses were overloaded as I took it all in and pulled myself together.

There was no training for this in journalism school, and Earl never had the chance to prep me for an interview of this magnitude. I was alone and had to rely on my instincts to get the job done, to get Jonus to agree to an interview on camera.

"Put your keys in this container and put your briefcase on the conveyor belt," the burly guard told me.

I did as he said and watched my briefcase pass through the detector without setting off an alarm. I was one step closer to Jonus. One step closer to solving the mystery. The first guard took me to another desk, where I was again checked in. A third guard then left the desk and waved me through another set of double doors.

"Are you nervous?" he asked, trying to break the ice.

"A little," I confessed as we made our way down the hallway.

"It's not so bad," he replied. "Once you get past his eyes."

I didn't know how to respond, so I just let it go. "The second door on the left," the guard told me as we headed further down the hall. He led me into a small conference room and told me to sit down on one side of the wooden table in the center of the room.

"I'll be right back with the guest of honor," he said, as he walked out. The door closed behind him.

I sat in silence, sure that my heart was going to blow out of my chest. I could feel the beads of sweat starting to form on my forehead. I fumbled for my briefcase, opened it and searched for a handkerchief or a napkin.

Nothing.

I ran my hand along my forehead, scooping up the sweat, and wiped it on my pant leg. As they say, you can take the boy out of the country, but you can't take the country out of the boy. Outside the door, I heard metal against the stone floor. *Ching. Ching. Ching.* And then the door opened.

I looked up as the guard led him in. A young man, in khaki pants and a matching shirt. My eyes went to the floor, and I saw the shackles around his feet. My eyes made their way up his pant leg to his wrists. He was handcuffed.

"You sit over here," the guard told him. Jeremy Jonus nervously made his way around the table and took the seat across from me. The guard reached for a key and removed the cuffs from this killer's wrists. Unthinkingly, he rubbed at the red blotches on both of his arms.

Our eyes met for the first time. It was like I was staring at his mugshot, but in real life. And then, the cold, gray eyes. Like those of a shark about to attack or be attacked.

Now I knew exactly what the guard meant. I just had to get past those eyes.

"Two hours, max," the guard said as he turned to leave the room. "I'll check in on you boys every now and then."

The guard was gone. I was left alone.

Just me and Jeremy Jonus.

There was a very awkward silence between us as I studied him and he studied me. I thought he was boyish and small compared to the size of his crimes. I wondered what he thought of me as his eyes examined me. He was the first to break the silence.

"So, what do you want to know?" His voice was deep and gravelly.

My mind raced. In my head, I could see the photos from the crime scene. Jimmy Ray, face down in the grassy ditch. The stab wounds in his back. The frayed rope tied around his wrists and legs. I saw Robbie Wilkins, face down in the snow, stained dark red from the blood that had flowed from the boy's wounds.

A calm passed over me and I stared Jonus down like he had stared at his victims before killing them.

"Just one thing, really," I said to him. "Why? Why did you kill these boys? You didn't know them, right?

"No."

I pressed further.

"I saw the autopsy photos. It was horrible. How could you do that to these kids?"

Jonus paused, as if searching for the answer. He responded in a bone-chilling tone that I will never forget.

"I really don't know," he said, almost apologetically. "All I can tell you is that for as long as I can remember, I've just had a need to kill."

There was another awkward silence between us.

The hairs on the back of my neck rose and a rage burned. It hit me again that we were alone. No one around us. No one to stop me if I chose to attack him. I wondered what the parents of his victims would do if given the same chance.

I snapped out of it. My attention was back on Jonus.

"Forgive me for being rude," I said to him as I reached across the table. "I should have introduced myself. I'm Mark Pettit."

He sat and then shook my hand. As I said earlier, I had decided before meeting him to neither condemn nor condone, to be objective.

"I think you know who I am," he said. "Jeremy. Jeremy Jonus."

Oh yes, I knew who he was, but there was a whole lot more I was going to learn about him. I didn't realize it at the time, but our lives were about to become entwined. Very much so.

Till death did us part.

"Okay," I said, continuing the interview. "How long have you felt this need to kill?"

Jonus' eyes drifted off as he continued.

"Since I was around six years old. I wanted to kill my babysitter."

"Why?"

"I hated her. She was always putting down my father. Telling me why my mother divorced him."

Now we were getting somewhere.

"Did you want to rape her, then kill her?"

"No. I had no concept of rape," he chuckled. "It was just simple. One minute she's there and the next she's not."

"Like turning off a light switch?"

An eerie smile crossed his face.

"This was in Burlington, right? Where you grew up?"

"Yeah. You should check it out sometime. You might find some pieces to the puzzle back there?"

He appeared to be opening a big door.

"Pieces to the puzzle? Like more unsolved crimes?"

"You're the investigative reporter," he said as if tossing a piece of cheese to a mouse in his cage.

"As a matter of fact, I did a little digging before I came to see you," I told him. "Turns out there are a number of unsolved crimes back in Burlington."

Jonus smiled and responded. "You don't say?"

"Does the Woodland Slasher ring any bells?" I said, looking down at my notes.

"Stupid name," he said. "The media can be so lame. No offense."

"None taken. Why don't you tell me what happened back there."

He obviously knew the story well.

"January 1990. There was this woman on her way to class at the local college. I walked up and stabbed her."

"Did you kill her?"

"No. She screamed and ran away, so I ran too," he said.

"Were there others?"

"Yes. A boy named Michael, later in March. I slit his throat with a hobby knife."

"Did he survive?"

"As far as I know," Jonus said. "It never made the news."

"Anything or anyone else?"

Again, Jonus smiled a creepy grin.

"Yeah. I stabbed a girl on a bicycle. She got away too."

I scribbled it all down on my notepad.

"And this is the first time you're telling anyone about these crimes?"

"You're the first person to ask," Jonus said.

I decided to move in for my own kill.

"There's another case that hasn't been solved back in Vermont. The murder of a young boy. Randy Statham. Very similar to what happened here in Nebraska."

Jonus' mood changed and he was ice cold.

"I think this meeting's over," he said.

"I think there's a lot more you want to tell me and maybe it could help someone else who's struggling with what you're struggling with. Uh, your feelings."

Jonus seemed to find the statement of interest.

"You think my story could prevent some other guy from killing people."

"I do. Sometimes you need to hear from someone going through what you're going through," I said.

I reached into my briefcase and pulled out a self-addressed stamped envelope and handed it to Jonus.

"I'd like the next interview to be on camera," I told him. "Use this envelope to write me back. People need to hear from you. They want to know why, and you're only person who can answer that question.

"I'll think about it," he said.

I scribbled a phone number on a section of my notepad, ripped it off and handed it to the killer.

"That's my home number," I told him. "You can call me collect."

"Give me some time to think about it," he said as he signaled for the guard.

"Take your time."

The guard entered the room and led Jonus away.

I sat back in my chair and soaked in the moment, wondering if it would be the first or last time that I met Jeremy Jonus.

The following Sunday morning, I lay in the bed next to Paulo, watching him sleep as the sun rose in the distance. One of the many things I loved about sleeping with him was that he never snored. It was just a smooth, steady stream of breathing. I sat there and looked at his beautiful face and watched and listened as he slept.

I was startled from my stare by the sharp ringing of the phone. DOH! The receiver was on the nightstand on Paulo's side of the bed. I tried to climb over him without waking him, but as I reached for the phone, my elbow swiped across his right ear.

"*Caramba!*" He blurted out, Portuguese for *damn it!*

"Sorry, baby. Just go back to sleep," I said as I picked up the receiver and placed it to my ear.

"Hello?" I whispered.

"You have a collect call from Jeremy Jonus, a prisoner at the Nebraska State Penitentiary," the operator said sharply in my ear. "Will you accept the charges?"

Without hesitation, I said, "Yes, I will."

There was a click on the line and then Jonus' voice.

"You set it up and I'll do the interview," he uttered in his low, gravelly voice.

I pumped my fist into the air with excitement, trying not to wake the sleeping beauty next to me.

The following Thursday, I sat across from Jeremy Jonus again. This time in front of bright lights and a camera. This interview would be on the record. I thought he might be nervous, but Jonus seemed to enjoy what was happening. His mood was light, bordering on cheerful.

As my cameraman finished setting up the lights, Jonus leaned in and asked me a question.

"What's up with the license plate on your car? The guard told me about it."

Simple enough.

"It's a vanity plate. It reads ANKRMN. You know, anchorman."

Jonus studied my face and replied.

"More like ANKRBOY."

His comment came out of nowhere. It made me smile. It was not the only question Jonus had on his list.

"So, do you have a girlfriend?" he asked.

"No," I said nonchalantly.

"A wife?"

"No."

He pressed harder. Hell, I was supposed to be the one inter-viewing him.

"What? A handsome guy like you should have girls crawling all over him," he said.

He was starting to get on my nerves.

"Just look at me and answer the questions. This is your chance to speak directly to the people of Omaha," I said sternly.

"Should I tell them I hated the place from the second I got here?" he said.

"Just tell them the truth," I replied.

"You got it, ANKRBOY," he said, trying to get under my skin.

"That's it, we're rolling," my cameraman said. It broke the tension.

"Here we go," I said as the camera rolled.

"Can't wait," Jonus said under his breath.

"I'm Mark Pettit, KN2-TV, here with serial child killer Jeremy Jonus on death row at the Nebraska State Penitentiary. Let's talk about your childhood."

"Nothing much to talk about. Parents divorced when I was young. I liked being a Boy Scout."

I corrected him, "An Eagle Scout, actually."

He nodded and continued. "That's correct. Couldn't afford col-lege, so I joined the Air Force. That's how I ended up at Offutt in Omaha."

"What did you think of Omaha?" I asked.

"Next question," Jonus said.

"I've heard that child killers aren't very popular in prison."

"You heard right."

"Do you ever go out into the yard where the regular prisoners are held?" I asked.

"Yes."

"What kinds of things do they say to you?" I pressed.

"Oh, statements like there ain't no paperboys in here."

He seemed sad now.

"Does that bother you?" I asked.

"You yourself said it. Child killers aren't very popular people," he replied.

"Has anyone ever tried to hurt you? Attack you?"

Jonus seemed taken aback by the question and paused.

"No," he said. "We all have to live with each other in here twenty-four-seven."

I knew it was a lie.

Like a lawyer in court, I would not have asked a question I didn't already know the answer to.

My mind flashed to that night.

The lights on Jonus' prison floor had been off for about an hour, and the young killer had finally drifted off to an uneasy sleep. It was his very first night on death row and he found it difficult to settle his mind.

The small bed, the hard mattress, the eerie sounds that emanated from the haunted halls all made it tough for Jonus to get comfortable, much less enjoy a deep sleep. Without question, the spirits of all those wronged by residents here were doing their best to ensure their tormentors got no rest.

Jonus was jostled from his shallow slumber by the jingling sound of keys. Metal against metal. Then, the first door to the area known as death row swung open. Light footsteps followed, and another unfamiliar sound, as if a chain were dragging on concrete.

Finally, the familiar squeak of a skeleton key sliding into the slot in Jonus's own cell.

"He's all yours, Horseshoe," Jonus heard a familiar voice whisper.

Then chaos.

Before he could react, Jonus found himself pinned down by a stranger, who, as it turns out, was convicted killer and fellow death row inmate, Walter "Horseshoe" Jankins. Jankins had been sentenced to die for the rape and murder of a twenty-six-year-old photography student. Jankins had gotten his "Horseshoe" nickname because he was a blacksmith at the Ak-Sar-Ben Race Track in Omaha. He used a horseshoe from the track to bludgeon his young female victim to death after he sexually assaulted her.

"No, no," Jonus pleaded as Jankins pounced on him.

His resistance was useless.

Jankins pushed Jonus' face against the wall. As he held Jonus' neck and head with one hand, he used the other hand to rip down Jonus' prison-issued underwear.

"Please, no," Jonus begged, just as his own victims had begged him before their lives were taken and also to no avail.

Jonus heard Jankins hock spit onto his hand and then the skin-to-skin massaging sound. Terrified, he braced as Jankins spread his legs and violently penetrated the young serial killer from behind.

"God! No!" Jonus screamed.

The rape lasted for maybe sixty seconds, before Jankins ejaculated in Jonus's rectum.

"Welcome to death row, bitch!" Jankins taunted Jonus as he rolled off him. A final insult to a brutal afront. He gave Jonus' head an aggressive shove into his pillow.

Blood seeped from the young killer's anus onto the sheets of his bed.

As Jankins was led back to his cell, Jonus heard the cacophony of applause from the other inmates.

"Welcome to death row, bitch!" the young killer heard another prisoner mock.

Tears streamed down his face. Jonus lay still in the bed he had made for himself. At last, he understood what it meant to be a victim of a violent crime.

I was told the harrowing story by a guard at the prison who asked to remain anonymous.

Now, we were back doing the interview.

I did not press Jonus further on the attack.

"Why did you confess?" I asked instead.

He squirmed a bit, then leaned in.

"Detective Riley told me if I confessed, they would get me help from a psychiatrist," he said, looking at me with a wanting understanding. "He said if I didn't, I'd be subjected to homosexual rape in prison."

The first part of the detective's statement never happened. The second part did. I saw no use in questioning Jonus further about the attack.

"My God, how do you do it? How do you wake up each day," I asked. "What do you have to look forward to?"

Jonus eked out an awkward laugh.

"Getting out. Having my case overturned." I found the statement remarkable.

"You actually think you're going to get out of prison?"

"Yes, what else?" Jonus replied.

"I think people are going to shudder when they hear you say that."

"I'm sure they will," he said.

"You haven't come to the realization that you're going to die in that electric chair, have you?" I said bluntly.

"No, I haven't," Jonus answered. "But if the State of Nebraska is bound and determined to execute me, what can I do? I'm not about to take my own life to cheat them."

I felt an odd urge of compassion for his hopeless state.

"Thank you for taking the time to talk with us," I told him. "Hopefully you've answered some of the questions people in Nebraska wanted answered."

A week later, KN2-TV aired my full interview with Jonus in a half-hour documentary. The segment ran the full thirty minutes without any commercial interruptions. We ended up garnering a 70% share of the audience watching TV that night.

The documentary helped propel KN2-TV to #1 in the local news ratings.

I took the next weekend off to spend time with Paulo. I was feeling more and more guilty about not wanting us to be seen together in public. I suggested we fly to Southern California for a weekend in Los Angeles, which Paulo readily accepted.

As we walked along the beach in Santa Monica, we talked about everything. Family, having kids, the future. It was the happiest three days of my life. I was deeply in love with Paulo and so wanted to reach over and hold his hand as we made our way down the sandy shore. But I didn't.

Yet, I wanted something to commemorate our trip.

"Hand me the disposable camera," I said to him. He reached down into our beach bag and removed the disposable camera we purchased at the hotel gift shop.

"Ma'am!" I said to a lady walking near us. "Would you mind taking our photo?"

Her face lit up as she took the camera from Paulo's hand.

I moved closer to Paulo. His face sparkled in the afternoon sunshine. He was as gorgeous as I'd ever seen him. I placed my right arm around his shoulder and squinted as we looked back at the camera.

"Big smiles on three," the woman said. "One, two, three." She snapped the photo. "One more!" she commanded. "Three, two, one." *Snap*.

Our moment in the sun was immortalized.

"That was beautiful," she said, handing Paulo the camera. "So sweet to see such brotherly love."

We smiled and I looked over at Paulo. I so wanted to tell the woman the truth. To tell her how I really felt. *That I was in love with this man.*

But I simply thanked her for her time.

As the woman walked away, I saw a distant look in Paulo's eyes as tears trickled down his face.

I was riding so high at work that I failed to see a very real turmoil churning inside him. Storm clouds were forming on the horizon, and it would be our last walk on the beach.

13

PRIVATE DANCER

"It's important for us to get you out in the community," KN2-TV's promotions director said as she handed out a single sheet of paper in the station's main conference room.

Janis was a small woman with long, blondish hair and spectacle glasses. She was a constant ball of energy, bouncing around the station with one idea and then another about how to promote the station. Janis had been brought in from Milwaukee, where she had helped take the station from last to first place.

Carol sat next to me with four other station employees, including the general manager, rounding out the group around a large wooden conference table in the center of the room.

I looked down at the paper in front of me which had a list of six events highlighted:

Cancer Society Auction
Fall Harvest Festival

Holiday Coat Drive
Spring Flower Festival
College Baseball World Series
Downtown Merchant Week

"The Cancer Society Auction is next week," Janis said, pulling the right section of her long hair back behind her glasses and ear. "They want you, Mark, to be one of the most eligible bachelors that they auction off." She smiled.

"Like a cow at the county fair?" I replied dryly.

Light laughter echoed through the conference room.

"No, silly," she said, "It'll be a lot of fun. They'll have around twenty-five of their top donors, most of them single ladies, bidding on you. Whoever pledges the most money in the form of a donation, gets a dinner with you."

It didn't hit me quite right.

"And, of course, the station will pay for the dinner," she assured me.

I looked at Carol with an uneasy glare.

"Of course, you don't have to do anything you're not comfortable with," she replied, seeing the concern in my eyes. "But I trust Janis. If she says it's all in good fun, I say why not give it a shot?"

I thought better of it.

"It's just a one-night thing," Janis said. "Once the auction is over, you head over to the restaurant. Have some wine, dinner and a little dessert and that's the extent of your commitment."

"They'll promote your involvement to their full list of donors and the station will get a full-page ad in the program. It's a win-win for all," Janis said, working to seal the deal.

"I'd prefer throwing out the first pitch at the College Baseball World Series," I said in jest. "I think I could do it lefthanded if I had to."

Janis met me with a blank stare. Of course, she had no knowledge of my baseball history or damaged right wing, but that was beside the point. She seemed genuine about the concept.

"Okay," I said. "I'll do it this year, but you better have some ringers in the audience so I don't sell for a hundred dollars."

"Oh, I'm sure you'll go for a lot more than that," Janis said in earnest.

Later at home, I told Paulo that I had agreed to take part in the event. I was surprised when he didn't object.

"It's all in good fun, right? You'll raise money for a good cause and some lucky lady gets dinner with you. What's the harm?" he said. "Maybe if I paid you to go out to dinner, you'd agree to be seen in public with me," he joked. But not really.

"It doesn't feel right for some reason," I replied. "I guess I'll do it. I can always say no next year if I embarrass myself and no one bids on me."

"Can I call in a bid if necessary?" Paulo said. "You got this baby."

The next Thursday night, I was dressed in my best suit, shirt and tie as I entered the lobby of the fancy Farnam Hotel. The hotel had been restored to its early 1930s glory after a fire gutted the property in the late seventies.

"Hello, Mark!" a perky lady with a clipboard declared as I passed two of the leather high back chairs in the center of the lobby.

"I'm Betty Brainard," she said, flashing a bright smile. "We are delighted to have you take part in this year's auction. I've already heard some of the ladies buzzing about you." She winked at me.

Oh, great, I thought to myself.

"It's a pleasure to join you this evening," I said instead, offering my hand.

"We have you down front with the other gentlemen," Betty went on. "There's an auctioneer who will take the bids. And the ladies will be able to tip you additional funds that will go to the society."

"Tip me? Like a waitress at the Dundee Deli?" I tried to joke.

"I suppose," she said.

Then a melodic sound of a triangle ringing.

"That's your cue," Betty said. "The auction is about to begin."

A swarm of ladies clutching their cocktails swooped in from an adjacent room.

"They were in the next room getting the ground rules," Betty assured me.

It looked like they were getting sauced to me.

"We like to get the evening started a little early with a few cocktails," Betty said. "It tends to loosen the purse strings, if you will."

I could see that. A couple of the ladies hooted and hollered at me as they passed by.

"I can see you're going to be mighty popular," Betty said as she led me to the front of the ballroom and near the stage.

"Right here," Betty said as she sat me next to three other guys. All of them looked as uncomfortable as me.

"Hi, I'm Gerald Lusk." He reached to shake my hand. "Jerry Lusk," the young guy said, dropping the formality.

I could feel the sweat on his palm. I was warming up myself. Jerry was my type to a tee. Slightly shorter than me, deep dark hair, blue eyes and a square chin. I pinned him at about twenty-five years old. He had dark, wire-rimmed glasses and could have passed for Clark Kent's little brother.

"My wife made me do this," Jerry said.

Whomp whomp.

"Oh, your wife," I said, trying not to look disappointed.

"My news director made me do it," I said. We shared a laugh.

"Oh, yeah," Jerry said with a smile. "I thought I recognized your name in the program, and now, seeing your face, it all makes sense." He blushed like a schoolgirl. "It's really nice to meet you."

Hmm. Jerry seemed a little too friendly, but he said he had a wife, so I decided to go with it.

"One dollar bid, now two, now two…" we heard as the auctioneer took to the stage. "Welcome to the annual Cancer Society Auction ladies!" the announcer boomed as the mildly intoxicated crowd roared in excitement.

The next thirty minutes were excruciating as the auctioneer worked his way down the list of four contestants. Jerry and I were last with our names ending in "L" and "P" respectively. The first guy, a nerdy but cute lawyer, went for seven hundred and fifty dollars and, as the drinks continued to flow, the bids inched higher. The second guy, a hunky chiropractor, went for eight hundred. Things started to really get uncomfortable as Jerry took the stage and the catcalls rang out from around the room.

"Six hundred dollars!" a lady shouted.

"Seven hundred dollars!" another fired back.

Two ladies rushed onto the stage. One placed a hundred-dollar bill in Jerry's coat pocket as the other reached inside his jacket and placed another Ben Franklin in his dress shirt pocket.

"Nine hundred dollars!" another lady shouted as she raised her hand and spilled part of her martini.

"One thousand dollars!" another woman shouted.

I caught Jerry's eye. He looked like a puppy in a window, excited but frightened by the attention of the strangers looking in.

"Do I hear twelve hundred?" the auctioneer boomed. "Twelve hundred dollars for Jerry and a steak dinner next door at Horton's!"

"I'll end it right here," a tall, wiry woman with platinum blonde hair, shouted. "Fifteen hundred dollars!"

The crowd went wild.

"Fifteen hundred, going once, going twice. Sold!" the man shouted above the screams.

Jerry faked a smile and started to walk from the stage, his buyer making a beeline toward him.

"Dinner time!" she yelled, followed by a cackling laugh. Margaret Hamilton grabbed Jerry's arm and led him away.

He turned and our eyes met again. He gave me the saddest look. I shrugged my shoulders as if to say, *It'll all be over soon.*

It was my turn to head to the gallows.

"And now, last but certainly not least," the auctioneer shouted. "His last name starts with a "P," so he's the last up for auction, but soon to be number one in the local news ratings…"

Clearly, Janis had written my intro.

"Here he is, KN2-TV anchorman, Mark Pettit! One dollar, two hundred, two hundred, the bidding starts at two hundred dollars," he said in his sharp cadence.

"Four hundred dollars!" I heard a lady shout.

"Six hundred!" another screamed.

It all became a blur as I tried to block out the sights and sounds before me.

I was jostled as a lady shoved several bills in my right front pocket. Another yanked at the back of my suit coat as if she were trying to rip it from my body.

"*A thousand* if he shows us his chest!" a frightening woman shouted from the middle of the room. She looked like someone's grandmother remembering a crust of toast during the Depression.

Then it happened.

I felt a woman's hand rip at the buttons on my dress shirt. The second button, beneath the collar and the first hole in the shirt flew off like it had been fired from a sewing gun.

I felt more cash slide against my chest. I had forgotten to wear a T-shirt under my dress shirt and my skin was now exposed.

"Woo hoo!" I heard a lady scream. "Fifteen hundred!"

I was mortified. I didn't know quite what to do, so I tried to shake it off by pretending I was a dancer in a strip club.

It only made things worse.

"Sixteen hundred!" a woman shouted as another came on stage to stuff bills in my now wide-open shirt.

"Eighteen!" I heard another woman scream.

The auctioneer, sensing my growing discomfort, stepped in.

"Okay, ladies! Show's over!" he said. "It's time to call it a night. Who will offer a record bid of two thousand dollars for a dinner with the young anchorman?"

"I will!" a lady with a fistful of bills shouted, silencing the crowd.

I looked down to see a fashionably dressed lady in a red pantsuit who appeared to be in her early forties. Her dark brunette hair was cut sharply just below her ears. Gold bangles dangled ever so slightly from her lobes.

"Going once, going twice, *sold* for two thousand dollars!" the auctioneer declared as I reached to retrieve my suit jacket. I struggled to re-button my shirt, which was torn during the excitement.

I felt degraded as I lumbered toward the waiting presence of my purchaser.

"Nancy Guthrie," the woman said as she gave me a hug. "How do you like your steak?" she whispered in my ear. "I like mine rare."

"Medium." I pulled away from her. She snaked her arm around mine and led me from the ballroom.

"You like red, correct?" she asked, catching me a bit off guard.

"Yes. Your outfit looks very nice."

"I mean wine!" she fired back, followed by a burst of laughter. "Why do I always go for the ones who need training wheels?"

We spent the next hour cutting at our steaks. Hers rare, mine medium, as we tried to make small talk.

"Did you play sports?" she asked as she sized me up.

"Baseball in high school and college. Gave up my dream of hitting fungo in the major leagues and wound up here," I said, trying to be funny. She didn't get it and looked at me like a puppy trying to understand her owner.

"My son plays football," she said. "Walk on quarterback at Nebraska."

"No chance for a scholarship," she said in a dismissive tone. "Luckily after his father died, the insurance money covers most everything."

I tried to make more small talk.

"Quarterback, wow," I said, wondering how he might look in a jock strap. "And what about you? What do you do for work?"

"Corporate lawyer, Kintak-Cooper." I never heard of the firm. "We handle a lot of Warren's stuff," she said with pride.

"Warren?"

"Buffet, Mark. Warren Buffet. He's one of the richest men in the world. He lives here in Omaha."

I nodded.

"Could I get you two something for dessert?" the waiter said. "Chocolate lava cake, Key lime pie?"

I shook my head. "Nothing for me," I said.

"I already have dessert," Nancy said with a wink to the waiter, well into the bottle of Sonoma County merlot she had ordered for the table.

As the waiter left, I rose from my side of the table and walked around to Nancy's side of the booth.

"It has been an absolute pleasure," I said, as she rose from the leather bench. "Thank you so much for your donation, Nancy. I'm sure it means a lot to the Cancer Society."

Before I could say another word, she pulled me toward her and kissed me on the lips. I felt her tongue against mine.

I stepped back.

"Whoa, Nancy, what are you doing?" I said, giving her a look of disdain.

"I paid two grand for this," she said with a lusty fire in her eyes. "I'm going to get my money's worth." She pulled me back toward her.

"Stop it!" I said a little too loudly. Nearby diners looked up before returning to their meals.

The waiter interrupted.

"Mr. Pettit, the valet has your car at the front circle," he said, looking down at a ticket. "Black BMW, right? License plate A-N-K-R-M-N."

"Yes. 'anchorman' is what it stands for," I replied defensively.

I took the ticket and looked back at Nancy.

"The station is covering the dinner and the tip. You don't have to worry about paying anything," I said. "You've done enough already."

With a disdainful glare, she slid back into the booth.

"Chocolate lava cake," she demanded of the waiter.

"Coming right up, Ms. Guthrie," I heard him say as I walked away.

I drove home in silence and a bit of shame. I had agreed to take part in the charity auction against my better judgment and was now regretting it all. I shouldn't have gotten caught up in the excitement, I shouldn't have put myself in that position. I should have stopped the auction when Jerry was onstage and rescued us both from a night of embarrassment.

But I didn't. Now I wondered what I was going to say to Carol and Janis the next day. I was sure they'd want a full report, and I was in a quandary about what to tell them. Perhaps, I should just lie and say everything went great and that the dinner was delicious and that Nancy was delightful.

I was still pondering the answer as I opened the door to my apartment.

There, to my surprise, was Paulo, shirtless, wearing gym shorts and holding two glasses of wine.

"Hey, Mister Fundraiser," he said with a smile. "How was your dinner?" He handed me one of the glasses as he kissed me on the cheek.

I didn't know quite what to say, so I didn't say anything. I walked through the kitchen to the parlor.

"How much did you raise?"

"Two thousand. Record bid for the auction," I continued, trying to justify the personal price I had paid to earn it.

"Two thousand dollars? That's fantastic! Why aren't you smiling baby? Did the lucky lady who won bore you to death at dinner?" he asked with his signature chuckle.

I didn't answer. I set my jacket on the counter and reached to remove my tie and unbutton my damaged shirt. Sensing something was wrong, Paulo pressed further.

"Mark. What's wrong? What happened?"

I was ashamed but didn't want to lie to him, so I halted and then replied.

"She made a move on me. It came out of nowhere and I didn't know what to do."

Paulo became quiet and sullen.

"A move? What do you mean, a move?"

"She kissed me. With her tongue," I confessed. "I was totally surprised and shocked."

"She kissed you?" Paulo said, his voice rising. "You let her kiss you?" he said even louder.

"No, I didn't let her kiss me," I fired back. "She just did it."

Paulo's face flushed bright red. He smashed his glass of wine against the wall behind me. Red drops splattered onto my white dress shirt.

I was in a bit of shock.

"I am so done with this fucking bullshit," Paulo exploded. I had never seen this side of him, his blood boiling beneath his beautiful Brazilian skin.

"Chill out. I didn't sleep with her. I pushed her off of me as soon as it happened," I tried to explain.

"I don't care, Mark! I don't give one shit what you did," he said. He paced back and forth before running to our bedroom.

I heard a rustling. The packing of a bag, then jeans slipping on his legs and the familiar sound of his belt buckle as he buttoned his pants. He returned from the bedroom holding his overnight bag.

"Baby, calm down. What are you doing? I asked as I tried to pull him toward me.

He pushed me away and said, "I'm done. Done." Tears were welling in his eyes.

I was frightened.

"Paulo, I told you nothing happened. I just let things go too far. On stage, with the bidding, all of it," I said.

"It's not about you," he shouted. "It's about me." Tears streamed down his cheeks. "I can't go to dinner with you. Hell, I can't even be seen in public with you! But some rich bitch can pay two thousand dollars and stick her tongue down your throat?"

He grabbed his car keys from the kitchen counter.

"I can't do this anymore, Mark," he said. "I'm sorry, but I'm done." He yanked his jacket from the closet and headed for the door.

"Baby. Stop! Please," I begged him.

"Not anymore," Mark. "I've had it with all of this!"

I grabbed at his arm before he reached the door.

"What do you mean, all of this?"

"*Entudo mentira!*" he shot back. "*Entudo mentira!*"

"What are you saying?" I said, trying to pull him toward me.

"It's all a lie!" he said. "A fucking lie!" he screamed.

"Shh." I whispered to him, hoping he had not disturbed the neighbors.

"*Quao rico? Quao rico?*" he cried.

"I hate it when you do this!" I lied. "Speak English!"

"I said, *How rich?* How rich? They pay you all that money to tell the truth and you're living a lie. Everything about your public persona is a lie," he said. "And I can't take it anymore. I want to live the truth." Each word broke my heart into another piece.

"I'm leaving, Mark. This is it. I'm sorry, but this is it."

He pulled away from me and headed out the door and toward the elevator.

"Paulo!" I shouted. "Come back here!"

I heard the neighbor's door open and then saw two eyes peering from the opening between the door and frame.

"It's okay, Ms. Jennings. I'm just saying goodbye to my friend."

I saw Paulo as the doors of the elevators opened. He entered, turned and held the door with his arm, as if he was waiting for me to join him.

Our eyes met for another sad connection. He lowered his arm and the door closed in front of him.

Then the neighbor's door closed and I was alone.

Again.

14

ONE LAST GOODBYE

Eight months had passed since Paulo left.

I tried calling him at his work and even called the Press Club trying to find him. No one would tell me anything. He had simply vanished out of thin air. I missed him terribly and he was on my mind as I entered Carol's office for a meeting she had arranged with me.

"You've seemed off the last few weeks," Carol said to me as she sat down behind her desk. "Is everything okay?"

"Yeah, sorry, Carol, just going through some personal stuff. Nothing major," I lied.

"Well, I don't mean to pile anything else on you," she said sincerely, "But, I have some news. I'm leaving the station." She looked at me with sadness.

"What happened?" I asked, instantly assuming that something bad had gone down.

"I've been offered my dream job," she said. Her face shifted from sadness to a warm smile. "I'm going home to Detroit. News director at the last-place station in the market. That seems to be my thing," she said with a chirp of laughter.

Startled, I replied, "Congratulations, Carol. Nobody deserves it more than you." I felt a bit sad myself now.

"I don't say this lightly, Mark." Her tone changed back to her signature, all-business cadence. "I don't get this call without you. I want you to know I sincerely thank you for the tremendous work you've done. You've changed my life."

"You hired me, Carol," I said. "I should be the one thanking you."

"We did it together. We're a team."

For a moment, I thought she was playing me.

"Hold on here, Carol," I said with a grin.

"What?" she asked.

"I'm not going to Detroit with you." I thought I was being slyly recruited to follow her to her new job. "The winters here are bad enough. I'm from Georgia, remember?"

She smiled, no longer able to keep a straight face. "I do, and that's where you'll be heading back."

"What?" I asked with a puzzled look on my face.

"You're going home too," she said. "I got a call from your agent this morning. She wanted my blessing before letting you know the news."

"What news are you talking about?" I hadn't received a heads up from my agent.

"You've been offered an anchor chair in Atlanta," she said, a huge smile crossing her face. "Congratulations."

For a second, I thought she was kidding. The news caught me completely off guard.

"What station?"

"Channel 4," she said with a big smile.

"What? Fearless4 News?" I said, no longer able to hide my excitement. "That was my favorite station growing up! I used to practice my standups in front of the mirror. Reporting live, Mark Pettit, Fearless4 News."

"You won't have to pretend anymore," she said like a proud mom. "They want you there sooner than later. Get with your agent and work out the details. We'll tell the rest of the team. Everyone will understand. They'll respect that this has always been your dream."

I was overcome with emotion and tears filled my eyes. All the hard work, all the pain. Finally, I was being rewarded.

Rising from her chair, Carol came around her desk. I stood before her. She pulled me close and hugged me.

"You've earned this," she whispered. "They want to meet you ahead of any official offer, but it's a formality. Take the next few days off and arrange your visit with the news director," she told me. "Steve Sherman. I've heard he's a really nice guy."

"Thank you. Thank you for everything, Carol," I told her as I wiped the tears from my cheeks. She pulled me close again, like a mother would hug her son.

The final lap for the dream team.

A few days later, I made my way to the airport in Omaha. I arrived just after six a.m. for my seven-thirty Eastern Airlines flight to Atlanta and headed straight for the shoeshine man. Years before, my grandfather told me the importance of clean shoes when meeting new people, especially in business. This coming from a man I never saw not wearing overalls and work boots.

"They look at your shoes before they look you in the eyes," Grandpa Pettit told me as if a business professor at Harvard. "Don't give 'em a reason to not look up."

I must have been around twelve at the time, but the discussion made an impact on me. That year for Christmas, I made him a shoeshine box at Vacation Bible School. I painted it bright red, and his eyes lit up when he opened it on Christmas morning.

"Good morning, sir!" the shoeshine man said as I approached his booth inside Eppley Airfield. "Where are you headed on this glorious morning?"

I've always been impressed by the joy in people you might think have mundane jobs. I found his attitude refreshing.

"I'm headed to Atlanta," I told him. "For a very important business meeting."

"Well sit right down here and let me get to work, young man," he said. He turned into a whirling mix of arms, shoeshine, brushes and rags. His feverish work ended in about ten minutes. He finished with a small toothbrush spreading a black liquid on the soles of my leather shoes.

"There you go, my man!" he said proudly. "If the shoes do any talking in the meeting, we gonna be just fine," he exclaimed with a smile.

I reached for my wallet and pulled out a crisp sawbuck. At the time, a shoeshine was around two dollars. I handed him the ten spot and reached to shake his hand.

"At least I know they'll look me in the eyes after they see the shine on my shoes," I told him. There was no need to elaborate on Grandpa Pettit's story. He knew what I meant. We parted with smiles.

A few hours later, I landed in Atlanta and after grabbing my bag from the claim area—I always check my bag!—I headed out to hail a cab.

"Waffle House on Clairmont Road," I told him like I knew where I was going.

Yes, you heard that right. Steve Sherman, the news director at the famous Fearless4 didn't want to meet at my hotel, or even at the station. He wanted to start our meeting over breakfast at the legendary Waffle House. Scattered, smothered and covered as they say in the South.

That was the kind of guy Steve was. Very unassuming and gentle, himself like a college professor. I arrived at the Waffle House to see him waiting in a back booth, wearing a white button–down shirt, red and blue tie and slacks.

I walked up to his table.

"Fancy meeting you here. And by fancy, I mean here at the Waffle House," he said with a childlike laugh.

Steve and I hit it off immediately. I liked his calm demeanor, which would come in handy at Fearless4, where they employed a range of news personalities. Some of them with very big personalities packed in tiny bodies.

"Your agent has been hounding me about you for a year now. She thinks you'd be a great fit at Fearless4," he said. "I think she might be right. We're looking for a solid investigative reporter and I know you like anchoring. So how about the best of both worlds," he teased.

"What do you have in mind?" I asked?

"Weekend co-anchor and lead investigative reporter," he said. "A buck twenty-five to start, up to one fifty in Year Three."

"A buck twenty-five?" I asked naïvely.

Steve let out another chuckle. "I guess I should speak English," he said, which hit me funny at the time. "One hundred twenty-five thousand dollars starting salary. We can up you to $150,000 by Year Three."

I almost did a spit take. I had worked my way up to an annual salary of $85,000 in Omaha, anchoring the five, six and ten o'clock news. One hundred twenty-five thousand was another stratosphere for me. However, at the time, it was not uncommon for the main anchors at the TV stations in Atlanta to make half a million or more.

Weekend anchor and lead investigative reporter was the way I had started at KN2-TV. I felt I had paid my dues and was finally ready for Atlanta. Steve and I finished our breakfast at the Waffle House, and he drove me into town to tour Fearless4. He led me in the side door, where employees entered and exited the building, and we made a detour into the lobby where he introduced me to the bubbly receptionist, Ann.

"Welcome to Fearless4!" she said with a bright smile. "Who's your handsome friend, Steve?"

"Mark Pettit. He's going to be our new investigative reporter and weekend anchor," he told Ann. "Save a place for his face up there on the wall." He pointed to three rows of oversized photos of the station's news talent.

I looked over at the wall and saw the faces of many on-air personalities that I had grown up with and had dreamed of becoming. As I told the *Calhoun Times* after I was hired by the station, it was like signing with the New York Yankees and playing with Joe DiMaggio. I should have referenced the Atlanta Braves and Hank Aaron. I blame it on youthful excitement.

The rest of the tour went well. Steve proudly walked me through the newsroom, stopping at the desks of the main anchors.

"John, meet Mark. Mark, this is Chuck. Guy, meet Mark." And on down the line. It was surreal. I was going home to Atlanta to play in the major leagues.

I put in my two weeks' notice at KN2-TV, and my tour of duty in Omaha was over. That was that. At the end of the two weeks, I was back at my apartment, boxes stacked all around me.

I looked around the rooms, which held a still sadness. I had spent so many nights here with Paulo and missed his face and his sweet laugh. I still had not heard from him since the night he left me standing in the hallway.

As I mentioned earlier, I tried calling him at the Press Club, but they said he had quit his part-time job there. I left clandestine voicemails on his machine at work.

Nothing.

He had left without telling me anything. I had a feeling though, as I picked up that morning's edition of the *Omaha World Herald*.

SAN FRANCISCO NOW GROUND ZERO IN FIGHT AGAINST AIDS, the headline said across page eight, buried deep behind stories about farmers and futures and the who's who of Omaha.

Everything was happening so quickly. A whirlwind, just like everything else in my life. I didn't even have time to read my mail. I picked up a chunk of unopened envelopes and stuffed them haphazardly into my briefcase. I could read the mail later. For now, I had one more stop to make before I left Nebraska.

The fertile farm fields laid out before me like a huge checkerboard as I made my way back to Lincoln. I had interviewed Jeremy

Jonus six times now over an eight-month period and spent many weekends traveling back to Vermont to piece together his troubled past.

I should have recognized the growing trouble at home and the rage that was slow boiling inside of Paulo.

"I don't like this," he had told me one of our ever increasingly rare evenings together. "I only see you late at night. I feel more like a hooker than your boyfriend," he told me, his eyes falling from mine to the floor.

"Baby, you know how hard I'm working," I tried to explain. "This book on Jonus isn't going to write itself."

I could see the hurt and anger in his face.

"He gets more quality time with you than I do."

Now, Paulo was gone, and I was on my way for what would be my final interview with Jonus.

It was the same routine as always. Front desk, guard desk, metal detectors, maximum security guard desk and finally the small conference room where we had met all six times before.

Once again, like Groundhog Day, the guard brought Jonus in to sit with me.

When the guard left, Jonus became animated.

"Did you happen to see *People Magazine*?" he asked out of the blue. "The one with Charlie Sheen on the cover?"

I hadn't seen the issue and said, "No. Why?"

Now, even more animated, Jonus replied, "He said he'd rather be in a killing scene than a love making scene. I'm in prison for thinking like that."

It was an odd exchange but opened the door for my first round of questions.

"Let's talk about your fantasies, like the one you had about killing your babysitter when you were six years old," I reminded him. "Do you still have those fantasies?"

Without hesitation, Jonus replied, "Yes. Often."

"And do they involve young boys?" I pressed.

He hesitated, as if he didn't want to answer, but couldn't help himself.

"Yes, some of the time," he confessed.

"And what happens when you have these fantasies?" I asked, trying to get to the effect of the cause.

"I usually jerk off," he said, matter-of-factly. "Sometimes I draw them out, so I can remember them later."

"What do you mean, 'draw them out?'" I asked, pushing my small tape recorder closer to him to make sure I captured his exact response.

"On paper, with colored pencils," he said. "I even have a red one for the blood."

What?

"My god, you're on death row and you're drawing out your fantasies of killing more young boys?" I asked incredulously.

"Yes," he said with a look of guilt. "The guards shook me down last spring. They found two of the drawings on my desk and confiscated them."

"So, the prison has the drawings?" I continued, an idea coming to my head.

"Yes, they took them to the warden," he said. "I got solitary for three days afterwards."

I couldn't hold back my judgment.

"You know this is fucked up, Jeremy," I said. "You know something's really wrong with you, right?"

He hung his head, ashamed of what he had told me.

"I do," he said, "I would really like to understand it myself."

I paused to think and then told him, "I have an idea. Tell the prison to release the drawings to me. I'll take them to an expert and get them analyzed and bring you the results," I promised him. "Maybe it will help you stop the fantasies."

He looked at me, his freaky eyes again meeting mine. He reached across the table and grabbed the yellow pad on which I had been taking notes. He tore a single page from the notepad and wrote a brief note which he signed.

"Take this to the warden and he should hand them over," Jonus said.

"Great. I'll do that and let you know what he says."

"I really would like to know what all this means." Becoming animated again he said, "What else do you want to talk about today?"

"Burlington," I said.

And then, cracking an odd smile, he said, "How was your trip and how were all my dear friends that I'm sure you tried to speak with?" His tone was facetious.

"I liked the city," I told him. "Idyllic, actually. Just not as innocent after you."

"As for your 'friends,' there didn't seem to be many," I reported.

"Tell me about it," he said. "I was what you would call a loner. I got bullied a lot and became even more of one."

"What else did you find from your snooping?"

This had become the pattern for each of our interviews. A high-level chess game, cat and mouse, and all the clichés that might apply.

"That everything you told me was true," I told him. "And the cops had no clue. I found the police reports, the clippings from the newspaper. Even talked with two of your victims."

This piqued his interest.

"Did they remember my face," he said coldly. "I hope so."

"Again, that's fucked up," I scolded him.

We had gotten to that point in our relationship. Both of us dropping our guards at times and saying things we probably shouldn't have.

"What did you tell the cops?" Jonus asked pointedly.

"Nothing," I said. "They can read it in the book."

"You know I'm not crazy about this book idea," Jonus fired back.

"The prosecutor was right, Jeremy. He said no one knows more about this case than you and me. It's time people knew the truth, the why you did all this. That's all I've ever been after. You know that."

"I believe you," he said.

This was the opening I had been waiting for and I pounced.

"Then tell me the truth. Did you kill Randy Statham?"

Jonus recoiled.

"I told you I didn't want to talk about Randy Statham!" he shouted, causing the guard outside the door to interrupt.

"Is everything okay in here?" he asked, looking at me.

"Yes. Everything's fine, officer," I told him. "The discussion got a little heated. I apologize."

The guard nodded and left the room.

Again, it was just Jonus and me.

"His parents are hurting, Jeremy," I said, leaning toward him. "They need closure. You're the only person who can give them that."

"I don't want to talk about it!" he said in a hushed but angry whisper.

"I walked the path that Randy ran around the lake," I said. "You remember his jogging suit, right? Gray, USA on the chest? The boy's bright red hair?"

Jonus looked down at his hands. He knew. I knew.

I pressed my case further.

"I saw the autopsy photos. It was awful," I told him. "Just like Jimmy Ray and Robbie. It was you, wasn't it, Jeremy? You killed Randy Statham."

Without pausing, Jonus reached for the small tape recorder in front of him and pressed the off button.

There was a tense moment between us. And then, the answer I had been waiting for.

"Listen, I like you. I trust you" Jonus whispered. "I can't lie to you. I can't say that I didn't do it, but the last time I pled guilty to anything I got the death penalty."

Silence.

After about fifteen seconds, I said, "Thank you for being honest with me."

"I felt like we've come too far for me not to be honest with you."

I shifted uncomfortably in my seat and then broke the news to him.

"I'm really going to miss our conversations," I said.

A puzzled look overcame his face. "What do you mean?"

"This will be the last time I get to meet with you in person," I confessed. "I've taken a job in Atlanta, with a station there."

Jonus became agitated. His eyes flashed anger.

"What?" he demanded.

"Weekend anchor and investigative reporter," I said proudly, not sure of why I said it the way I did.

"That's it?" he shot back to me. "I tell you everything and you're just going to leave?" he said, his cheeks now aglow in red.

"It's not personal, Jeremy," I tried to explain.

"Actually, it is," he said. "I don't want you to go."

I felt incredibly awkward and started to gather my things.

Then, he pounced.

"I know what you are." His voice had a demonic tone.

"Excuse me?" I replied, not sure where he was going.

"You don't go any dates, you never talk about any girls," he said.

My eyes narrowed as I listened to him.

"You're some kind of homosexual, aren't you?" he said aggressively.

I was shocked by his words. Had I done something to lead him on? Yes, when I first saw his mugshot, I was in a guilty way attracted to him. When I saw the photo of him as an Eagle Scout, I was attracted to him.

But no. He was a killer. You can't be attracted to him. He's a killer.

I wasn't going to play his game. I leaned in and whispered to him.

"You know what they say, Jeremy. It takes one to know one," I said, recalling the old saying of when one suspected homosexual defends himself from another.

He sat back in his chair with a smug look on his face.

The prison guard interrupted the exchange.

"That's two hours, gentlemen. Wrap it up."

Flustered from it all, I grabbed at the papers in front of me, rearranging the stack of unopened mail I had stuffed into my briefcase earlier.

"So, that's it? You're gone?" Jonus said.

"I'll be back in touch," I said, trying to jam the lid shut on the briefcase, the latch catching on the stack of mail inside. It wouldn't close, so I just picked it up and placed it under my left arm.

I didn't realize it at the time, but a piece of the mail fell from my case. Jonus saw it and placed his foot over it on the floor.

"I'll miss you," he said, as he reached to shake my hand for the last time.

I awkwardly returned his shake.

"I'll miss you too," I said.

It sounded horrible as soon as the words left my lips, but I had formed an odd bond with Jonus. And we were now the two keepers of his last secret.

We shared a last glance, a capital goodbye.

The guard led me from the room.

CHAPTER

15

IN A DELUXE APARTMENT

The move to Atlanta went smoothly.

I found an apartment in a brand-new community not far from the station and moved what furniture I had into what they called the "penthouse unit." It was on the top floor but overlooked busy I-85. At night and sometimes in the very early morning hours, I could hear cars whizzing by on the pavement below.

Darling, I love a penthouse, but not with an interstate view.

It didn't really matter, as I had no friends in the city and a name to make for myself as Fearless4's new investigative reporter and weekend anchorman. Like before at KN2-TV, I poured myself into my work, trying to forget about Paulo and trying not to act on my raging homosexual hormones.

Steve called me into his office on the first day I started and said something that very few reporters would hear in today's TV newsrooms: "Take your time," he told me. "We want you breaking stories that matter. We want you to build relationships, to make sources, to do really solid work."

So that's what I did. I even went so far as to have little stickers printed out with my name and my direct phone line printed on them. Everywhere I went, I handed out the stickers. To police officers on the streets, detectives at police stations, receptionists, FBI agents, GBI agents, anyone who might know anything when news broke.

Never Fear: Mark is Here! the stickers said. *When news breaks, call me first!*

It worked.

I started getting calls with tips and story ideas from all sorts of people. Everything from a pastor in Gainesville molesting young boys at church to city workers slacking on the job. The latter would win me my first Emmy Award.

Men at Work was the title of the series.

My photographer, Dan Johnson, and I spent weeks following lazy city workers, doing everything but their jobs. Buying liquor during the workday, sitting by campfires in the woods, everything but working.

Our hidden camera footage was riveting and led the nightly news for almost a week. Atlanta's then-mayor, Maynard Jackson, was livid over the coverage and called me personally to ask to review the footage.

I still remember him barreling into the station with two aides by his side. Maynard was a big, bold man and with a personality the size of Lake Lanier. We sat together in an editing booth at the station and watched the hidden camera footage roll.

After about fifteen minutes, he had seen enough.

"Where do you want to do the interview?" he asked me. "Uh, the lobby? Conference room? Anywhere you want, Mayor."

I scrambled to the assignment desk. "He's really upset," I told the lead assignment editor. "He's agreed to an interview. I think we should lead the eleven o'clock news."

And we did and Mayor Jackson did not disappoint, blasting the city's public works director.

"If *he* is not taking care of business, then *he* has got to go!"

Not long after, the city official in question was gone and our series beat out three other solid segments to win the coveted Emmy for investigative reporting. Again, keep in mind, this was when investigative reporters were given weeks, if not months, to work on a story. Not expected to slice and dice a ninety-second story across multiple newscasts and social media platforms.

It was real investigative reporting against some of the city's best reporters like Richard Belcher and Dale Russell, who both recently retired (still at the top of their games).

When I wasn't working at the station, I was working to finish my book on the Jonus case. I had naïvely taken the Nebraska prosecutor's advice and jumped into writing the book, with no real knowledge of what I was doing. Luckily, the small Nebraska publisher who signed me to write the book had paid for an editor to help guide me. I worked for a solid year, diligently banging out copy on my Brother typewriter and ended up sending my editor around two hundred pages of typewritten text by US Mail.

A few weeks later, the package came back to me.

It was like Jack the Ripper had reviewed my copy. There was red everywhere. Notes of disdain. Notes of encouragement.

Be more descriptive here! Be more specific here! Do you have a source for this?

And then the big red circle at the top of Chapter Ten.

??? my editor wrote next to the circle. *Is this a confession?*

> I can't lie to you. I can't say that I didn't do it, but the last time I pled guilty to anything, I got the death penalty.
>
> —Jeremy Jonus, death row interview
> at the Nebraska State Penitentiary

Yes. I included the quote in my book and, yes, I considered it a confession.

A day after I received the package from my editor, I got a message on my answering machine from my publisher, Jerry Kronenburger.

"Mark, Jerry Kronenburger. We have to talk about your book. Please call me at your earliest convenience."

It sounded ominous and urgent. Jerry left his office phone number, which I pretty much knew by heart at this point, and I called him the next morning.

"Mark, are you sure this is what Jonus told you? This is some serious shit," he doubted in his distinctive nasally tone.

"I have it on tape, Jerry," I replied confidently. "Well, almost all of it."

"That's what I was hoping you'd say," Jerry replied, "Because this is explosive, Mark. He's basically confessed to a third murder. You need to be ready when this book comes out. Everyone is going to come after you. After us." His voice indicated concern.

Jerry was right.

The book came out and we sold 2,500 copies within two weeks. I went on a book tour in Omaha with no books to sign. People were wrapped down the halls outside the mall bookstore.

I was signing IOU's, promising them a signed copy of the book from the next printed batch.

I did manage to save more than a hundred copies of the hardback version of the book for a signing in my hometown of Calhoun. My mother sat beside me, smiling brightly as I signed copies of my book for friends, family members, former schoolteachers, anyone and everyone who came out to the event, benefiting the local Calhoun Gordon County library.

About an hour into the event, I looked up and saw a slightly familiar man near the back of the line, holding a copy of my book that he had purchased that night.

That man was my biological father, Olen.

My heart almost stopped as he approached the table where my mother and I were sitting. Before addressing me, he walked around and hugged her. They exchanged awkward pleasantries and then Olen turned back to me.

It's hard to describe our relationship, because, honestly, there wasn't much of one. I had been born out of wedlock, the result of a heated fall to winter relationship and several romps at the "Sugar Shack" in the woods, as my mother referred to it.

She told me stories about Olen. That he was a good man, smart, talented and creative. But a man with a drinking problem. He would bring home a six pack of Miller, "The Champagne of Beers," and sit in front of the TV with little to no interest in me or my mother. On several occasions, I remember Olen picking me up from my mother's place with my Uncle Rusty riding shotgun. Them in the front seat of the car, laughing and singing and me and a case of Miller in the back seat, hanging on for dear life.

"I'm really proud of you, son," he said to me as he opened the book to the title page. "Writing a book is a really big accomplishment. You should be proud of yourself too."

My mind drifted back to a Christmas morning at my Grandparent's house when I was eight or nine years old. I loved going there for Christmas. I would get to stay the night with three or four of my other cousins. I can still hear the laughter from the kitchen as my aunts worked with Grandma Pettit on our Christmas meal. I loved how we'd all open presents, sometimes, a simple pair of socks from my grandparents (there were a lot of us!) and how happy I was. And I remember the time Olen showed up with nothing to put under the tree.

After we had opened our presents, he came up to me and reached into his pocket.

"I have something for you," he said proudly.

He then handed me a pocketknife. At first, I was excited. It didn't need to be wrapped. It was a present from my dad. And then, I flipped the knife over to admire it from the other side and that's when I saw the writing on the case holding the blade: *Merry Christmas from your friends at Mauldin's Feed & Seed.*

My young heart sank. It wasn't a gift from my dad. It was an afterthought from a man distracted by drinking with no time for his bastard son.

I snapped back to my senses and reached for the pen on the table.

To Dad, I wrote on the page beneath my name, *Good News Always.*

Yes. Sadly, I gave him the generic salutation that I wrote out to the common strangers who approached me with their books or their boarding passes.

I might as well have written, *Merry Christmas from your friends at Mauldin's Feed & Seed.*

A few years later, Olen lay dying in the Veteran's Hospital in Atlanta. He had finally reached the end of the party line and, as his liver and heart were failing him, my Aunt Faye begged me to go visit him.

"Please, go see him," she implored. "If you don't, you'll regret it for the rest of your life."

But I couldn't. Or I wouldn't. I was still angry. Still hurt. He never showed up for anything in my life. Not one birthday, not one baseball game. Not our high school play. Nothing.

And the one time he did show up, it was to regift me with a pocketknife. I had no reason to visit the Ghost of Christmas Past. I didn't go see him and he died in the hospital. And my aunt was right. I regret my decision to this day. Yes, Olen was a lousy father, but he deserved better from his lousy son. I at least had the decency to help my older stepbrother plan my father's funeral.

People and absent parents weren't the only ones who took an interest in my book. So did a publisher and the police.

Call Elisa Waters, the "While You Were Out" message read by the phone on my desk in the newsroom. *Fawcett Books,* with a 212 phone number. I dialed the number and Elisa answered on the second or third ring.

"Our president read your book on a plane," she said to me. "She's actually from Nebraska and was familiar with the case. We'd like to buy the paperback rights to your book, if they're still available."

"Elisa, that sounds great. But honestly, I've never heard of Fawcett Books," I confessed. "Could you tell me more about your company?"

There was a brief pause on the line and then she dropped the bombshell.

"We'd be the largest publisher of paperback books in the world," she said calmly. "Perhaps you've heard of Danielle Steel?"

I had heard the name.

"Romance novels," Elisa told me. "She's on her way to selling billions."

"In that case, count me in," I told Elisa.

It was a smart decision. We went on to sell 85,000 copies of my book around the world in just six months. It went on to be a best-seller and #1 on another list, the FBI's.

"We want to talk with you about your book and the quote," the agent told me over the phone. "And if necessary, we'll come after your notes with a subpoena."

He wasn't joking.

"Mark, this is Ann at the front desk," the receptionist said after I answered her call at my desk in the newsroom. "There are two agents here to see you," she said with concern in her voice.

"Ask them who they represent." I could hear a muffled sound, like the palm of her hand placed over the speaker of the phone handset.

"One of them is with the FBI. The other says he's with the Vermont state police," Ann said.

"I'll be right there," I told her.

I grabbed my employee ID badge and headed to the lobby. The two agents were looking at the oversized anchor photos on the wall as I interrupted them.

"I look much better in person, don't you think?" I said, trying to break the ice. The FBI agent was in no mood for foolish conversation.

"We'll make this brief," he said. "We want your notes and your tapes from your interviews with Jeremy Jonus. We can do it the easy way or the hard way." He gave me a serious look.

"Are you threatening me?" I said to him, which I believe caught him off guard. "Because if you are, this conversation is over. I'm not giving you anything. If you want to talk with Jeremy Jonus, I think you know where you can find him."

"We thought you might feel that way," he said, as he handed me an envelope. I took the envelope, opened it and pulled the oversized letter out.

SUBPOENA it read across the top of the document. I scanned it. "…any and all notes, tape recorded interviews…" was all I needed to see.

"Meetings over, G-men," I told them. "My attorney will be in touch."

It was a bluff. I didn't have an attorney.

I made my way back to my desk in the newsroom and punched in the number of my agent in DC. She picked up right away. "Kris Keckler. How can I help you?" she said in rapid fire response.

"Find me a lawyer," I told her. "We've got a problem with my book."

Kris was a big, broad-shouldered woman who suffered no fools. "What's the problem?" She asked.

"It's the FBI. They want all my notes and the tapes from my interviews with Jeremy Jonus. They just served me with a subpoena here at the station," I whispered into the phone.

"Fuck that!" she said, her back now up. "Don't give them shit. All a journalist has is his or her word with sources. If you give up that information, no one's going to trust you with interviews down the road."

"You're preaching to the pope, Kris," I said. "I told the agents who came here today that they'd be hearing from my attorney. The problem is, I don't have an attorney."

After a couple of beats, Kris collected her thoughts.

"I've got an idea," she said. "Frank Deekins is a very well-known media lawyer up here," she continued. "He represents the *Post*, Associated Press and others. He owes me a favor," she said with an awkward laugh.

"A favor?" I asked. "What, are you sleeping with him?"

"I wouldn't call it sleeping with him," she replied right away. "Just a little fun here and there." She laughed.

"Whatever it takes, wherever news breaks," I replied with a chuckle, repeating a famous news slogan.

Whatever she had to do, she did and a few hours later I was on the phone with the DC media attorney Frank Deekins.

"You've got a bit of a problem, Mark. We can fight it tooth and nail, but you've got books for sale in airports across the country. You've made these guys look really bad as you got a confession that they couldn't get, and you can bet they have bosses up their asses over this," he said.

"What's your gut on the case?" I asked him point blank.

"My gut is that we cut a deal. No notes, no tape recordings," he said. "Kris is right. If you give those up, you're risking your career. Nobody's going to want to talk to a perceived agent of the government. But maybe we give them what they need: that confession."

"What do you mean?"

"We limit your testimony to just what Jonus told you," he counselled. The quote at the top of Chapter Eight. You testify to the veracity of the statement and that's it."

"I don't have a dictionary close by, Fred," I said. "Can you define the word 'veracity?'" I asked. "And it's actually Chapter Ten in the paperback."

"Simply put, 'veracity' means the accuracy of fact," he said. "That you believed what Jonus told you to be the truth. That's it. No notes, no tapes, nothing else. Just confirm what he told you and that you took it as the truth."

I was on the spot. I didn't have a treasure trove of cash to mount a legal fight, but I didn't want to risk a future as a rat. A journalist no one could trust with an interview.

"Jonus is going to lose it," I told Fred. "He trusted me and now I'm going to fuck him over in court?"

"He fucked himself, Mark," Fred said. "You just reported the facts. He's the one who killed those boys. That's not on you."

So that was the deal we cut with the FBI and authorities in Vermont. I would take the stand to testify against Jonus in the new murder trial, but my testimony would be very limited and focused primarily on the words Jonus spoke himself.

It was early October as I made my way north to Burlington. Winter had not begun to squeeze its sub-zero grip and it was a balmy sixty-five degrees as I landed at Burlington International. I picked up my overnight bag from baggage claim and made my way outside the airport. Detective Pete Kenton was waiting for me in an unmarked police car.

Kenton had led the investigation into the death of Randy Statham, the twelve-year-old boy Jonus was now charged with killing. Like the investigators in Omaha, Kenton and his fellow officers had tracked down hundreds, if not thousands of leads in the boy's death but had come up empty.

They were not privy to the clues that I was provided by Jonus allowing me to connect the dots to a series of crimes in and around Burlington that had led up to Statham's murder.

"Welcome to Vermont," he said, as I loaded my suitcase into the back seat of the cruiser and slid into the passenger's seat of his black sedan.

"Thank you, sir," I said. "It's nice to be back."

"You should have told me you were coming the last time you were here," he said. "We might have been able to piece things together before your book came out. That book caused me some serious heartburn."

"I'm a reporter, Detective Kenton," I said. "I don't work for the police department like you. I work for the people who count on me to report the truth."

"No hard feelings. We both have the same goal: solving this murder," he summarized.

"I thought I'd show you around town before we head to meet with the DA." he said, as he pointed his car toward the lakefront.

"That would be nice," I told him. "I didn't have a lot of time for sightseeing the last time I was here. I tried to talk to as many people as I could who knew Jonus and Randy."

"So you walked the trail, right? Where the boy's body was found?"

"Yes sir, I did," I told him. "It was eerily similar to walking the crime scenes in Omaha. It was horrible, what Jonus did, to all those boys."

Kenton was to the point. "So you believe he killed Randy Statham?"

"The book speaks for itself sir," I told him. "I'm going to tell the jury what Jonus told me and that's it."

We drove in silence for the next ten minutes.

Burlington was originally a lumber town and was still suffering from its foray into the oil and gas business. The riverfront had been ravaged by oil leaks and sludge, remnants of the more than eighty above-ground storage tanks that used to dot the waterway.

By the mid-eighties, it became a disaster area with barbed wire and fencing around the storage tanks making the area all but inaccessible. A historic Supreme Court ruling led to a reclamation effort along the waterfront, which would eventually restore the area to its natural beauty.

For now, the transformation had not happened, and the place looked sad.

As we approached the courthouse, Detective Kenton briefed me on what was to come.

"Ms. Lechevsky is the assistant state's attorney for the district. She's the one who brokered the deal with your attorney. She will handle the questioning for the state. Hank Horan will question you for the defense. Be careful. He's a wily son of a bitch," Kenton said. "I've had to deal with him a thousand times over the years."

I nodded in quiet acknowledgement.

To my surprise, there were no reporters waiting for us at the courthouse as we arrived.

"Where's the media?" I asked the detective.

"Dumb bastards are about to miss the biggest story of the year," Kenton said, in his deep Irish brogue.

He was right.

I was ushered into the courthouse and no one from the media was there to witness it.

Just after three p.m., I was called into the courtroom. As I entered, Jonus turned his head from the defendant's table. Our eyes met and his stare burned like the afternoon sun on my face.

He was not happy, and he was about to get a lot unhappier.

For the first forty-five minutes, I was questioned by Ms. Lechevsky. She worked diligently to paint me as an expert on the Jonus case. Her aim was to convince the judge to allow my testimony. Then, Hank Horan stood and faced me. The red of his tie was only surpassed by the red in his cheeks, an angry red and I braced for impact.

"The simple fact of the matter, Mr. Pettit is that you were brokering information for the police," he said. "Isn't that right," he yelled.

"Objection, your honor!" Ms. Lechevsky fired back. "Mr. Pettit is a reporter, not an agent of the government."

"Sustained," the judge said, not looking up from his legal pad.

"Let me ask it in a different way," Mr. Horan said. "Did you tell Jeremy Jonus that his interview with you would be used against him in a court of law?"

"Objection, your honor!" Ms. Lechevsky said sternly. "Both sides have stipulated ahead of this trial that Mr. Pettit was not an agent of the government and did not coerce Mr. Jonus in any way."

"Sustained," the judge said, now looking at Horan.

"Did you forget the terms of the agreement, Mr. Horan? It has been clearly established that Mr. Pettit is not an agent of the police. He is a reporter. His job is to ask questions," he continued. "Your client made the decision to answer those questions. And, that is why we're here. Because of the answer to a very important question."

And that was that. Horan sank into his seat and the judge dismissed court for the rest of the afternoon.

The next morning at nine a.m., the judge ruled that my testimony would be allowed and ordered the trial to continue. I steeled myself for the onslaught of questions that were to come from Hank Horan.

Instead, he let his assistant do the questioning.

She was unprepared and disorganized. So much so, that she didn't even ask me if I had written down the quote in question, much less question whether Jonus had stopped the tape recorder before responding.

Jonus never had a chance. He was convicted for Randy Statham's murder and given another life sentence on top of his death sentence.

As court concluded, I gathered my papers, placed them into my trusty Samsonite briefcase and headed out the door. As I made my way outside, I looked to my right and saw sheriff's deputies walking Jonus down the sidewalk and toward a waiting patrol car.

Once more our eyes met. He paused, almost causing the deputies to trip into him. I stopped as well, and we stared at each other for what felt like an eternity. His eyes were red with a rage and anger like I had not seen before.

Then, his head dropped, and he continued on the path to the patrol car.

I saw Hank Horan heading to his car and walked quickly to catch up with him.

"Mr. Horan, I said. "When this is over, I'd really like to speak with Jeremy again."

He looked at me like I had three heads.

"You can talk to him after the State of Nebraska executes him," he said as he slammed the trunk of his car.

No further questions of this witness, your honor.

There was really nothing left to say at that point. I turned and walked back over to Detective Kenton who was waiting for me on the sidewalk.

"I told you he was a wily son of a bitch," he told me.

"Maybe not so much of a defense lawyer," I replied.

Detective Kenton drove me to the airport. I boarded my flight back home to Atlanta. There was an even bigger story waiting for me back there.

And adventures I had not planned for.

CHAPTER

16

SECURITY FOR SALE

A s I mentioned before, sources are everything to a good investigative reporter. The right tip at the right time can uncover an iceberg of information.

I hit that iceberg in 1990.

"I can get you uniforms, employee badges, access codes to restricted areas, just about anything you want," the man said to me over the phone. "If you've got the money, I've got the keys to Hartsfield International."

Keep in mind, this was a full ten years before 9/11.

"I don't believe you," I told the man, trying to call his bluff. He didn't take the bait.

"Four fifty gets you a pilot's uniform, a baggage handlers uniform and the code to the tarmac at Concourse A," he said calmly.

At the station, my news director, Steve Sherman, sat next to the station GM, who sat next to two lawyers in what they called "the

177

boardroom." It was a large conference room with a boardroom table just off the GM's office on the second floor.

I sat alone on the other side of the imposing table, trying to make my case.

"If this guy's telling the truth, Hartsfield is the Swiss cheese of airports," I told them. "This is major-league stuff."

The GM shook his head.

"I don't know, Mark," he said. "The whole thing sounds fishy. There's no way you wouldn't get caught if you tried to sneak into that airport."

"You could go to jail if they did catch you," one of the lawyer's chimed in.

I thought for a moment and then had an idea.

"Okay. Let's tell them before we do it," I suggested. "Let's go to airport officials, the FAA and the FBI. Tell them what we think we have and see what they do about it."

I could see Steve was picking up what I was putting down.

"I like it," he said. "Let's take this in two steps. Tell them what Mark has uncovered and see how they react. If they don't act, maybe we move to Step Two," he said.

"Which is?" the GM asked.

"We turn him loose and see what happens," he said, looking toward me.

I shrugged my shoulders in agreement.

"Delta is going to shit its pants if we do this," the GM said, looking at me with dead seriousness. "And Eastern is already on the brink. Are you sure about this?"

"It all looks legit, Harry," I said. "I'm nervous about it too. I don't want to go to jail, but that airport could be a target for terrorists. Don't we have a responsibility here?"

"What do you think, Erik," the GM asked, looking at one of the attorneys.

"It's risky, Harry. We'll have to take this all the way to the general counsel's office at corporate. This could have a material effect on the company's stock price," he counseled.

Steve looked at me with concern and jotted a note on a piece of paper and slid it over to me. I tried to be cool as I read it.

Are your nuts up in your ass right now?

That was Steve, always the jokester, even when our careers were on the line.

I couldn't hold back and let out an awkward laugh.

"He said he was nervous," Steve said, coming to my defense in a crime of his making.

"Let's take a parallel path," Harry, the GM said, looking first at the lawyers and then at me. "You guys run it up the flagpole at corporate. You start with the FAA and Delta. Tell them what we have and let's see how it plays out."

That's what we did.

My first call was to Jack Barker, the regional spokesperson for the Federal Aviation Administration. He wasn't exactly thrilled to hear from me or to talk about the evidence we had uncovered indicating a serious breach in security at Hartsfield.

"You people in the media are like stolen cars," he said dismissively, "So easy to take for a ride."

I pressed him further.

"With all due respect, Jack," I told him (with no respect intended as I thought he was an asshole), "I think you're wrong on this one. I think I can use this stuff to get on an aircraft and at least onto the tarmac."

Again, he rebuffed me. "Listen, son, I've been doing this since before you were born." This much, at least, was true. If there was a security problem at Hartsfield, I'd know about it. I wouldn't need a rookie TV reporter like you to inform me."

I bit my tongue and pressed on.

"Okay, Jack, but you better give your bosses in DC a heads up. If this blows up, it'll be on you," I warned him.

"You let me worry about my bosses, son," he said, talking to me like I was a teenager.

"See you on the news, Jack." I hung up the phone.

A spokesman from Delta Air Lines was kind enough to meet with me in person at their corporate office not far from the airport.

I could see Delta jets taking off and landing as I waited in a small conference room for the spokesman to join me.

"Good morning, Mark. Gary Allen, head of corporate comms," he said as he entered the conference room. "This is Mary Lange, one of our senior attorneys. I thought it might be good for her to sit in on our briefing," he said.

I shook Mary's hand as we all sat down at the conference table.

"So, what do you think you have, Mark?" Gary asked as our conversation began. I reached into my briefcase and pulled out the baggage handler shirt that we had purchased as part of our package from the confidential informant.

"Working on your Halloween costume already?" Gary said, trying to ease the tension in the room.

"We also bought a pilot's uniform," I told him. "And we have what I've been told is the access code to at least one of the secure doors leading to the tarmac."

As we talked, I could see that Mary was taking detailed notes.

"First of all," Gary began, "What you've shown us could have been purchased at any thrift store," he said looking down at the baggage handler shirt. "And the access codes to doors are changed regularly. It's a matter of standard procedure."

"That's not what I've been told," I responded. "According to our sources, some door codes haven't changed in over a year."

"Well, your 'sources' are mistaken," he said, giving me the brush-off. "We take security very seriously, as I'm sure you can understand, and I can guarantee you any code you have been provided, will not open an access door at Hartsfield International."

I wrote down exactly what he said on my note pad: *will not open an access door.*

"What else can we help you with, today?" Gary asked with an awkward smile and sounding like a customer service representative.

"Just one last question, Gary," I said. "What if I were a terrorist?"

He and Mary both looked at each other and then back to me.

"Well, that's just silly. If you were a terrorist, you would have been arrested before you got to this floor," he said confidently.

"Oh, really? Just so you know, I flashed an ID badge we purchased and just walked right past your security guards downstairs."

Again, a troubled look crossed his face.

"Just kidding, Gary," I said, as the air returned to the room. "We're saving that for the real test at the airport."

"Good luck," he said. "Be sure to have a good bail bondsman's number in your wallet."

And that was the end of our meeting and the beginning of the biggest story I would ever break in my career, even bigger than Jeremy Jonus.

Or at least I thought.

We spent the next several weeks plotting just how we'd test security at Hartsfield International. I was assigned a photographer, and I would serve as both producer and reporter on the investigative series.

"Just tell me what you need, within reason," Steve told me, "And we'll work to make it available for you to do your work."

"I'm going to need a pilot's flight case fitted with a hidden camera," I told him. "I think Bruce should dress as a tourist with a home camcorder. We'll need wireless mics so we can all communicate as I try to access the tarmac."

"We can make that happen," Steve said.

"I need the art department to help me recreate the ID badge we bought from the informant. The one we have is pretty banged up," I told him. "I watched the security lines at the airport. It looks like employees just flash their badges and walk in. The guards never really look that closely."

"No problem," Steve replied. "What else?"

"We'll need a make-up artist and maybe someone to dye my hair darker," I told him. "The FAA and Delta know what I look like and might put out an APB."

"Done," Steve replied.

"What else?" the news director asked.

"Got the name of a good bail bondsman?" I said, half-jokingly. "The Delta guy warned me that I could get locked up for this." I was starting to doubt whether we should go through with the story.

"This is unbelievably risky serious shit, Mark," he said. "You don't have to do it."

"But what if I was a terrorist, Steve? I don't know if people are using this stuff to move drugs, or what. But what if they wanted to put a bomb on one of those planes? Or blow up a terminal? What if that happens and we had withheld this information, or at least not tested it?"

"Then, I guess that's our answer," he replied. "This is why we hired you, Mark, to break big stories. Just tell me how much time you need."

"Give me three months," I told him. "I think I can get in twice."

"You really think you can breach security twice at that airport?" he asked.

"Once is going to be tough enough," I said. "Twice? You might want to call the Vatican. We just might have a miracle on our hands."

Steve's face turned serious again.

"If you pull this off, we could lose you," he said. "Kris will be getting calls from all the networks."

It reminded me of the look on Earl's face in Chattanooga when he took the message from Carol at KN2-TV.

I can't quite explain it, but I had always had a special bond with the news directors I had worked for. Maybe it was because they took a chance on me or that they trusted me to take risks and chances that might pay off in ratings.

Or, maybe I just liked them, and they just liked me.

That, too, would change in time.

But for now, I had news to break. And a huge risk to take.

I had moved into a nice two-bedroom condo off of North Druid Hills Road, just north of Midtown and about two miles from the TV station. The first time I walked into the unit, there was something about it that I loved. It was beautifully renovated, with French doors that opened onto a deck with a gorgeous garden, and a hot tub lodged in the corner of the wooden deck.

A bachelor's paradise. Or make that a gay man's paradise.

As I made my way up the stairs to the second floor, I noticed the framed photos along the wall. The photos were all of handsome men. Some in ski suits, visiting what looked like a glamorous, snow-covered locale. In other photos, the men wore tiny bathing suits, which I would later know to be called Speedos.

"What do you think of the place?" My realtor said, disturbing me from my voyeuristic dive into the current owner's private life.

"I really like it," I said. "I love the style and the finishes."

"I thought you would," she said. "Peter has great taste."

"Peter?" I asked.

"He's the owner of the unit," she said. "He and his partner Mike did the renovation themselves."

His partner. Mike.

Now I understood the finishes. And the photos.

"Actually, Peter will be back in about ten minutes, if you'd like to meet him," she said.

I felt uneasy, like I had been violating Peter's privacy. Or maybe I was nervous about him. Another gay man.

It takes one to know one.

"Sure, why not?" I wondered if I should just leave before he got back.

"He can answer any questions you might have about the renovation or the garden," she said. "Did you notice he had everything labeled?"

"It'll all be dead within six months," I told her. "You realize how much I work?"

"I do," she said. "But now you'll have roots in the city. And a place to share with that special someone."

I didn't realize it at the time, but Jane, my real estate agent, was a lesbian, and she had seen right through me from the beginning. I began working with her mother, Beth, but we never really clicked on locations.

On one of our first tours of potential homes, Beth loaded me into her Lincoln Continental and headed way out to Stone Mountain, far from Midtown, where I instinctively wanted to live not really knowing that's where the gayborhood was.

"I'm not sure about this neighborhood," I told her as we drove down the tree-lined, suburban streets.

"Okay, Maaaark," she said in her classic Southern lady drawl. "I just have to ask ya. How much money do you make a year, honey?" Her demeanor had a hint of provincial apology, the topic of coin still a taboo no matter how germane it was to the conversation.

"One thirty-five this year up to one fifty next year," I replied, not sure if it was the answer she was looking for.

She whipped the big Lincoln Continental around in a nearby driveway and sped out of the neighborhood and back onto I-285, heading back to town.

"Right church. Wrong pew," she said with a wonderful laugh.

Beth apparently saw through me as well, quickly put two and two together and handed me off to work with her daughter, Jane.

"I think you two have a lot more in caaaahman," she said. "I love working with you, Maaark, but Jane knows more about your community than me."

At the time, I thought she meant where I would live. Later, I would understand she meant where I belonged.

Suddenly, a doorbell.

"That must be Peter," Jane said, as she headed for the door. "You go ahead and look upstairs and then come down and meet him. I think you two will hit it off."

I finished my tour of the upstairs level of the townhome. Like downstairs, it was gorgeous. Beautiful woven carpets in the two bedrooms, light tile and a glassed-in shower in the master bathroom. The shower looked like it was big enough for three or four people. I should have picked up the clues to a happy gay man's life.

But I digress.

On the nightstand in the main bedroom, I saw more framed photographs. Handsome, happy men smiling in what exotic locations. In one of the photographs, a good-looking older man had his arm around the shoulder of a younger blond-haired man. They both radiated happiness and I could sense a love between them.

I was shaken from my forbidden daydream by a familiar voice.

"Mark! Mark!" I heard Jane call from downstairs. "Peter's here."

I gathered myself, taking one last look at the smiling faces on the small, framed photos. The men resembled the families in the generic photo you'd see in a new frame. I scooted down the stairs and into the open living area below.

And there he stood before me: the older, handsome gentleman from behind the glass in the frames.

"Mark, this is Peter, the owner of the home. Peter, this is Mark, who we hope will be the new owner of the home," Jane said enthusiastically.

Peter extended his hand.

"You look familiar," he said.

"So do you. Uh, I mean, I saw you in some of the photos, uh, not that I was looking, they were just out…" I stammered.

"It's quite alright," he said. "I put the photos out because they make me happy and remind me of all the good times Mike and I had together," A wistful smile crossed his face.

Had together?

"Mike passed away this summer after a brief illness. The place is too big for just me, so I'm downsizing to a smaller condo in a Midtown high-rise," he said.

"Again, haven't I seen you somewhere?" he quizzed.

"Fearless4," Jane chimed in. "Mark's been there about a year. He's an anchorman and the lead investigative reporter," she boasted.

"That's it!" Peter said. "You did that story on the lazy city workers."

"Won himself an Emmy for that one," Jane said again.

"Very impressive," Peter complimented me.

"Mike was a writer too," he said. "Very talented." His voice trailed off. "It was very sudden. AIDS is a horrific thing."

Chill bumps ran up my arms and down my back.

AIDS?

They had looked so happy in the photos. So healthy.

I thought of Rock Hudson. How people only saw the movie star looks and not the horrors of how he died.

"The market's a little soft, so I lowered the price," Peter said, trying to change the subject. "You'd be getting one of the nicer town-homes on the cul de sac for under market price. How about I pour us all a glass of wine and give you a tour of the garden? Mike and I built it together."

I almost broke into tears and am close to tears now writing about it. From the outside of the home and inside the framed photos, everything looked perfect, but now, I knew things were not as they seemed from afar, from the other side of the glass on the frames.

"A glass of wine sounds great, right, Jane? I'd love to hear more about the garden and Mike."

"I'm always up to put down a little wine," Jane replied with a hearty laugh. She reminded me so much of her mom. Huge person-alities but very different people.

"I've got a nice Sauvignon Blanc from Australia," Peter said, "Let me grab it from the kitchen."

I caught his reflection in the mirrored wall behind the dining room table. He appeared to be in his early forties, fit, trim with broad shoulders. His dark hair was splattered with a little salt and pepper. His eyes were deep set and a beautiful greenish gray. I remembered seeing him in the tight blue swim trunks in one of the photos in the staircase.

I could see what Mike saw in him. He was handsome, gracious and seemed kind. I sensed he was dealing with a deep sadness. It made me like him even more.

There was a loud pop from the kitchen, and I heard the clink of glass against glass as Peter gathered our beverages.

"To the garden!" he said. "I can't wait to show you the hibiscus and the old magnolia tree along the back fence."

Talking about the garden seemed to bring Peter back to his happy place. It made me smile seeing him smile, especially after what he'd been through with Mike.

"We would have gotten married back here," he said as he flung open the French doors to the wide wooden deck that overlooked the garden. "If that type thing wasn't illegal here in the great state of Georgia," he said with a laugh.

I walked through the wide-open doors, across the deck and kneeled in the garden to read several of the small metal placards next to each planting.

A-G-A...

"Agastache," Peter said from the deck behind me. "Hummingbirds love those! And the ones next to them are black-eyed Susan's. Butterflies can't resist them." He smiled as he poured the wine.

I had never really stopped to think about something as simple as a yellow flower with a black center bringing so much joy, but I could see it on Peter's face. It stirred something inside of me. A longing for my own home, my own joy, my own Peter. Someone I could plant a garden with and hopefully live happily ever after.

This is where things started to go sideways.

I bought the townhouse and moved in a month later. Peter proudly handed me the keys to the property at the closing.

"I hope it brings you as much joy as it brought us," he said, tears filling his pretty eyes. "There were some holes left in the walls behind the photos. Just tell me what color you want, and I'll have my guys repaint the entire place. It'll be my gift to you."

We stood in a bit of silence and then he leaned in and hugged me. I hugged him back.

"I wish you much happiness, Mr. Anchorman," he whispered in my ear.

"Thank you, Peter" I said, not really wanting to release my grip from around his broad shoulders. I missed Paulo so much. I missed his body against mine, I hadn't been held like he held me in a very long time now.

After a bit too long, I released my arms from around Peter's back.

"You remind me of Mike," he said. "He was so smart and so handsome, just like you."

My heart ached. For Peter and Mike.

And for Paulo and me.

CHAPTER

17

PICKING UP STRANGERS

t seemed the small, windowed boxes were on every corner in and around neighborhoods close to the TV station. They were hard to miss as I drove to and from work or on my errands around town.

One day, I stopped and opened one of the boxes and pulled out a free copy of *Creative Loafing*, the city's "alternative" newspaper. And by alternative, I would call it the wild child younger cousin of the city's major daily newspapers, the *Atlanta Journal* and the *Atlanta Constitution*. Yes, in the heyday of print journalism, Atlanta had both a morning and afternoon edition of a newspaper owned by the moneyed Cox family. They also owned WSB-TV, the staunch rival to my own Fearless4.

While the *Journal* and *Constitution* cranked out a steady stream of traditional news, a conservative mix of local, state, national, politics, entertainment and sports; *Creative Loafing* was grittier and more in-your-face, along the lines of the *Village Voice* in New York. Yes, I enjoyed the aggressive, gonzo journalism favored by the paper, but there was something else that also grabbed my attention.

Each week, about two-thirds of the way through the paper, things took a decidedly raunchy turn. There were ads for the adult bookstores and bars along the city's famous Cheshire Bridge Road, ads for telephone psychics and the like.

And then there were the personal ads near the very back of *Creative Loafing*. Lonely people searching for other lonely people in thirty-to-forty-five words or less. Each week, these personal ads became my private obsession.

Especially the section entitled "Men Seeking Men."

The ads were written in shorthand: "masc" for "masculine" or "bi" for "bisexual," sometimes "dom" for "dominant" or "sub" for "submissive." What always got my attention were two simple words: seeking same.

Those words were the equivalent of a romantic S.O.S. *Please, is there anyone out there?* As Freddie Mercury would say, *Somebody to love?*

"How are things coming with the airport story?" I heard the voice say, startling me from my private reading session in the break-room at the TV station. I awkwardly moved the newspaper, trying to cover the personal ads with my leftover sandwich that I didn't have time to finish at lunch.

"Uh, really good," I stumbled as Steve sauntered over and sat down at the table across from me. "I think we should go for a test run next week," I told him. I tried to move the newspaper farther beneath the sandwich wrapper so he wouldn't see the header of "Men Seeking Men."

"Gotta love *Creative Loafing*, right?" he said.

I nodded.

"CB Hackworth is a trip," he said, referring to one of the newspaper's best writers who had recently become its editor. CB was known for his straight-to-the-jugular approach to news gathering, which I admired.

"What's your favorite part of the paper?" Steve asked me.

"Uh, I like the music reviews," I said, not sure how to respond. "And where to go on a date," I stumbled. What was I supposed to say? *I love the ads where the guys are looking for guys, Steve!*

"Cool," Steve said. "How about we plan to meet tomorrow to talk about the airport story? This test run stuff makes me nervous."

"You and me both," I confessed.

The next afternoon at two p.m., my photographer, Bruce Mason, and I met with Steve in his office.

"Pettit's a pussy," Bruce blurted out about a minute into the discussion.

That was his style. Hilariously funny and gruff. Bruce was tall, lanky and oddly handsome. His eyes were set widely apart, but they were steel blue and encased with rugged sockets. Bruce was the kind of photographer that hangs out on the landing blade of a helicopter shooting the reporter/pilot from outside the aircraft. Sometimes, without his safety harness properly configured inside the chopper, as once happened.

Steve and I both looked at Bruce incredulously.

"A pussy? Really?" Steve asked, then breaking into his signature cackle of a laugh.

"Yes," Bruce said. "He's been sitting on this shit for three weeks now," he said, producing a piece of paper from his pocket with 6-8-2-8-8-1 written in bold black ink.

"That's supposedly the code for the security door at Gate A-18," he said. "It was a gift with purchase along with the pilot's garb and the baggage handler blouse Pettit is supposed to wear when we try to crack security at the airport.

Hell, they've probably changed the code three times by now. Mr. Calhoun is scared to try it," he said. "That's why I called him a pussy."

In today's business culture, we would have both been walked to HR and given sensitivity training.

"Are you scared?" Steve asked me, seeming concerned.

"A little," I admitted. "This is a big fucking deal, guys."

"See, he's a pussy," Bruce retorted, his face breaking into a big smile. I felt like fraternity brothers plotting a panty run with the RA.

"Ok, screw it" I said. "Let's go for it. Who cares if I go to jail?"

"How fucking awesome would that be? You'd be all over *A Current Affair*," Bruce said with delight, referring to the famous precursor to *TMZ*.

I was committed now. The question was, would I go to jail if things went to hell in a handbasket?

We were about to find out.

In the bedroom of my new condo, I sat on the bed and pulled up the pants on the Eastern Airlines pilot's uniform that we had purchased as part of the investigation. Black, straight cut polyester with a hint of gold fabric raced down each leg. I zipped up the pants and latched them just above my hips. A perfect fit. Whew.

I slipped on the white dress shirt and whipped the dark black tie around my neck and scooted into the bathroom so I could look in the mirror and properly knot it. I was surprised at how authentic the attire made me look like a pilot. I walked back into the bedroom and plucked the suit coat from the closet and slipped it over my shoulders.

Again, a perfect fit, right off the confidential informant rack.

I looked down at the nightstand and picked up the Eastern Airlines pin and placed it just above the pocket on my jacket. I checked out the three golden stripes on the sleeves of my suit coat. The stripes signified co-pilot, second-in-command of the aircraft.

Slowly, I reached for the final component of the uniform. I placed the heavy hat on my head and looked in the mirror. A little goofy, I thought, but felt I just might pull it off.

"Come on down, Rapunzel!" I heard Bruce shout from downstairs. "Let's get this party started," he said.

"You won't be the one going to jail, you prick," I shouted down to him. "I want to look good in the mug shot."

I then walked downstairs to find Bruce wearing shorts and a Hawaiian shirt. He was supposed to dress like a tourist, and he certainly looked the part.

"Where the fuck did you get that get up?" I asked.

"Straight out of my dad's closet," he replied. "He's got about ten of the exact same shirts. I didn't think he miss one of them," Bruce said with a laugh.

"What's the plan?" I asked.

"We're going to take MARTA from the Lindbergh station. It'll be too risky to park at the airport and we might not be able to get away. I've got your pilot's case with the hidden camera in the trunk of my car. You just have to get through security without them confiscating the gear," Bruce finished.

Bruce had the perfect temperament for the assignment. The bastard wasn't afraid of anything.

We got to the MARTA station around nine thirty. It was going to be one of two test runs at the airport. If, by chance, we got through with me dressed like an Eastern pilot, we were going to try again with me dressed as a baggage handler from Delta.

If we got busted on the first try, there wasn't going to be a second one.

No pressure.

As we got on the train, Bruce handed me a small earpiece and a battery pack that powered our wireless microphones. "Put this in your ear and the battery pack in your pocket," he said.

I wrapped the earpiece around my right lobe and inserted the small listening device. I then flipped on the battery pack.

"Test, one-two, test," I heard Bruce say into our earpieces.

"Big Bird to Big Pussy, come in," he said, cackling.

Yes, Bruce coined my name long before the any of the Sopranos.

"Go fuck yourself, Big Bird," I replied back.

Newsroom banter and playfulness was one of my favorite parts of the job. It was a way for us to show affection to each other without getting too attached. You never knew which one of us would be getting the axe, so you didn't want to get too close. As they say, news directors can only change two things: the news set or the news staff.

It was also a way for us to deal with the pressure. And, right now, the pressure was dialed up to about eleven.

As the train chugged along through Midtown, Bruce laid out the ground rules.

"As soon as we get off the train, it's like we don't know each other," Bruce said. "Don't even look at me. If you make it through security, I'll follow behind you and meet you at A-18."

Yes, at this time, people were allowed to meet traveling passengers at the gate. Something that would never happen in today's hyper-secure world of airports.

We arrived at Hartsfield. Bruce and I bounded off the train and up the ramp for the main entrance to the airport.

I drew a deep breath as I approached the employee lane of security just past check-in. I reached in my pocket and retrieved the fake ID badge that the Fearless4 art department had made for me. It was an exact replica of the damaged ID that we were able to purchase as part of the overall package.

As I got within about five feet of the security guard manning the line, I flipped and flashed the badge toward him. Without hesitation, he waved me through the turnstile.

"Good morning, sir," he said. "Have a nice flight."

My heart was racing at this point, and I kept on walking, deciding not to look back for my co-worker. As I approached a newsstand to my left, I turned and just as I did, I saw Bruce's big head coming through the crowd. It was hard to miss him in that Hawaiian shirt.

We had cleared the first hurdle and had officially violated the first level of security at Hartsfield International. With each step I took down the concourse, my heart pounded along with the sound of the huge pilot's case slapping against my leg. In the distance, I could see my ultimate destination: Gate B-12.

I decided to step to the side of the concourse to test the hidden camera. I sat the pilot's case down at my feet, opened the lid and reached inside the leather box-like bag and pressed the record button on the camcorder. I closed the lid, picked up the case and pointed it back up toward the concourse.

I did my best to shoot footage of Bruce as he walked down the hallway. I thought I had captured the footage, but there was no way of really knowing until we got the tapes back to the station.

If we made it back to the station.

Hoping I had gotten the test footage, I sat the case down, opened the leather top panel and stopped the recording.

"Excuse me captain!" I heard a woman's voice say from behind me.

Oh shit!

"Sir, sir," she said, chasing me down. "Can you tell me how to get to baggage claim?"

I was caught off guard by the question and pointed toward the far end of the concourse.

"Are you sure you work here? That's where I just came from," she said with a confused look on her face.

"Uh, I mean, that way," I said to her, pointing in the opposite direction this time.

The woman looked at me strangely but kept moving.

I pressed forward with my eyes focused on the prize: Gate B-12.

Within a few minutes, I arrived at the gate. The area was packed with people. I looked for a seat, but there was none available, so I walked over and leaned against a wall. In another couple of minutes, Bruce arrived in his shorts and shirt.

He walked over to a bank of pay phones and looked over to me. I pretended to look at aircraft taking off and landing in the distance.

After a couple of minutes, I glanced looked over at the doorway of B-12 and watched as several airline employees punched in codes on the door. Each time the door opened and the employee walked through the opening. I walked over to the large window facing out to the lines of planes and saw that the door in question led directly onto the tarmac.

This was my chance. I looked back at Bruce and mouthed the word "roll."

There was a big enough crowd to provide a distraction and I accepted the fact that the code I had purchased a month before probably wouldn't work, so the worst thing that could happen would be the door wouldn't open and that would be that.

"Good morning, sir," a flight attendant said as I started making my way to the door.

"Good morning," I replied without looking her in the eye.

6-8-2-8-8-1. 6-8-2-8-8-1. 6-8-2-8-8-1.

I repeated the code three times as I got closer to the door, and then a fourth.

6-8-2-8-8-1.

It felt as though my heart would explode as I reached the door and looked down at the lockbox in front of me.

Without hesitating further, I slowly punched in the numbers.

6-8-2-8-8-1.

As my finger pushed the final 1, I heard a loud click.

And much to my shock, the door opened.

Imaginary alarm bells started ringing in my ears.

HOLY SHIT! IT WORKED!

I had no time to look back and hoped that Bruce had captured footage of me opening the door and heading onto the jetway. My footsteps sounded like loud drumbeats as I made my way down the narrow hallway and out another door that led me to a stairway and straight down to the tarmac.

I paused, lowered my pilot's case, opened the top portion of the attaché and again pressed the record button inside the box. I adjusted the contraption that held the camera up to a small hole on the side of the case which provided the opening to capture footage.

It felt as though I was in a dreamlike state as I made my way from the staircase and onto the tarmac. My gut instinct was to pretend like I was inspecting the aircraft, so that's what I did.

I walked beneath the huge wings of the plane, pointing the opening of my case down and around the plane hoping I was getting quality footage.

"Good morning, sir," I heard from behind me. I looked back to see a worker carrying baggage up to the aircraft.

"Good morning," I said back to him.

I couldn't believe the plan had worked! I was now on the tarmac, having violated security not once, but twice. I decided to look back up at the large glass window overlooking the pavement below and there he was.

Bruce, in his flowery Hawaiian shirt shooting away on his camcorder. Tourist turned investigative journalist. Bruce gave me a thumbs up and I knew things were going well.

I decided to take our plan to the next level.

My eyes found the staircase leading up to the opened door of the aircraft. Without another thought, I pointed the hidden camera forward and made my way up the stairs. Again, it felt as though I was dreaming. Everything had worked exactly as planned. The question now was would I be able to get aboard the aircraft.

In less than fifteen seconds, the answer was yes.

There was no one there to stop me, so I boarded the aircraft. In the distance, I could hear what sounded like vacuum cleaners or air vents and air rushing through the hull of the aircraft. There were no passengers on board and no crew members, at least not in the main cabin.

I heard voices to my left and turned and started to walk through the first-class section of the airplane.

Then, I saw a man's arm in the cockpit.

It was a maintenance worker, sitting in the right front seat looking at the gears and dials of the aircraft. To his left was another maintenance worker doing the same on the left side of the cockpit.

I sat my pilot's case down on the carpet beneath my feet. I opened it and saw the red light was still flashing. Then, the worker in the right seat spotted me and I stopped dead in my tracks.

"Just keeping the seat warm for you, sir!" he said to my immense relief. I started walking toward him, hoping the hidden camera would capture the interaction.

"No worries. Your job is more important than mine," I said as I continued making my way to the front of the plane. I paused and then stepped into the cockpit with the two workers.

"We'll be out of your way in two minutes, sir," the guy to my right said. "Just doing a final check of the flight deck."

"Again, no problem. We won't leave until you say we're cleared to go," I told him, trying to come up with my best pilot's jargon.

And then I had an idea.

"Hey guys," I said. "My daughter is working on a project for school. Sorta like, 'A Day in the Life of Daddy,'" I lied. "Would one of you guys mind taking a photo of me up here?"

As I waited for an answer, I stepped back down to the pilot's case. From the lower right side, I pulled a disposable camera. The kind that produces that zippy sound as you advance the film.

"I'd be happy to," the guy to my right said, scurrying out of the seat and past me as he grabbed the camera.

He stopped about two feet behind me and turned to me facing the cockpit. He raised the disposable camera and took aim.

"Three, two, one," he said, before pressing the button and immortalizing my day as a federal scofflaw.

"OK, one more!" he said, and I heard the crank of the film. Once more, he lifted the camera.

"Three, two, one," click. "Got it," he said. "I hope your daughter gets a good grade on her project," he said with a smile.

"She just passed with flying colors," I told him.

Then, coming to my senses, I realized I needed to get off the plane.

"Need to grab a bite before we take off, guys," I told them. "Thanks for all you do to keep us safe up there." I pointed to the sky.

I turned and made my way back down the cabin, picked up the pilot's case, and headed out the front entry door. I jogged down the stairs and back on to the tarmac and traced my steps back up the jetway. I prayed the door would open when I got to the top.

As I got within inches of the door, I extended my hand and turned the metal handle.

Please, God, I thought.

And, with a turn, the door opened. I walked back into the crowded waiting area of the gate. I looked up to see Bruce holding the camcorder in one hand and a big thumbs up in the other.

We did it!

I walked over to Bruce and took off my hat.

"Got it all!" he said triumphantly. "But I think we can do better. Let's do it one more time."

"Fuck no!" I said. "Let's get out of here!"

I think Bruce realized what we had and the risk we'd be taking if we tried it again.

"If you're waiting on me, you're backing up!" he said.

We made a beeline for the escalator and made our exit to the waiting Plane Train below. We rode in excited silence all the way back to baggage claim, where we boarded the MARTA train and headed back to Buckhead.

Mission accomplished.

Later that night, I sat at home alone celebrating with my third Jack & Coke.

I had just reached what could have been the height of my career and had no one to celebrate with. No one to kiss goodnight.

I reached for a pad and pen from my briefcase and sat down at the dining room table and wrote out the following on the paper beneath my hands: 27-year-old white male. Bi-curious. Straight acting. Seeks same for fun and maybe more. Mark. P.O. Box 11512, Atlanta, GA 30329.

The next morning, I placed the ad copy and a check for fifteen dollars into an envelope and mailed it to *Creative Loafing*.

My life was about to change.

CHAPTER

18

ONLY THE LONELY

"Hey Mark, It's Steve at the station. It's pretty important. Call me as soon as you can."

I played the voicemail message again on the recorder in my kitchen and tried to decide if I should call Steve back or head to the station and meet with him in person. I was just back from a bike ride to the post office and was sweating through my shirt and bike shorts.

I sat the stack of letters down on the counter. My ad had run in *Creative Loafing* for a week, but my post office box was full of letters and notes from guys whom I suspected were just like me. In the closet, but desperate for a connection.

I stuffed the bounty into my backpack and peddled home. It was less than a mile from my townhouse to the post office. After I listened to Steve's message a second time, I reached into the stack and pulled out one of the letters. I opened it and read it to myself.

"Hi Mark. My name is Scott," the letter began. "I'm a lawyer for the State of Georgia. As you might expect, I can't be out at work, so when I saw your ad, I thought I would respond. I don't think I'm 'bi-curious' like you as I pretty much know what I want. I'm 5' 9", 165 lbs. with brown hair and blue eyes. Bottom if it gets to that," he wrote.

That was something I would come to learn about gay guys. It's important to get things straight, so to speak, from the start.

A weird guy I would meet down the road once told me, "Don't leave the bar with a guy until you know all the answers to your questions. There's nothing more awkward than two bottoms trying to bump pussies."

Crass, but correct.

Scott finished his letter sweetly.

"Let me know if you'd be interested in meeting up for a drink. It's really difficult to meet quality guys out there. I'd like to think I'm an exception to the rule. Anyway, my number is enclosed if you want to give me a call. —Scott."

I folded Scott's letter and placed it back in the stack. I would decide how to respond later. I grabbed a quick drink of water from the sink, picked up my keys and headed for the garage. Obviously, Steve's message was urgent. I thought it best that I go see him in person.

I arrived at the newsroom around four thirty. It was a Tuesday, my normal day off and, as usual, the place was hopping with reporters, anchors, photographers and editors getting ready for the five and six o'clock news.

It was unusual for me to be dressed in anything other than a suit and tie. one of the editors, Benita, a vociferous Latina firecracker, let me have it the second I walked past her.

"Ah… caliente, papi!" she said to me. "Wait till Rob Stinson gets a load of that tight ass."

Rob Stinson was the producer of the six o'clock news and there were rumors that he was gay. I found Rob attractive. He was a couple of years older than me, with thick dark brown hair and puppy dog eyes. I could see his well-developed chest beneath his dress shirt and his biceps bulged as he banged at his typewriter. When he would get up and down from his desk, I would sneak glances of his butt. Nice and bubbly. Like two small cantaloupes.

I was both mortified and flattered that Benita might think Rob would be attracted to me. In today's corporate climate, she would have been in counseling for what she said about him.

"Horrible about what happened to Bruce, right?" One of the assignment editors said to me as I walked past the desk in the center of the newsroom.

I didn't know what he was talking about.

"Pettit!" I heard Steve shout from outside his office. "Come see me," he said.

I walked into Steve's glass office.

"Shut the door," he said. I did as I was told and sat down in the small side chair in front of his desk.

"Listen, we're going to have to delay the work on your airport security story," he said. "Bruce was in a really bad car accident last night."

My heart sank.

"Broken back and pelvis," he said. "Car crash as he was heading home after the eleven last night. It's really bad. They say he might not walk again."

What?

Just days before, we were laughing and romping around the newsroom, like two school kids. Bruce's laugh still rang in my ears.

With my story on hold for a bit, I decided to focus on other things.

I sat across from Scott, my new pen pal at a "straight bar" in Buckhead. He looked as nervous as me, but I found him very attractive and there was a good energy between us as we sipped our drinks.

"I recognized you as soon as you walked in," he said. "Pretty brave that you'd meet me out in public," he said, making me even more nervous.

"Look, this has to be just between us. My bosses have no clue. My straight friends have no clue. But to be perfectly honest," I told him, letting down my guard, "I'm lonely. And I'm horny."

He laughed and I laughed. Our eyes met and the hint of a spark flew.

"I think I can help you with the last part. But you need to know, I'm not really looking for a boyfriend," he said. "I just got out of something that didn't end well. He cheated on me with one of our best friends. Well, I thought he was a friend." His eyes fell to his drink in front of him.

That was another thing I learned about gay guys. There's a very thin line between a friend and a fuck. Once the line is crossed, it can be tricky.

"I live about a mile from here," he said. "Do you want to come over for a little fun?"

For the first time in a while, I felt the bulge build between my legs and the urge build in my body. I wanted to rip his shirt off of him right there and throw him down on the table, but I pulled myself together.

"Can I park at your place?" I asked him.

"Sure," he said. "I have two spots in the garage."

Thirty minutes later, I had him pressed against the headboard of his bed, banging him from behind. Luckily, he had condoms, as I honestly didn't expect things to get physical and didn't leave home with any "party supplies," as they say.

I tried not to think of Paulo as I banged Scott. In my mind, I knew it was just sex, but in my heart, I felt a sense of betrayal. No, I hadn't seen Paulo in two years now, but I felt a strange allegiance to him.

Still, I was twenty-seven and horny, so I let Scott have it.

"Damn man," he said after we finished. "You're aggressive."

"I'm from the country," I told him. "Everything's a little rougher there." We shared a laugh, and I leaned in and gave him a kiss. It was nice, but it wasn't Paulo. And I wasn't in Nebraska anymore. Sexual beggars couldn't be choosers at this point.

"I'd be open to more fun every now and then," he said. "If you are."

I thought for a second and then said, "Sure. Work is my main focus, but I'd be up for a distraction with you every now and then."

He leaned in and kissed me.

"You're really handsome," he said as he looked me in the eyes. "And you're good in the sack."

"Thanks. Sorry if it was a little rough," I told him. "It's been a while."

He smiled.

"I'll live," he said. "You've got my number. Maybe next time, we can meet at your place?"

What the hell?

"Okay," I told him. "I just ordered a waterbed."

Water beds were all the rage in the late eighties, so I thought I'd see what all the fuss was about.

"Aye, aye, captain," Scott said.

I leaned in and hugged him.

"Good night, counselor," I said. "Have a good day at work tomorrow."

That was my first trick in Atlanta.

It would certainly not be my last. I still had a stack of mail waiting for me back home.

A couple of days later, I went to visit Bruce in the hospital. I arrived to find him in a weird contraption that held his legs up from his body and I could see that his left arm was in a cast. The accident had left him in terrible shape, and it made me sad to even look at him.

He was groggy, perhaps drugged, as I sat down in the chair next to his bed.

"I'll give you two a few minutes to talk," his mother said, as she gently touched Bruce's forehead before leaving the room.

I waited a few seconds and then said, "How are you feeling, Brewster?"

He drew a deep breath and replied, "How does it look like I feel, asshole?"

I couldn't hold back and laughed out loud.

Even with a broken back, pelvis and left arm, Bruce's wit was not to be hospitalized.

He smiled. "It sucks, man. My whole fucking body hurts." Then he asked, "What about the airport story?"

"Don't worry about the airport story. We can pick back up on that when you're feeling better," I said, trying to comfort him.

"When I'm feeling better?" he whispered. "That could be months, man, if not years."

He seemed disconsolate, and it made me sad too.

"Get Johnson to pick up for me," he whispered again. By Johnson, he meant Dan, one of my best friends in the newsroom and the photographer who shot with me on the *Men at Work* series.

"He's the second-best photog in the station," Bruce said. He cracked a smile that seemed to shoot pain throughout his body.

"Ok. Let me talk with him," I said. "For now, don't you worry about it. You just need to worry about getting better."

"They said I might never walk again," he replied. I noticed a tear slipping from his big right eye. It was heartbreaking as Bruce was always the tough guy. The jokester in the newsroom. But this was no joke. It hurt me to see him in this condition.

"You'll be walking and kicking ass soon," I said, trying to comfort him.

"Get with Johnson," he said. "Don't be a pussy."

We both laughed and I told him I'd think about it. Bruce's mom returned and I decided he needed some rest, so I excused myself and went home.

"Hey, can I talk to you for a minute," I said to Steve as I poked my head in his office this next afternoon.

"Sure," he said. "Come on in."

I sat down in front of him.

"I went to visit Bruce yesterday," I told him. "It's really bad. I've never seen him that down."

"But he was adamant that I press forward with the airport investigation," I told him. "How would you feel about letting me work with Dan Johnson on the next phase of the story?"

"Sure," Steve said. "You guys did a great job on *Men at Work*. Is Bruce okay with it?"

"He's the one who suggested it," I told him.

"Then, get with Dan and let's move this thing forward. What's the next step?"

"Up next on the bingo card is Delta," I joked. "I've got the baggage handler uniform. I'll just need another ID badge and we can give it a go"

"You've done it once," he said. "If you do it again, we're going to have a massive story on our hands. If you get caught, it could get really messy. Don't get caught."

Damn. I needed a drink.

I went home and poured two. And opened the next letter.

"Hi Mark. My name is Erik. I'm 27, 6' 1", 185 lbs. I have blond hair and blue eyes."

I sat Erik's letter aside and opened the next.

"Hello Mark. This is Mike. I read your ad in *Creative Loafing*. I'm 24 years old and just finished my third year of law school at Emory."

I pushed Mike's note to the left of the pile, "the follow-up list," and reached for the next envelope.

"Hi Mark. My name is James. I'm 26 years old. 5' 10", 168 pounds. I have dark brown hair and blue eyes. Your ad sounded interesting, so I thought I would write you back. I like to play golf and am a huge Bulldog's fan. My number is enclosed. I hope to hear back from you."

There were thirty-two responses to my first ad in *Creative Loafing*. I was blown away. Were there this many guys out there? All in the same position as me? Caught up in lives and jobs that did not allow us to pursue love, outside of personal ads?

A couple of other responses drew me in.

"My name is Diego. I'm 28 years old and about six feet tall. My hair is black and my eyes are brown. I work in marketing, for a skin care company. Don't worry, I speak perfect English!" he added. "Let's have drinks." He left his home number.

Something about Diego sounded interesting, so after a couple of days of thinking about it, I called him. He suggested we meet for a drink at a neighborhood bar in Midtown called Blake's.

It was a Thursday night after work. I pulled into the parking lot across from the bar and noticed the rainbow neon above the door.

My heart banged against my chest as I neared the entrance to the bar.

My mind flashed back to me sitting in the car outside the Max in Omaha. It was a similar scene now, a gaggle of young guys laughing as they got in line ahead of me.

I could hear the *thump-thump-thump* of a disco beat emanating from inside the bar. From the window, I saw videos flashing on oversized screens. Men were laughing and I was drawn to the darkness.

Yet, I felt a strange awkwardness as well. Like I shouldn't be in this place. That danger lurked beyond the door and up the stairs to the dance floor and the outdoor balcony. Something pulled me inside and my eyes scanned the bar.

About six feet tall. Black hair and brown eyes.

And then, a gentle touch on my shoulder.

"You must be Mark," the dark-haired stranger said. "My name is Diego. You know, from *Creative Loafing*."

"Yeah," I answered. "I'm Mark. Nice to meet you, Diego."

Now, I could see why he worked for a skin care company. His face was glowing, smooth and sexy. We stood in a moment of uncomfortable silence. That weird moment, when things could go one way or another.

"How about that drink?" I asked him. "I'm parched."

"Same here," he said. "You have great eyes."

"Thanks," I said. "So do you. Let's see what's behind them."

He laughed. I laughed and we headed up the stairs to the bar and the outdoor patio. We ordered one drink, then two, then a third.

That's why I can't remember if he told me his dad had married a woman from Kentucky or Kansas.

We mainly talked about Diego, his family and his job, and I tried to say as little about myself as possible. I told him I was a writer. He didn't press further. It was the most substantial conversation I'd had with another gay man since Paulo.

It was getting late, and I was definitely buzzed.

"I could talk with you all night." I smiled. "Well, honestly, I'd want to do more than talk," I said, trying not to be too forward. "But I've got to be at the station early tomorrow. I'm working on a big story."

Fuck. I let it slip.

"Fearless4," he said. "I've seen you on the news. I didn't want to press you on it as I didn't want to make you uncomfortable," he said with a kind smile.

"Thank you," I said. "I'm not really good at this bar stuff."

"I have an idea," Diego said. "My friend Patrick is having a dinner party on Friday night. Nothing major. Eight or ten guys. Why don't you join us?"

I thought about it for a minute and then said, "Sure. I'd like that. Let me know what I can bring."

"Just a smile and that bubble butt," Diego said with a chuckle. "I think you're going to be popular with my friends."

As it turned out, that dinner party would be a major life event. Patrick became a good friend and through him I met Rick, Ace, Mark and Glenn, who became my closest of friends.

Through it all.

19

DO ASK, DO TELL

I know what you're probably thinking, or questioning, so let's go ahead and get it over with.

Yes, I've slept with women.

At least a dozen, maybe more. I tried. I wanted to be straight. I wanted to get married, have a family, grow old with the right girl. The only problem is that would have been a lie which would have ultimately led to betrayal, heartache and, without a doubt, a broken home and family.

The simple fact is nothing felt like it did being with the right guy. You know it in your own life. When it's right, it's right, and you can't fake attraction or love. Straight or gay.

If I could have faked it and wanted to run the risk of heartbreak, Eva might have been the one.

She was beautiful, bright and bubbly. Five-five with blond-ish-brown hair that fell just below her ears. Her eyes were bright blue, the kind of blue you'd see on Lamborghinis. She had one of those laughs that made you happy when you heard it. We met at Fearless4 where she worked in the promotions department, and we spent a good bit of time together.

As friends. Or so, I thought.

One Christmas, Eva helped me shop for presents for my family. My mother told me the only thing she really wanted that year was a Dirt Devil vacuum cleaner. A red one. Eva and I scoured several department stores and finally found one at Service Merchandise and hauled it back to my condo to wrap with the other presents.

We were on the floor, near the Christmas tree with paper scattered all around us. I remember the wine bottle was sitting just to my right, almost empty. "Silver Bells" played across the speakers in my living room. It was magical and fun, two friends enjoying the Christmas spirit.

Then it happened.

Without warning, Eva leaned in and kissed me. Her hand slipped onto my thigh and down to my crotch. I didn't mean to, but I recoiled back from her.

"No. Eva." I said. "Stop."

Suddenly it was as if "Silver Bells" had skipped on an old Victrola and the moment of fun and Christmas cheer came to a screeching halt.

"What's wrong?" Eva asked, her face now contorted. "We've been having so much fun. I thought you liked me too!"

I tried to console her. I extended my arm to hers and she turned away from me like an angry two-year-old child. She rose to her feet and as tears streamed down her beautiful cheeks, she continued her outburst.

"What's wrong with me?" she yelled. "Why does this always happen to me?"

She began to pace around the room. I had never seen her like this.

"Eva, please calm down," I said as I rose to my feet and moved toward her.

"There's nothing wrong with you," I said, trying again to comfort her. "I do like you, just not like that."

The words I'm sure millions of young girls, and boys, have heard throughout love lives eternal. Words that echo in hollowness and let down.

Just not like that.

There was a moment of quietness between us and then I could see the lightbulb going off in her eyes.

"Wait a minute," she said, a calming force seeming to overtake her body. "Are you gay?"

Her question hit me like a freight train. I'm sure my face dropped before her eyes. I didn't know quite what to say, but I knew I couldn't tell her a lie.

"There's nothing wrong with you," I began. "The problem is me."

The answer set her off again.

"I knew it!" she screamed at the top of her lungs. "The way you dress, the way you take care of yourself. The reason you never talk about any girls!"

Again, I stepped toward her, trying to get her to calm down.

"Please, Eva, don't tell anyone about this conversation. My family doesn't know, my closest friends don't know. I haven't even come to terms with it myself," I said, now starting to become emotional myself.

She didn't want to hear it and turned away from me.

She quietly grabbed her coat from the corner arm of the couch, put it over her shoulders and walked out the door. I watched her go, frozen in thought and watching in horror as my secret life was beginning to unravel.

I tried again to suppress my urges and dove deeper into my work. Eva ignored me at the station, barely looking at me when she came in and out of the newsroom from time to time. Still, I had no time to dwell on it. The moment had come for Round Two in trying to crack security at Hartsfield International Airport.

"There, that should do it," the hair and make-up lady said as she combed what looked and felt like dark brown shoe polish across my head. She was doing her best to give me somewhat of a disguise for the next part of my airport security investigation.

The part of a Delta Air Lines baggage handler.

After the lady finished my hair, she dabbed a light film of make-up across my face and used a brush to stroke a red powder across my cheeks. I reached for the Delta baggage handler shirt we had purchased from the confidential informant and snapped the fake ID we had designed over the left pocket of my shirt.

I reached for my aviator sunglasses and placed them over my ears.

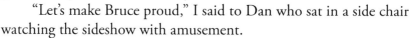

"Let's make Bruce proud," I said to Dan who sat in a side chair watching the sideshow with amusement.

"Dude, you are so going to get busted," he said with a laugh. "You look like you're eleven years old."

I released an uneasy laugh as well.

"Screw you and the Georgia Bulldogs," I said knowing how much Dan loved his beloved 'Dawgs.

"We might not make it to the airport to the make-up lady," Dan said. "Mr. Calhoun's about to get his ass kicked."

Again, we laughed. I knew he was nervous too. If I got caught trying to violate security at Hartsfield, there was a decent chance he would get caught too.

Dan and I pretty much repeated the steps that Bruce and I had followed on the first, successful attempt. We parked our news car at the MARTA station just off Piedmont Road. Dan was in jeans and a flowery shirt like Bruce had worn. Again, the idea was for Dan to blend into the crowd of vacationers at the airport and for him to get footage of me as I attempted to gain access to the tarmac at Hartsfield.

We made our way from the Plane Train and up to the security checkpoint. I was in panic mode that one of the guards might recognize me from when I wore the pilot's uniform as I approached the employee entrance.

I reached into my right pocket and pulled out the fake ID badge and stepped closer to the checkpoint.

"Hey!" a guy shouted from behind me.

Again, panic set in as I looked over my shoulder.

"Here," he said, "you dropped your Chapstick."

Good God!

"Thank you," I said, as I reached back to grab the small tube.

"I like that cherry flavor too."

"Sir!" I heard a woman say.

I turned and the security guard was waving me toward her.

This was the moment of truth. The second bite at the airport apple. I raised my fake ID and flashed it toward her, hoping she didn't look too closely.

"Next!" she said, waving me past her and through the turnstile.

I had to be sweating through my shirt at this point. I looked back and Dan was making his way through security.

"Meeting my wife at the gate. She's coming back from a Mary Kay convention in Texas," I heard him lie.

We both made it through security and headed for the moving sidewalk and the train that would take us to our ultimate destination.

Gate A-18.

It was the secret code to a second door at the airport. Surely, it wouldn't work, right? Like Bruce, Dan paused at the bank of payphones as I passed by him.

"A Mary Kay convention? What the fuck was that about?" I whispered.

Not missing a beat, Dan replied, "I said that in case someone asks where you got that rouge on your cheeks," he laughed.

Always the class clown.

"As Bruce would say, let's get this party started."

He knew what to do and pretended to test his camcorder. He wanted to be ready when his lovely wife, the fictitious Mary Kay representative disembarked from her flight from Texas.

After a quick hand off of our communications tools, Dan made his way past the rows of chairs and up against the full wall of glass, so he'd have a clear shot of the tarmac and the Delta jets below.

I took a deep breath and walked toward the security door. 7-4-2-6-1-5. 7-4-2-6-1-5.

Only a few feet from the door now, I reached for the listening device in my left pocket and placed the small end of the IFB into my right ear. I flipped on the battery pack that powered the small microphone attached to the inside of my shirt and slipped the pack into my back right pocket.

7-4-2-6-1-5. 7-4-2-6-1-5.

I reached the door and prepared to punch in the security code—thinking for sure it wouldn't work a second time. Surely, they had caught on to me after the first time? Slowly, I punched in the numbers.

7-4-2-6-1-5.

Click! Just like before, the code worked. I opened the door and made my way down the jetway. I felt an incredible surge of adrenaline as I reached the second door that led down the steel staircase that led to the pavement below me. In the distance, I could see the big Delta jet. My eyes scanned the area for trouble as I landed at the base of the stairs. I reached into my pocket and retrieved my aviator sunglasses and placed them over my ears.

"Testing one-two, testing," I said, trying to make sure the hidden microphone was working.

"Give me about fifteen seconds and I'll look back at the window," I said, my voice just above the humming jets that sat at their gates. "Give me a thumbs up if you can hear me." I hoped that Dan could make out what I was saying.

The Delta jet was now about twenty feet in front me. All of a sudden, a luggage cart sped past me and pulled up to the airplane.

A worker jumped out and pulled a long conveyor belt from under a door on the side of the jet. I could see that this was where baggage would be loaded onto the plane.

The worker parked the cart filled with bags near the jet, jumped off the tractor pulling the cart and headed back toward the gate and underneath the awning.

I knew it was now or never.

"Get ready to roll," I said down into my shirt, again, hoping Dan could hear me. "I'm going for the luggage."

My shoes felt like they were again loaded down with concrete as I walked toward the conveyor belt. Just before reaching the belt, I pulled down a small black bag on the cart. Then grabbed a second suitcase. I made my way to the other side of the belt, facing back toward the glass wall at the gate in hopes that Dan could get a good shot of me with his camcorder.

"This is Fearless4 investigative reporter Mark Pettit, handling baggage at Hartsfield International Airport," I said. "Luckily for Hartsfield and the passengers soon to board this airplane, I'm not a terrorist."

I placed the suitcases on the conveyor belt and turned to walk back toward the gate.

"Please tell me you got all that," I said into the hidden microphone.

I looked up to the gate to see Dan waving enthusiastically.

"Every second of it," he said into my earpiece.

"Great!" I said, "Let's get the fuck out of here!"

I bounded back up the staircase, back through the jetway and then back out into the crowded gate area full of passengers.

I saw Dan and waved him toward the hallway. He caught up with me and we made a beeline back to the train hoping to escape without being confronted. Sweat beaded through my cheesy make-up and I tried to wipe the rouge from my cheeks, then down the side of my pants.

"The next stop is baggage claim," the computerized voice said aboard the train.

"Almost there," I said to Dan. "We just need another ten minutes and I think we're free and clear," I whispered.

"Oh, God, I forgot to press the record button!" Dan said, sending a shock of fear through my system.

"Just fucking with you, man," he said with a laugh. "I got it all."

I wanted to smack him in the mouth and kiss him on the lips for getting the footage, but I just smiled and stood silently as the train came to a stop. The doors opened and we bolted from the tall escalator that would lead us back to the MARTA station, and hopefully to freedom.

We paid our fee at the turnstile and headed onto the platform.

The next train arrives in sixty seconds, said the words on the video screen. It seemed like six hundred seconds as Dan and I waited and watched for our getaway vehicle. *Ten, nine, eight*, the monitor counted down. *Three, two, one*, the sign read as the train came whizzing in and to a gentle stop in front of us.

Dan and I boarded the train with about a dozen other passengers and, within another fifteen seconds, were on our way back to Buckhead.

We had done it. Again. We had done the unimaginable: we had violated security a second time at what would become the world's busiest airport. Of course, we had no way of seeing into the future or visualizing the World Trade Center towers collapsing before our eyes a mere ten years later.

But we both knew we had a whale of a story on our hands.

Now, we just had to get the whale on the boat and the story on the air. I didn't realize it at the time, but I was about to become the story behind the story.

"That's it!" the promotions director said as the camera flashed.

"Step a little to your left," the photographer said. "Cross your hands and hold the pilot's hat below your waist."

Click. Click. Click.

The camera rolled and the lights in the canopy-draped casings flashed. We were shooting promo photos for the advertising campaign which would promote my series *Security for Sale*.

"Now, look back like you're watching the plane take off," the promotions director shouted.

"Damn. What are we shooting?" I smirked. "*Gone With the Wind II?*"

Out of the corner of my eye, I could see Eva standing to the right of the photographer. On her clipboard she took notes in between takes of the photography.

"I think we've got what we need," the photographer said, finally ending the drawn-out production.

I tried to catch up with Eva as she scurried off the set.

"Eva," I called out to her.

She turned and for the first time in weeks, looked me in the eyes.

"I'm so sorry about that night. I really care for you and would love for us to continue our, uh, friendship," I said, tossing a bit of a Hail Mary.

"I have all the friends I need, Mark," she said coldly. "I think it's best we just stay co-workers."

I nodded and turned to walk away.

"Your secret is safe with me," she said. "I at least appreciate your honesty."

20

WHITNEY HOUSTON, WE HAVE A PROBLEM

"Hi, Mark. It's Steve. It's about your airport series. Can you get to the office, ASAP?"

Another voicemail on my machine on my day off. Never a good sign in TV news. I had errands to run and letters to respond to, but I packed my trusty Samsonite and headed to the station.

"Steve is up in Harry's office," the assignment editor on duty told me. "He told me to send you up there when you got here."

I trudged through the newsroom and out the back door and up the stairs to the second floor where all the executive decisions were made. I turned the corner to see a cadre of attorneys sitting with Steve and the station GM.

"Hey Mark," Steve said weirdly, "Thanks for coming in on your day off."

"No problem, Steve. What's up with my series?" I said, cutting to the chase.

"We've got a few questions," one of the attorneys piped in.

"Objection, your honor!" I quipped, "Who is this guy?"

Harry looked at me and then the lawyer.

"Greg Price, managing partner at corporate's law firm," he said, his eyes shifting from side to side.

"Delta is extremely upset with you, uh, the station. They're tossing around their weight. We got a call from the district attorney's office in Clayton County. They're considering pressing charges against you and the station," he said.

"Pressing charges?" I fired back. "We told them what we had! I met with Delta in person. They told me what we had was junk. That was before I handled baggage under a 757."

"Let's just all take a breath," Steve said, trying to be the voice of reason.

"What do you guys suggest we do?" he said, looking at the lawyers.

"Our best advice is hold the story," a stern looking woman with heavy framed glasses said. "Let things cool down a bit."

"Hold the story? My face is on page three of every *TV Guide* in Atlanta. We've run a week's worth of ads in the *AJC*. We have radio ads on half the stations in the city. If we pull the story, I'm going to look like a fool. *We're* going to look like fools," I said.

"The heat is just too hot," Harry said under his breath. "Let's just hit pause. Let things die down a bit and then revisit this."

The lawyers nodded their heads in agreement.

Of course, word spread quickly and the next morning my TV guide ad was plastered in color on the front page of the *Atlanta Constitution* and that evening in the *Atlanta Journal*.

WILL STATION RUN AIRPORT SERIES?

FEDS SAY REPORTER MIGHT HAVE VIOLATED SECURITY LAWS.

On the jump page (where the story continues deeper in the paper), the newspaper's editors stabbed me with their poison pens: SERIES: REPORTER MIGHT HAVE BEEN BILKED, SOME SAY.

The infamous "some say." That's code for journalistic laziness or sources that don't exist.

The headlines continued: EXPOSE ON AIRPORT SECURITY TEMPORARILY GROUNDED BY STATION.

I was getting hammered by competitors and critics.

"He's obviously been sold a bill of goods," an unnamed federal source told the *AJC*.

"I've worked in seven markets and never seen that before," said the news director at a rival station.

So for a week, I dangled in the journalistic winds, my reputation and reporting skills battered in the process.

Finally, the station regained its backbone and balls. My story was slated for air on the following Thursday during the six o'clock news. Once again, heavy promotion of the series ensued. I was prepared for the massive blowback that might come after the story aired.

But air it did, for what the *Washington Journalism Review* called "a riveting twelve-minute report" on the six o'clock news, something that would be unheard of in today's ninety-seconds-or-less slice-and-dice-across-multiple-social-media-platforms manner of reporting.

The next day, the story made *USA Today* and was covered by the *Associated Press*, which meant the story got picked up across the country.

One day, the tide turned.

"Reporter should not be penalized for doing his job" read the headline in the *Atlanta Journal* above an editorial written by the legendary Durwood McAlister:

"It is not up to the FBI or the FAA to decide if Mr. Pettit had a 'legitimate' news story. If they did not find his evidence of an international ring selling security items persuasive, so what? The fact remains that the reporter breached their security.

He did so, not for the purpose of planting a bomb, but to determine if it would be possible for a terrorist, with more deadly purposes in mind, to do so. That is something the public has a right to know."

The FAA's Mr. Barker denied media suggestions that the government tried to pressure (the station) from airing the story.

"That's a bunch of garbage," he said. "There is indeed something rotten about this affair. But it smells more like an attempted cover-up than media garbage."

"GET THAT REPORTER FOR IMPROPER EXPOSURE IN A RESTRICTED AREA!"

And, in a stunning move, the *Atlanta Journal* ran an editorial cartoon showing Hartsfield officials with their pants down around their ankles as a reporter and his photographer tried to question them.

"Get that reporter for improper exposure in a restricted area!" the caption under the cartoon read.

As the kids say today, mic drop.

Over the next several days, I continued to release details from our *Security for Sale* investigation and airport officials were forced to admit that 1,600 airline employee uniforms and more than 2,000 identity badges were "missing" or unaccounted for.

As the shoes continued to drop on airport and airline officials, the Clayton County District Attorney's Office made its decision.

Clayton will not prosecute reporter who broke security, the Associated Press reported.

Clayton says it won't hound reporter for airport violations, but it does want details, blared the headline above an article in the *Atlanta Journal.*

"It must have been tough for the writer (who shall remain unnamed) to be objective," he later told the *Washington Journalism Review.* "There's no question they ran it for the ratings. I think the most serious crime in this field is to tell the public something that is not true," he added. "I think that's been violated. He also scared the hell out of a lot of people."

Again, I'll remind you (and the writer) this was ten years before 9/11. People should have had the hell scared out of them. As I told *WJR* at the time, "This story is as solid as any that I have done." I dismissed the writer at the Atlanta paper and the other reporters who had blasted me as "cynical journalists." I told *WJR,* "Why take the word of the government? What are we supposed to do, all sit back and take what they tell us? Why don't we just put Richard Nixon back in the White house?"

Ode to Dan Rather.

In the same article, my news director Steve Sherman told *WJR,* "I don't know the source, but I trust my reporter."

That's what a real news director does. He backs his reporters when they know they've done great work. Not long after my investigation aired, Steve was elevated to a job in corporate and his replacement was named.

Tom Blasek.

Simply put, he was no Steve Sherman. He was a weirdo and someone I didn't trust the minute he walked into the newsroom. He promptly moved into Steve's old office and hung a piece of paper on the wall behind his desk.

What part of no don't you understand?

We'd be in his office watching the six o'clock news (as we all used to love to do with Steve) and it was running insults from Blasek.

"He looks like a fucking Nazi," he said of one of our best reporters as he broadcasted live from the scene of a breaking news event.

"She has a face for newspaper," he said of a female reporter.

I grew increasingly uncomfortable with Blasek but tried to mind my own business and continue to do good work at the station.

I spoke to my agent, Kris, about my uneasiness with Blasek.

"Just try to roll with it. He's like a wrecking ball. Once he does the damage corporate needs done, he'll be gone," she counseled me.

Meanwhile, my homelife was miserable and I continued to make mistakes.

"Come to Backstreet with us," my friend Diego said to me one night at dinner. "Rick and I are going on Saturday." We were eating at Roasters, a rotisserie chicken restaurant not far from Lenox Mall in Atlanta at the time. It's where all the gays went for a somewhat healthy meal. Diego always ordered the same thing: grilled chicken breast, no skin, rice and steamed broccoli.

The waiters all knew him by site and by order.

"Princess Platter?" they'd each ask every time it was Diego's turn to order. He'd always smile and hand them the menu without even looking at it.

Backstreet was the famous gay dance bar in midtown that had a simple slogan: "Always Pouring." That's right, you could get yourself a Jack & Coke at nine in the morning if you wanted it. And you know by now, I liked a Jack & Coke every now and then.

So, reluctantly, after I finished anchoring the eleven o'clock news that Saturday night, I agreed to meet Rick and Diego at the bar. I still remember that night. After I got off the news, I changed into a starched buttoned-up long sleeve shirt, t-shirt, jeans and loafers. I knew the minute we made it through the front door of the bar that I was sorely overdressed.

"It's Raining Men" blared from the speakers in the front bar area and trust me it was. There were hot shirtless guys everywhere, and there I stood looking like a turd in a punchbowl. I looked over at Diego, who removed his black T-shirt as he bellied up to the bar with his rippling abs.

Dear God, what am I doing here? I thought to myself.

But an hour later, I didn't give a shit anymore. Diego had convinced me to take half of an Ecstasy pill and I was on the dance floor, shirtless with him and Rick dancing my ass off to a disco beat. At around four in the morning, I looked down at my belt, where I thought I had looped my starched buttoned-up shirt only to see a sweaty piece of leather clinging to my Levi's. My fancy shirt was nowhere to be found, and I could not care less.

It was one of the most fun and freeing nights of my life.

But again, there were eyes in the crowd. Ones that had certainly seen me on Fearless4 News. I was becoming reckless, and it was only a matter of time before the jig was up.

About six months before my contract expired at the station, Blasek asked to meet with me and, of course, I agreed. I walked into his office, which still felt odd that he was in there instead of Steve, closed the door behind me and sat down in front of his desk.

"We're going to be making some pretty significant changes as it relates to on-air talent," he told me.

Uh, oh.

"Chet's out. Joe's out and probably Jeanne, too," he said of three of our top on-air personalities. "We're cutting the six o'clock news from an hour to a half-hour. Corporate's got a new show coming that's based off of the newspaper," he said, speaking of a national daily print publication that was owned by our parent company.

"As for you," he said, "I like you. In fact, you just might be the best reporter in the newsroom. So, keep doing what you're doing, and you'll be fine."

I felt that deep unease in my gut, but I nodded in agreement. It was best that I keep my head down and do what was asked of me.

"One other thing," he said. "John's going to be taking some time off over the holidays. We're going to have you anchor all the main shows."

What he was saying was that I would be working every holiday. Thanksgiving, Christmas, New Year's.

"You're the back-up anchorman," he said. "That's what you have to do if you ever want a seat at the main desk."

So I did it. And pretty much every holiday, I worked and came home to an empty condo. I grew more and more depressed. I might have been smiling on the six o'clock news, but I was dying inside.

Diego offered me more artificial encouragement.

"Why don't you try a little coke with us one night?" he asked. "I think it'll lift your mood," he said. "Maybe a little K, too?" K was the codename for the drug Ketamine. "Rick's got a hook-up."

And by "hook-up," he meant a dealer.

"No, man, I'm good," I told him, regretting that I had even tried Ecstasy. "I'm just not into drugs."

Diego nodded, but he knew that I was really struggling with my sexuality and the conflict it presented at work.

I could feel my personal prison closing in around me. Soon drugs would release me from the bars. Or so I thought.

I pressed on. Through the end of 1990 and into the spring of 1991, things were rocky at the station. Four more of our top on-air personalities were let go or their contracts not renewed.

Before the upheaval, we were a strong #2 in the market. Our weekend news, that I co-anchored was often coming in #1 but in general the station was slipping, and everyone knew it.

And then, on April 24, 1991, my world came to a halt.

"See me before you get started on anything" the message read on my desk. It was signed by Blasek.

I picked up the note and tossed it onto the desk of my cubicle. I walked slowly toward Blasek's office, but was stopped by Doug, one of our assignment editors.

"He's upstairs with Harry," he told me. "He asked me to send you up when you got in."

I wasn't sure what to make of things as I made my way up the stairs and toward the GM's office. Harry spotted me through the glass wall in his office and motioned for me to come in. I walked the few short steps down the hallway and turned into his office.

Blasek sat at the side conference table in Harry's office. In front of him, there was a blue folder.

"You wanted to see me?" I said as I entered the room. It was solemn and tense.

"Sit down, please Mark," Harry said. I felt like I had been called into the principal's office and he had been joined by the school superintendent.

"What's going on?" I said as I sat down at the table across from Blasek.

"We received a letter," Blasek said, not looking up from the table. "A disturbing letter. From Jeremy Jonus, about you."

A letter from Jeremy Jonus? What the hell was he talking about?

"About me?" I repeated.

"He's brought up some, uh, troubling accusations against you," Blasek said.

"Well, I did cause him to get convicted of a third murder," I said. "He's probably still really upset with me."

Ice cold. No reaction from my bosses.

"What did he say?" I demanded, "I'm sure there's an explanation for whatever he's brought to your attention," I said, looking directly at Blasek.

"It's not what he said," Blasek said, reaching down to the folder in front of him. "It's what he sent us."

With that, he opened the blue folder revealing two handwritten letters and a small photo.

I tried to quickly look down at the materials but couldn't quite make them out.

"We're going to need you to explain this," Harry, the GM said.

I reached for one of the letters and the small photo.

My heart sank into my stomach.

The photo was of me and Paulo, shirtless, arm in arm on the beach. My emotions boiled over and I could feel the tears slipping from my eyes.

I then reached for the letter.

It simply read, *ANKRBOY HAS A SECRET.*

As I soaked in the words, I placed that letter down and reached for the second. The penmanship was elegant, and the letter was obviously written with care.

For the first time in over two years, I heard Paulo's voice as I read the letter.

Dear Mark,

I hope this letter finds you well. Things are good here in San Francisco. I'm settling into my new job here at the clinic, literally the front lines of the epidemic. At least I feel like I'm helping people.

The only thing missing is you.

I'm heartbroken at the way things ended. What we had was real. I hope you are ultimately able to live your truth. To be honest, finally, with and about yourself. Enclosed is a memento from our trip to the beach. It's the only photo I have of us together. I thought you might like a copy.

Take care and stay sweet.

All my love.
Paulo.

Tears fell from my eyes and onto the paper, blotting the ink.

Jeremy. I squeezed my eyes shut, trying to figure out how.

Then I remembered. Our last meeting until our day in court. The rush of jamming my attaché shut, my mail sticking out, my holding the briefcase underneath my arm and getting out.

So Paulo's letter fell and Jeremy, clever bastard, slipped a foot over it for a rainy day.

I was overcome with emotion. Paulo's words and Jeremy's revenge and betrayal of my secret and the impending collapse of my own existence.

"What is all this?" Blasek asked me.

There was so much I wanted to say. So much I could say. I could have defended myself; I could deflect. I could lie. But in that horrible moment, I found courage.

"The truth," I replied to Blasek as tears flooded my face.

The GM and Blasek sat in silence, looking at me with cold, robotic eyes hiding what felt like some unspoken rage.

"I'm sorry Mark, but this just won't play with a lot of our viewers. You're a great reporter," Harry said somewhat sincerely, "But we're going to have to move on."

Then, Blasek dropped the hammer.

"We won't be extending your contract," he said. "You have two months to go on your current agreement. HR has a check for you. Pack up your desk and security will be waiting to escort you out."

Security? To escort me out?

I was in a daze but gathered myself and walked out of the office. The HR director was waiting with the envelope as I exited the room.

"We're going to miss you around here," she said as she handed me the envelope containing the check.

I looked up and across the way, I saw Eva standing outside her boss's office. She was a mess. It seems the news had spread to others before it was delivered to me. I looked at her momentarily, then continued my way down the hall and down the stairs back to the newsroom.

Dead newsman walking.

As I arrived at my cubicle, I found a small box, about two-by-two feet waiting for me. Clearly my exit had been thoroughly planned in advance. News spreads quickly, especially in a newsroom and I could hear people buzzing as I stuffed the items around my desk and into the box.

I could feel a presence behind me and turned to see Wayne, the station's head of security waiting for me.

"I just need to grab my jacket and my keys," I told him.

His eyes darted from mine.

Across the newsroom, I could see people starting to form a line, as Wayne led me from the office.

A handshake from Ken, one of the best reporters I had ever worked with. A pat on the back from Johnny, the weatherman.

"We'll miss you, Cutty," said the weekend sports anchor. It was a running joke and some silly movie reference for us to call each other Cutty each time one of us saw the other.

"I'll miss you, too, Cutty," I said in a fog.

I said my goodbyes to my co-workers as I worked down the line and toward the side door of the building.

At the end of the line, my dear friend and colleague Kay Flowers stood with tears flowing down her beautiful face. She had married my co-worker, Dan Johnson, in 1987 and it broke my heart to see her crying.

I paused as I reached her, and we hugged each other goodbye.

Wayne gently touched me on my shoulder and pointed me to the door that led outside of the building and down to the parking garage where I had left my car.

As I opened the door, the bright sunlight of that spring morning hit my face. It was like a vampire awakening. I continued to walk in a daze, pausing briefly to look back toward the lobby where the receptionist Ann always held court.

I saw her wiping her eyes as maintenance workers pulled my oversized photo down from the wall where it had been placed three years before with the other key on-air personalities. In a painful insult to injury, I watched as one of the workers made the final tug of the foam core, removing the image from the wall. In its place was a clean patch of paint, my negative shadow remaining.

He then bent the board, breaking my photo in half. Then, with the air of a distant memory, he tucked it under his arm and walked out of the lobby.

The dead cat was out of the bag.

The next morning, the headline in the *Atlanta Constitution* read: PETTIT THE LATEST CASUALTY IN STATION REVAMP.

At first, I tried to laugh it off, joking with the paper's gossip columnist about the message on my answering machine.

Hello, this is Mark. Yes, it's been quite a week. Thanks to your overwhelming response I've designed this message to answer your questions. To hear more about my TV problems, press 1 now. To hear more about my personal problems, press 2 now. To make a deposit into my checking account, press 4 now.

But, in reality, it was no joke. There were no offers from other stations.

As I stated earlier, my agent was blunt.

"There's nothing I can do for you now," she said into the phone. "They don't put guys like you on the evening news."

When it was just affecting me, I was okay with it. But then things took a turn for the worse in my hometown.

"I walked into the beauty shop and it was like I was a stranger," my sweet mother told me on the phone. "People look the other way when they see me in the grocery store."

And then she told me a story.

"A woman at work once asked me a question," she said. "She asked me what I would do if you came home with a black girl?"

I almost interrupted her, to say how inappropriate the question was, but before I could, she said something amazing.

"I told her if Mark loves her, I love her. It's as simple as that."

I choked up as she finished the story. My mother was as country as a cucumber, but her love was unconditional. That was not the case with others in our community.

My stepfather, Max, who raised me since I was two years old, was scheduled for open heart surgery at a hospital in Rome. My younger brother, Jeff, and my Aunt Flonnie and I were by his side as he was being wheeled down the hall on a gurney toward the operating room.

I looked up to see the preacher from my church in Calhoun walking toward us. I thought surely he would stop to speak, perhaps lead us in prayer as Max entered surgery. But, instead, the pastor walked right past us without speaking a word.

It was something my aunt never forgot.

"He's no man of God," she told me later. "You are more of a man than he is."

My aunt knew the truth about me now but, like my mother and like Max, her love was unwavering. After he recovered from his surgery, I remember sitting with Max out in the front yard of his home where we had grown up.

He began to cry as we sat together.

"Is it my fault?" he asked, trying to come to terms with the news that I had shared with him about my sexuality.

"It's nobody's fault, Maxie Doodle," I told him, using the pet name I had given him as a boy. "It's life, and I'm going to live it the best I can."

He nodded his head and pulled the handkerchief from his pocket and wiped away his tears.

"You know people are talking about you, about us," he said.

"I do. I'm sure it's a shock to people who thought they knew me," I said, somehow trying to justify it.

"Don't let it get to you," I told Max. "You're a good man and you've been a good father to me."

Again, he nodded.

"Thank you. I've tried."

The way my family was treated and me struggling with my situation led me into a deep depression. I was drinking way more than I should and was hungover the Saturday morning I went in to get my hair done, or should I say dyed.

I had started getting gray headed in my early twenties and it freaked me out. At around age twenty, I started getting it dyed both in Omaha and later in Atlanta. Depending on the daylight, my hair ranged in color from Auburn Autumn to Nutmeg Brown. It never looked natural, and it was a bitch to keep up the routine.

"Baby! You gotta quit this shit!" the shampoo lady told me at the beauty shop (as my mama always called it) as she used a warm rag to try and scrub the remnants of the remaining dye from my forehead.

It looked terrible, so that night I sat at home alone, drinking heavily again.

At about ten-thirty, the phone rang, catching me off guard as I dozed in front of the TV set. Against my better judgment, I answered the call.

"Hello," I said, trying not to sound drunk.

"Hi Mark," the man said before pausing. "It's Luke. Luke Lawson."

I didn't know how to respond.

"I'm sorry to call you so late," he said, his voice now starting to crack.

"It's okay," I told him.

"Listen, I heard what happened to you. With your job," he said, "And I just want you to know how sorry I am. For what she did."

I could hear him crying now.

"What are you talking about?"

"Katie is the reason for all this," he said.

"I don't understand."

"She knew about us, Mark! She followed us to the motel."

"What?" I said again.

"How do you think you got the job in Omaha, Mark? It was Dave Farrell. Katie took photos of us at the motel and sent them to Dave. She blackmailed me. And you."

Suddenly, I was there. In the darkroom with Katie. I watched her hand slip into the vat of liquid before her. Her eyes were fixed and glazed as she moved her hand across the paper in the water. Clearly, the image came into focus.

It was me, kissing Luke on his lips.

Katie removed the paper from the liquid, watching as the last drops fell from the corner of the image. Her eyes were filled with an uneasy rage. She then used a clip to hang the photo alongside two others on a line across the small room.

"It's all a lie," I heard Luke say.

I was now back in Atlanta, in my home, on the phone with Luke.

"Omaha. All of it," he said as he sobbed.

"All she wanted was two kids and a country club membership," he said. "When she got that, she was gone. She told all her friends about me. And about you. The station fired me. My life has been a living hell since."

"Luke. I'm so sorry," I said.

"She killed us both," he said as he hung up the phone.

Later that night, I had a horrible dream that at the end of the call with Luke I had heard a gunshot. Him blowing his brains out, with me on the phone with him. It had shaken me terribly and now as I stood in front of the mirror.

In horror, and in pain.

I walked back into my room and removed the framed publicity photo from a shelf near my bed. My mission was clear. I had to free the man trapped behind the glass.

I stared at myself again in the mirror, disgusted.

Then, I lifted the framed photo above my head.

CHAPTER

21

ANGEL OF THE MORNING

Back to Palm Springs.

As I said earlier, the last thing I remember was darkness and then silence. That eerie quietness that I imagine comes between life and death. A slow ride to the next realm. The only question is whether the elevator is going up or down. *Ding. Ding. Ding.*

I'm not sure how long I was out, how many floors I was riding on the elevator, but then, shockingly, I was back. Sort of. It was all a slurry blur of sounds and images.

And then a loud, familiar voice. And accent.

"Step back! Get away from him!"

The voice sounded like an angel. Okay, great, at least the elevator went in the right direction. I tried to open my eyes but everything about it hurt. My head. My stomach, my entire body ached. Then, I felt a warm, oozing liquid slide down my back. Another, foamy like liquid slipped from my lips and I heaved.

"I'm a doctor!" the voice said, "Someone call 911!"

Again, things happened so quickly, and I was so groggy. I didn't know how to respond or what to do. From behind me, I felt someone or something lifting my body. Could this be The Big Guy pulling me through the pearly gates?

Warm, firm hands came around my waist and up to just below my stomach. Then, a violent squeeze. Then another.

I felt the vomit churn in my lower abdomen, and then as it raced up my esophagus and out of my mouth. Oh boy.

BLWWWWWWLLLK! BLWWWWWWLLLK!

The stranger's thrust had conjured the demons from their depths. I heaved again and threw up on my stomach and white pants. And not just regular vomit, the kind Kenny has on *South Park*. The remaining crowd around me scattered.

"It's me, baby," I heard the stranger whisper in my ear. "It's me, Paulo."

What?

Okay, I was in Heaven.

"I need you to take deep breaths," the voice told me. "You have to breathe." I did as I was told and puked again. A gut-wrenching blast that again covered my stomach and pants.

"That's it," the voice said. "Get it all out."

Who was this stranger? I had to know. I raised my hand and wiped the rest of the liquid from my mouth. I then turned my head slightly and the stranger's face became clear. It was Paulo. I had not seen or heard from him in three years now. But it was him. In the flesh, and here to save me.

He pushed me up and forward and then scrambled in front of me.

"I'm going to lift you onto my shoulder now. *Nao vomite em mim!*" he said sternly.

"What?" I asked. "You still can't speak English?" Once a smartass, always a smartass, even in a near death experience.

"Don't throw up on me!" Paulo said as he lifted me onto his right shoulder.

"Get out of the way!" he yelled. I came to just enough to see a sea of white, or the wake of a sea of white.

Bam. Bam. Bam. My head bobbed on the soft cotton of the shirt on Paulo's back. Again, I smelled his familiar scent. Those berries and that woody dirt smell that I loved and missed so much.

He carried me farther. I felt a change in the temperature as he darted through a side gate on the veranda and out into the parking lot just outside the resort. The night was crisp and I felt the oozy substance on my back hardening.

Bam. Bam. Bam. What seemed like ten more steps, where he stopped.

"Ugh!" he groaned as he lowered me from his shoulder onto a curb or the sidewalk. I wasn't sure which. He darted back onto the veranda and a bar near the sidewalk.

"Bottled water," I heard him order.

After another few seconds, he returned and handed me the bottle. I took the water from his muscular hand as my eyes traced the muscles in his forearm back up to his chest.

Unlike the other party revelers who shunned fabric for skin, he was dressed conservatively in a white shirt, opened from the neck to his tight waist.

"What happened?" I asked.

"People said it was that guy from New York. That he spiked your water. Why the fuck did you take water from a stranger?" he scolded.

"Because he was hot," I said. "Well, I was hot. You know what I'm saying."

He wasn't amused.

"This isn't funny, Mark. You could have died in there."

I was now firmly back among the living, but still confused. I gulped the water like a hostage held captive for weeks.

"What are you doing here?" I asked him.

"I'm here with friends from Palm Springs," he said almost apologetically. "Just to get away from San Francisco for a few days. You can only stand the front lines for so long. I'm not into this circuit scene."

"Speaking of that, did you save my wings?" I asked, almost serious. "Those things cost me fifty bucks. I was hoping to get a couple of wears out of them."

We shared an awkward but familiar laugh. And then sat in silence.

I had forgotten how beautiful he was. His kind eyes, that sharp straight nose that drew me down into his warm smile.

"Do you have a boyfriend now?" I asked, deciding to put myself out of my misery before I fell for him all over again.

"No," he said to my surprise. "How about you?"

I shook my head. "No. Just a couple of friends with benefits. That's it," I told him.

He nodded in agreement.

"San Francisco, huh?" I said judgmentally. "So, that's where you ran off to without telling me."

He hung his head and the smile left his face.

"There was no future with you," he said. "So, I decided to move to San Francisco. For my career and the cause."

I knew what he meant. That was the kind of person he was. The kind to run to a fire when others run away at the mere smell of smoke. Even if it means running away from something wonderful, and by that, I mean me.

"I heard one of the guys say your name and that you were from Atlanta," he said. "That's what got my attention. That's why I came running over to you. Just in case it was you."

His words melted my arctic heart.

"Yes, I'm back home in Atlanta now. I got a job in TV news there. Well, I had a job in TV news there," I said, not really wanting to get into the details.

"Wow. Too ironic," he said. "My dad took a job at the CDC about six months ago. My parents live in Decatur now."

I couldn't believe my ears.

"What?" I asked. "Your parents moved to Atlanta? That's perfect!"

"What do you mean, 'perfect?'" He asked, looking at me like he didn't understand the word.

"Uh, I mean, if you're burned out in San Francisco, maybe you could try Atlanta," I said. "To be close to your family."

And then, I blurted it out.

"And me."

He looked at me the way a puppy looks at its owner. *Are we going out? Are you offering me a treat? Did I chew up your shoes? You shouldn't have left them out!*

"I don't understand," he said.

"It would be perfect!" I said, no longer able to control my excitement. My hope and dream. "We could finally be together. We can be real boyfriends now."

The words hit him hard. There was no acknowledgement in his manner, no smile on his face or in his eyes.

Harshly he said, "No. We can't."

I put my salesman hat on, like I used to do in the morning editorial meetings at the station when I was lobbying for the lead story on that night's newscast.

"Why not?" I implored. "I don't have to hide anymore. I got a job in PR. Fuck, everybody's gay!"

I laughed. He didn't.

"We… uh, I can't," he said. I thought I saw tears slip from his eyes.

"This is what you always wanted!" I pressed on. "Us to be together, open and honest. What are the chances I would see you here and be saved by you at this party?" I said, choking back tears, trying to convince him.

"That has to mean something, right?"

A hushed, life-altering pause, and then he said it.

"I'm HIV-positive, Mark" he said.

The words struck us both like a meteor in the desert night, shattering my heart.

"No! You can't be! You're a doctor! You're trying to cure it!" I screamed, as if pressing my case before God.

I began to weep as emotions overcame me.

"I can count on one hand the number of times I've had sex without a condom," he said, tears now visibly streaming down his face. "And you were one of them."

"But, no! I'm negative," I said. "I promise you. I just got tested last month."

"It's not you, Mark," he said with a resigned tone that shook me. "It's a guy named Jim from Chicago. I met him at a medical conference. It was just one time. One night. He didn't have condoms." He was choking back emotion and trying to stop the tears.

"I made one mistake and now I'm going to die for it," he said. "At least he had the decency to call and tell me once he found out he was positive."

I mustered every ounce of compassion I had in me.

"Baby, no," I whispered to him, as I reached for his hands. "They're going to find a cure for this. You're going to find a cure for this. You just have to keep taking care of yourself."

Our eyes met. A haunting stare I will never forget.

"The doctor has me on this new combo drug. I take it twice per day," he said. "Eight in the morning and eight at night. I can't eat dinner before eight o'clock at night."

"Table for two at my place?" I whispered. "Eight fifteen? Every night? Move in with me, Paulo. We can have the life we've always wanted," I begged him.

"I've been thinking about changing jobs," he said. "Getting out of San Francisco."

I leaned over and pulled him toward me.

"You were here for a reason tonight," I whispered as I kissed his smooth face. "God sent you to save me and to bring us back together."

"It could take me a couple of months to find a job," he said, looking at me with a glint of hope in his eyes.

"I got a couple months' severance when the station let me go," I told him. "I can take care of us both until then."

He lifted both hands and clasped the sides of my face and then leaned in and sweetly kissed me.

"Oh, God!" he said. "Your breath smells terrible."

We both laughed. Like we used to laugh.

"If I do this, there's just one condition," he said. "If I get too sick to take care of myself, I'm moving back home with my parents. They know everything at this point." He lowered his eyes, hinting at shame.

"That won't happen, baby," I reassured him. "Maybe we'll get a puppy. A stray, just like you and me."

"One step at a time."

"Let's start with tonight," I said. "Come stay with me. I have my own room at the hotel."

"Thought sure you'd get lucky," he replied with a smile.

"Turns out I did," I said.

He then reached for his back pocket and pulled out a flip phone.

"Let me call my friends," he said.

I couldn't believe how the night had begun and now how it was ending.

A month later Paulo moved to Atlanta and into my townhouse just off of North Druid Hills. At first it was bliss. Surprisingly easy. Like we had never been apart after our breakup in Omaha.

We shopped for furniture and art together. He brought a sophisticated style and touch to our home.

I felt like I was living a dream. Perhaps I was.

"Let's go on a real date tonight," he said one Saturday afternoon. "I want us to go see *Ghost*," he said with a childlike smile.

"Sounds scary," I joked.

"It's a love story, silly," he said. "It'll be sweet."

And he was right.

You know the story. Patrick Swayze plays Sam Wheat, a banker who falls madly in love with Demi Moore's Molly Jensen. Sam is murdered by his friend, and sleazy business partner, and is left to roam eternity as a powerless spirit.

Early in the movie, Molly is working on a piece of clay pottery while Sam sleeps. Suddenly, her jukebox changes records and the Righteous Brothers' "Unchained Melody" begins to play. Sam wakes and walks in and stands behind her.

"What are you doing?" he asks.

"I couldn't sleep," she says, as she continues to work on her sculpture. Swayze slips his arms around Demi's waist and slides up closer to her. He reaches to touch her hand and the sculpture collapses.

"Oh no, I hope it wasn't a masterpiece," he says.

"It's not now," she says as they share a sweet laugh.

"Can I help?" Swayze says as he moves closer to Demi the music grows louder.

I need your love. I need your love.

"Just let the clay slide between your fingers," she says.

As their hands intertwined around the clay, Paulo reached for my hand. It was one of the nicest moments of my life.

I squeezed his hand hard.

It was in that moment, as "Unchained Melody" rang through the theater, that I finally knew the meaning of true love.

...are you still mine?

Paulo leaned his head over on my shoulder and we continued to watch as Swayze and Demi were covered in clay.

Godspeed your love, to me.

Unfortunately, every dream and every good movie comes to an end.

A few weeks later, I came home from work and as I entered the living area of our townhome from the garage, I heard Paulo singing. At the top of his lungs.

Don't cry for me, Argentina.

As I entered the dining area, Paulo emerged from the kitchen holding two cocktails.

"What are we celebrating?" I said with a smile.

"I'm dying, Mark," he said in a matter-of-fact tone. "The medicine's no longer working. The doctor has given me three months, six months, tops," he said.

I froze. Not sure what to do in the moment, I tried to comfort him. Give him hope.

"No. Don't give up," I said, my emotions beginning to get the best of me. "We can beat this."

"Shh. No baby." he said. "That's it. I'm dying."

As I began to cry, Paulo leaned in and gently kissed me on the cheek. With his left hand, he tried to wipe the tears from my face.

"We can't give up!"

"We talked about this in Palm Springs. I told you if this day came, I would move home with my parents. That's what I'm going to do. You can move on with your life," he said as his eyes fell to the floor.

"No! This is *our* life." I pulled him close to me, I wasn't going to let him go a second time.

But the choice was not mine.

That weekend, I watched him load what belongings he had into his car and stood in silence in the driveway as he pulled away.

I tried calling him every day, but his phone went straight to voicemail. Finally, after about three months, I just gave up.

My heart and my home were shattered.

I was three drinks in on a lonely Friday night when the phone rang at my home. I reluctantly answered on the fourth ring.

"*Boa noite, Marcos,*" the woman said in a meek voice. "Good evening, Mark. This is Helena, Paulo's *mae*. I'm so sorry to bother you on a Friday night," she apologized. "But Paulo asked that I call. He would like to see you tomorrow afternoon, if you could possibly visit our home."

I was surprised but elated to get her call.

"It's urgent," she said.

"Of course, just tell me what time."

"*Fou da tarde,*" she said. "Uh, I'm sorry, four thirty." She gave me their address and I wrote it down.

I could barely sleep that night, tumbling around. I had horrible dreams about Paulo. In one of the dreams, he was being chased by a monster and I couldn't do anything to save him. I might have slept an hour the entire time.

The monster in my dream was nothing compared to what I was about to encounter.

Right at four thirty, I arrived at Paulo's parent's home. It was a beautiful Tudor home in an upscale neighborhood in Decatur, where many doctors and executives from the CDC lived. Paulo's father had been working in Atlanta for more than a year now.

I had been to their home once before.

Paulo had invited me to have a traditional Sunday dinner with the family. In addition to Helena, a beautiful, trim and proper lady with flowing black hair, I met Paulo's father, Francisco, who appeared to be in his early sixties with his dark hair being overtaken by silver. He was fit and handsome, no surprise, knowing how good Paulo looked in his birthday suit. I also met Paulo's older sister, Julieta. She was two years older than Paulo and had earned her PhD in psychology. She had moved with the family to Atlanta, where she had joined the faculty at Emory University on a work visa.

They were all courteous and kind to me, but they didn't ask very many questions about me or about my relationship with Paulo. There was just an unspoken easiness about us. That was fine with me.

For dinner, Paulo's mother and sister had made us *feijoada*, a sumptuous and hearty stew made with various cuts of pork and cooked with cabbage, carrots and tomatoes. It was served, in the traditional Brazilian manner with fried kale, rice, bacon and slices of orange. It was my first time trying *pão de queijo*, the famous cheese bread enjoyed in Brazil. I think I ate five or six balls at dinner.

"Eating like this is what put me in husky jeans in high school," I said with a laugh, which no one really understood but me. They all laughed anyway.

This time, there was no joy as I entered their home.

"Thank you for coming, Marcos," Paulo's mother said. "If you would follow me, I will take you to Paulo's room."

Her odd choice of words hit me. I followed her down a long hallway with a nice red and blue oriental rug that ran down the middle of the floor. She paused just before a door to the right near the end of the hall.

She turned and looked at me with the saddest eyes I think I have ever seen. Then, she knocked at the door.

"*Ola Paulo. Marcos esta aqui,*" she said. *Mark is here.*

She opened the door slightly, peeked in and then stepped back to allow me to enter.

"I'll let you two speak alone," she said, as she caressed my back, leading me into the room.

I felt a coldness fall over me. And then, like the clicking of a timebomb, I heard the tick, tick, tick of a grandfather clock. *Tick, tick, tick.* It was haunting to me, but I tried to ignore it and entered the room.

My eyes fell to the king-sized bed on the wall before me. And there Paulo was. Gaunt and thin. I held back tears. It was awful. He had lost what appeared to be every ounce of body fat, and he had little to lose in the first place. Paulo's face looked like a skeleton and reminded me of the famous painting *The Scream*, by Edvard Munch.

I approached the side of Paulo's bed, not sure what to do.

"Hello, handsome," he whispered. "Thank you for coming."

I walked toward him and slowly eased down to sit next to him on the bed.

"Now you see why I didn't return your calls," he said. "I didn't want you to see me like this."

It was the most devastating moment of my life.

I didn't know what to do. I leaned down and kissed him on the cheek. He lifted his frail arm and wrapped it around my shoulder. He was comforting me. That was Paulo. So gentle, so kind.

"I have a favor to ask," he whispered in my ear.

"Anything, baby," I whispered back.

"Will you help my parents get me into the bathtub?" he asked. "All I want is one more hot bath."

"Give me just a minute," I said, as I walked back toward the hallway. I opened the door and was about to yell but I realized that would be bad manners. Instead, I walked down the corridor to find Paulo's mother.

"Please. He'd like a bath." She leaned in to hear me, my words were weak. She led me to Francisco and the three of us formed a silent procession to Paulo's room.

Helena stroked his cheek as Francisco and I carried Paulo down the hall in the sheet from his bed. He was so light. We were able to lower him into the bathtub without strain. Paulo looked up and smiled. He closed his eyes. The scene felt baptismal.

I heard the door click quietly behind me. Paulo and I were alone.

As he soaked in the warm water, I reached for the shampoo. I squeezed a quarter-sized amount in my hand.

"Do you remember our trip to the beach?" I asked as I rubbed the liquid between my palms.

"Of course," he whispered. "I will never forget it."

"And you remember everything we talked about?" I asked.

"I do," he said. "Every word of it."

I decided to ask a follow-up question from our discussion at the beach. Something that had haunted me since that day.

"Do you think we would have had kids?" I asked him as I massaged the shampoo into his hair. Several strands of his once beautiful locks slipped from his scalp and through my fingers. My throat burned as I forced my sorrow down.

He paused ever so slightly, then replied.

"I do," he said, a smile crossing his sunken face. "Twin boys. Jack and João," he said. One classic American, one classic Brazilian name for each son.

His words caused me to choke. I tried to hold back the tears.

My mind drifted off in a sweet dream. We were chasing the toddlers in our backyard. They had his hair. My head. Oversized and bobbing as they laughed and chased our new puppy. A dog we had adopted from a shelter.

"Who wants birthday cake?" my sweet mother yelled from the back deck, holding her famous double chocolate fudge surprise on a plate in her hands.

"*Eu faço!*" Little João screeched in Portuguese. "*Eu taço!*" little Jack shouted.

Like father, like son.

Now, Paulo's mother joined my mother on the deck. In one hand she held a large "3" that she placed on the chocolate cake. Paulo's father soon joined us on the deck, where he grabbed the lighter from the side of the grill. With a big smile, he pulled the trigger on the lighter and pressed it to the wick at the end of the large candle.

"*Feliz aniversario!*" Paulo's parents sang, as my mother joined the chorus, "Happy birthday to you!" and then together, as one happy family we sang.

"Happy birthday, Jack and João! Happy birthday to you!"

The little boys danced in delight and then ran for their grandparents and the cake. My eyes met Paulo's with love and happiness.

Back in the bathroom, I looked down at Paulo's face, his eyes closed. No joy to be found. I ran fresh warm water from the faucet and across his head.

"Thank you for doing this. All I wanted was this bath and to see you one last time," he whispered.

We sat in silence for the next half hour or so as Paulo soaked in the water. Afterwards, his father and I lifted him from the tub. I used a fluffy white towel to dry him down. His body hung like a scarecrow in his father's arms. Once he was dry, I took him from his father's arms and walked him back and laid him in his bed, which Helena had refreshed with soft white linens.

I pulled the sheet and blanket up to his chin. I leaned down and gave him a final kiss.

"One last thing," Paulo whispered. "Promise me you'll get that dog."

As I wept, I nodded my head. I lingered for a moment more and then rose from the side of the bed. I hugged Paulo's parents and went home, where I fell into a coma-like sleep. There were no bad dreams this time, just peace sweeping over me.

The next morning, at around eight-thirty. I got the call I had dreaded.

"*Bom dia, Marcos*," she said. "It's Helena." As she choked back tears, she spoke softly into the phone and my right ear.

"*Paulo foi ficar com Deus*," she whispered. *Paulo has gone to be with God*. I was not prepared to hear those words and almost doubled over in grief. I thought he would last another week, maybe two. Not less than twelve hours.

I took it as a sign. He at least waited till after eight in the morning.

"*Por favor*," she said. Which I understood. "*Voce vai falar com Julieta?*" she asked. I understood Julieta and simply replied, "Yes."

"Hello Mark," Paulo's sister Julieta said as she took the phone. "We are all heartbroken. I know you are as well."

I could no longer hold it back and began to softly cry.

"He told *mamae e papai* how special you were to him," she said. "We know he loved you very much."

Now, I could no longer control my emotions and just sat there and sobbed.

"Would you do us the great honor and help us plan his arrangements?" she asked. "He told us you two had talked about it. We figured you would know what he wanted." Julieta was now weeping herself.

We were strangers and now a family united in devastation.

"Of course," I told her. "He wanted a simple wooden coffin. He said cherry. And he loved roses. We planted red ones in my garden."

A few hours later, Julieta and I were sitting in the office of their local parish priest. He was an older man of about seventy-five who sat stoically behind his desk in a black shirt and black pants. His starched white clerical collar was so bright it almost blinded me.

"Are you his brother," he asked me?

"No. Just, uh, a very close friend," I lied to him.

"*Gostariamos de um servico tradicional*," Julietta told him in Portuguese. I could sort of make out what she told him. "Traditional service," at least.

"And for music, we have just one request," she then said, in English, so I would clearly understand.

"Would you please have them play "Unchained Melody?"" she asked. "By the Righteous Brothers?"

The priest looked at her with confusion and disdain.

"Unchained Melody," I piped in. "It was our, uh, his favorite song."

The priest looked at me crazily and then, back to Julieta.

"*Nao tocamos esse tipo de musica nesta igreja*," he said.

"What did he say," I asked Julietta.

She did not answer me.

Instead, she rose, her face flush in anger.

"*Entao, queremos ter o seu culto nesta ingreja!*" she said.

Then she looked at me, knowing I had no idea what she had told the priest.

"I told him that if they didn't play the song, we wouldn't have Paulo's service in this church!" she said, tears streaming down her beautiful, porcelain-like face.

"I did not mean to upset you," the priest said, now in perfect English. "Let me speak with the music director."

"Very well," Julieta responded. "Let me know and we'll make our final plans."

The decision was made to have Paulo's funeral at the church.

It was a funeral like I had never experienced, except for the one for the mother of my high-school friend Kevin. He was African American and the service for his mother must have lasted four hours. Lots of shouting, wailing but somehow spiritually cleansing.

I left with a sense of joy and happiness for a life well-lived.

At Paulo's funeral, flowers surrounded him inside his coffin. A small lamp sat at the top of it, near his head. What appeared to be an assistant to the priest, sprinkled water on Paulo's casket, a ritual intended to ensure safe passage to Heaven.

As the priest finished his final prayers, the pallbearers walked up and surrounded the coffin. The lid was closed and an elegant blanket of roses were placed on top of the beautiful cherry wood casket. I sat to the left of Julieta, on the aisle of the second pew in the church. Paulo's father sat to the right of his mother.

Then, to my surprise, the organist took her seat, on a padded bench in front of the large instrument in front of her. As she gently pressed the keys, the familiar, haunting song softly lofted throughout the chapel. Our song.

"Unchained Melody."

Oh, my love, my darling,
I've hungered for your touch,
A long lonely time...

As if in slow motion, a totally hellish, but heavenly experience wrapped in one, I extended my left hand and placed it on Paulo's coffin as it passed.

Time goes by so slowly,
And time can do so much.
Are you still mine?

The pallbearers paused for a moment, recognizing its significance.

I held my hand there for three, maybe five, seconds.

I need your love.
I need your love.

As the song reached its crescendo, I released my grip from the side of Paulo's casket, hung my head and cried.

Slowly and softly, I felt Julieta's hand reach for mine. I squeezed it tightly, just like I had Paulo's hand at the movies the night we watched *Ghost*.

Godspeed your love to me.

CHAPTER

22

THE COMEBACK

A fter Paulo died, I began to turn my life around slowly.

I secured part-time work at CNN anchoring the news during overnight shifts.

Mark Pettit
CNN Center

"It's always primetime somewhere!" Bob Fernad told me before offering me the job. Bob was an executive vice president at the network and old school when it came to TV journalism. He actually sat next to me on set during my audition for the job.

"It'll remind you that I'm always watching," Bob joked as the prompter rolled.

I passed Bob's audition and rotated between the network's domestic and foreign channels. I remember on my first night anchoring CNN International, the teleprompter went dark just as I was supposed to report breaking news involving Russian president Mikhail Gorbachev and Georgian leader Eduard Shevardnadze.

It wasn't pretty. I mispronounced Shevardnadze's name at least three times in what should have been a thirty-second reader.

Maybe it was a sign.

I made the decision to transition from TV news to public relations and accomplished the successful leap in no large part thanks to Jane Shivers, who hired me at Ketchum Public Relations in Atlanta. Imagine a nice version of Meryl Streep in *The Devil Wears Prada*. Jane was sharp, sophisticated and intelligent. We hit it off immediately.

Through industry contacts, I secured interviews with the major PR firms in town. The majority of them reminded me of law firms, with older white men in paneled offices cutting deals in hushed tones on their office phones.

But Jane and her agency were different.

The first time we met, Jane greeted me warmly in the lobby outside her office. She was striking, with reddish-blonde hair and sparkling eyes. She wore a tight black leather skirt and a bright red sweater.

She looked like two million bucks. Ketchum's office was glass walled, open and bright. The employees were young, hip and energetic. Straight out of Central Casting.

"Wow, you look great!" were the first words I ever uttered to Jane when I saw her.

"Flattery will get you everywhere!" she laughed as she led me into her office for the interview.

Jane reminded me of Carol back in Omaha, but in a more polished manner. She had cracked the old boys' club, and Ketchum was among the largest PR agencies in Atlanta. Jane was a bit of a health nut.

When we entered her office, I saw shelves in a closet filled with what looked like packets of herbs and spices.

"I've got echinacea if you've got any hint of a cold. I've also got vitamin C, zinc, and quercetin. And be sure to get your flu shot," she said as we sat down for our discussion.

The interview went well, and, by the end of our discussion, Jane made me an offer.

"I usually make people take a personality and writing test as part of the interview process," she said. "But you can clearly write, and I think you have a great personality. So that's that."

We shared a hearty laugh and Jane walked me around the office. It was jam packed with people, sometimes two to an office.

"We've been growing fast and are about out of room in our current space. You won't really have an office."

"All I need is a chair and a desk," I told her, "I don't need an office. I need to learn your business and that's what I'm going to do."

I think Jane liked my attitude, and I certainly liked hers. I focused my energy on my new job. Things went smoothly for the next two years at Ketchum. I was also able to start living my life openly and honestly.

One day, I asked to meet with Jane and told her I was gay. I had recently started dating someone seriously and I wasn't going to make the same mistakes I had made with Paulo.

"Like that was going to make any difference in our relationship," she said recently of our discussion back then. "I also remember you telling me you were going to stop dying your hair," she wrote. I could hear her laugh through the email.

And then, another life-changing event happened. Ketchum landed a new client: MCI, the underdog rival to the monopolistic AT&T.

I was brought in as part of the Ketchum team to coach senior executives at MCI on how to deal with the media. One of the first executives I was assigned to was Tim Price, who would later go on to lead the entire company.

Several weeks after I began working with Tim, he said, "You should be working for us," and offered me the chance to join his team in Atlanta running PR for the Business Markets group.

I was just thirty years old and had no real management, much less budget, experience.

Jane was so sweet about the whole thing. She allowed me to take the job and helped me move my things into my new office out at MCI.

"My knees buckled for you," she later told me about the size of the job. But I was young and naive and jumped in with both feet, not without having a candid conversation with Tim before I took the job.

"I'm dating someone," I told him, "And it's a man."

Tim didn't flinch.

"That's great. I want our employees to be happy," he said.

"And, I don't agree with MCI's drug testing policy," I told him. "I think it's a way to weed out people with pre-existing conditions. It could be especially troublesome for people with HIV."

Tim paused for a moment and then said, "I agree."

That moment was pivotal as I had everything to lose in a new job but didn't care. If MCI was going to hire me, they were going to get the real me. I was going to speak my mind and tell the truth from this point forward.

It was a smart decision.

"I want people who tell me what I need to hear, not what I want to hear," Tim told me at the time.

Working at MCI was incredible. On many occasions I flew with senior executives onboard one of the company's private jets. I remember once it was just Tim and me flying to New York for an event. We landed at Teterboro Airport in New Jersey and the car took Tim and me to our hotel in New York.

"Enjoy the rest of your evening," I said to Tim at the front desk and headed to my room.

I walked in to hear the phone ringing. I walked over, sat my suitcase down by the bed and answered the phone.

It was my boss, Kevin, who reported to Tim.

"What are you doing?" he asked. "Get back down to the lobby. Tim wants to spend time with you!"

I ran back down to the lobby and ended up having a wonderful dinner and conversation with Tim. He was one of the smartest men I had ever met and had the most advanced vocabulary of anyone I knew.

I went on to have a fantastic five-year run at MCI and met some of my life-long friends including William Pate, Jonelle Sullivan, Alex and Karen Rogow and Ed Bergstraesser. The list of colleagues who became friends is so long I don't want to run the risk of leaving anyone off, so I'll stop here.

Everything went great at MCI until the day Bernie Ebbers, the then-CEO of WorldCom announced his hostile takeover of the company.

I remember seeing him during an interview with CNBC.

"I tried to call Bert Roberts [then-CEO of MCI] this morning and he wasn't in the office yet." Ebbers said in his sleazy southern drawl. "When he's working for me, he'll be in the office at eight a.m."

My skin crawled and I knew that I could never work for Ebbers. Luckily, I had made decent money at MCI and had accumulated a sizable amount of stock options. I decided to take the money and run and made yet another life-changing decision.

I started my own marketing agency called Creaxion.

Like "Creation" but with an "x."

My thinking was the intersection between creativity and execution. A stylized "x" became our trademark. I started with four clients at my dining room table and, along with my business partners, grew the business steadily over the next twenty years. During that time, we worked with some amazing clients including the Coca-Cola Company, Chick-fil-A, Delta Air Lines, Honest Tea, Porsche Cars North America, Intercontinental Hotels, Exhibition Hub and Segpay, our longest running client of more than fifteen years.

One Wednesday, April 22, 2015, I returned to my desk in the office and found an email in my inbox.

It was from Mark Pimentel, the General Manager at CBS46 in Atlanta.

> Hi Mark,
>
> We never worked together but I appreciated your work from afar. I know you have moved aways from news reporting and have a second career, but I have a proposal for you to consider. It's not a big-time thing, but it is an opportunity. It's not news reporting, but it is journalism. I got your contact information from Steve Sherman, a longtime friend. Could I buy you breakfast sometime soon and talk with you for 30 minutes?
>
> MP

I re-read the email and then closed my laptop. An opportunity. It's not news reporting, but it is journalism.

The following week, I walked into the Silver Skillet restaurant at our agreed upon time of seven thirty a.m., Mark was sitting in a booth across from the main counter and waved me over.

"It's good to finally meet you in person," he said. "As I said in my email, we never worked together, but I was a fan of your work."

I shook his hand and sat down on the bench across from him.

"Whataya have, sweetheart?" the waitress said as she scurried over.

"Two eggs over light with sausage," I said, "wheat toast, no butter. And some iced tea with lemon if you have it."

The waitress jotted it down and scampered off to place my order.

"I'll get right to it," Mark said. "We have this idea I'm calling *Just a Minute*, along the lines of the editorials that we GMs do from time to time."

"Here you go, Sugar, unsweet tea with lemon," the waitress said as she interrupted us.

"My goal is to bring back ten to twelve of the best TV personalities in Atlanta news to deliver the commentaries. I'd like you to be one of them," he said.

I looked at him with a bit of surprise.

"You want me to be one of them?" I asked.

"Yes," he said. "I always thought you were a great writer, and I feel you might have something to say, something to add to the overall discussion as part of the team," he said.

I was flattered by Mark's statement but felt I should just stop him right there and end the discussion. Surely there was a mistake.

"Mark," I'm really flattered that you'd think of me," I told him. "But don't you know my story?" The waitress slid my plate of breakfast in front of me.

"Of course, I know your story," Mark replied. "Mark, my son is gay. It doesn't matter anymore. What matters is that you have a voice and I think you should use it."

His words caught me completely off guard and I almost burst into tears.

"You'll get sixty seconds to talk about whatever you want," he said.

"Anything I want?" I asked, making sure I heard him correctly.

"Yes," he said. "I want open, honest dialog in these commentaries. I want to challenge our viewers to think and to be open to differing opinions," he said.

"It pays one hundred dollars for each segment," he said. "Not much, but a little grocery money."

"That's actually six thousand an hour," I joked.

We shared a laugh and an instant connection. I liked him. And I liked his honesty, especially about his own son.

"Let me think it through. If I do this, I want the commentaries to be relevant, as you said, to make people think. Who else do you have on the team?"

He rattled off a who's who of the best people I had ever seen in Atlanta journalism: Amanda Davis, Sally Sears, Paul Crawley, Angela Robinson, Lyn Vaughn, Kimberly Kennedy, Ken Watts, Bill Nigut and Cynthia Tinsely. It was an all-star team of Atlanta news veterans.

And Mark wanted me to be among them.

I agreed to take on the assignment and, as fate would have it, had lunch with Ed Buckley, a client who happened to be one of the best civil rights attorneys in Atlanta. Over our salads Ed blurted out something fascinating.

"This gay marriage thing is going to be crazy," he said, speaking of the impending Supreme Court decision on marriage equality. "Keep your eye on Anthony Kennedy," he said. "He's going to be the swing vote and my gut is 5–4, he'll go with the majority."

I looked at Ed with what I'm sure was a look of a crazy man.

"Google him and Gordon Schraber," Ed said.

So, I did just that when I got back to the office. I put two and

two together and thought maybe, just maybe, Ed could be right. I thought about it overnight and the next morning, I emailed Mark Pimentel and told him I wanted my first *Just a Minute* commentary to focus on gay marriage and Justice Kennedy's potential pivotal role in the Supreme Court's decision.

257

"Go for it!" he said.

And so, I crafted my sixty second opinion and two days later, stepped on the set at CBS46 to record my segment.

This was the anchor lead-in (how the main anchors introduce a story or segment):

"As early as next week, the U.S. Supreme Court is expected to rule on the landmark issue of marriage equality.

"Two questions are before the court. The first: Should all Americans, including same-sex couples be allowed to marry under federal law and protection? The second question is whether states that do not allow gay marriage should be forced to recognize legal, same-sex marriages performed in other states?

"In tonight's *Just a Minute* segment, investigative reporter and best-selling author Mark Pettit tells us there's someone special behind the potential swing vote in the case."

Mark on Camera:

You've probably never heard of him, but Gordon Schraber could play a major role in the U.S. Supreme Court's decision on marriage equality.

Schraber was a well-known lawyer from Sacramento and widely believed to be a closeted gay man. He was also a mentor to Supreme Court Justice, Anthony Kennedy.

Schraber recruited Kennedy to be a law school professor and testified on Kennedy's behalf at his confirmation hearing in Washington. They remained life-long friends.

Kennedy is no doubt a "conservative." He was recommended as a Federal Court Judge by then governor Ronald Regan and nominated to the Supreme Court by President Gerald Ford.

But, just a minute…

Despite his conservative background, Justice Kennedy has consistently ruled on the side of equality for gay Americans and some speculate he will write the court's opinion when it rules on marriage equality later this month.

Again, remember the name Gordon Schraber.

His relationship with Kennedy confirms what we know: that judgments, even at the Supreme Court level, are based on personal experiences. Once you know, love, or respect someone who is gay, things change. They become more than gay people, they become real people. Sons, daughters, co-workers and friends. All of us are just trying to get by and, if we're lucky, to get married to the person we love.

Gordon Schraber died just short of his seventieth birthday in 1997. He was never married.

As he ponders this historic decision, I'm confident Justice Kennedy is thinking about Gordon Schraber and I'm hopeful he'll have the courage to do the right thing and vote for marriage equality.

By doing so, he will not only be making history. He would be making his mentor very proud.

I'm Mark Pettit.

After taping the segment, I stepped off the set to warm handshakes and greetings from the crew.

"That was really insightful," Ben Swann, one of the main anchors, said about my segment. "It'll be interesting to see how this plays out."

I had planned to be in New York that weekend to visit friends for Gay Pride. On the evening of June 25th, I pinged Mark Pimentel at the station and told him I would take a suit and tie with me just in case there was a decision from the Supreme Court.

I arrived at the airport in Atlanta and as I reached my gate, I saw people huddled around TV monitors, watching CNN. There were cheers and applause and I moved closer to try and make out what was happening.

BREAKING NEWS! The red banner screamed under the anchor's face.

SUPREME COURT UPHOLDS GAY MARRIAGE IN 5-4 DECISION

Oh my God!

I couldn't believe my eyes, but thankfully I had believed Ed Buckley. As he predicted, Justice Anthony Kennedy had cast the swing vote.

I reached for my phone and texted Mark Pimentel.

"Call me!" he said.

"If you're up for it we can do a live shot back to the station from New York," he said. "The desk is working now to book a window with CBS," he said.

"Of course, I'm up for it!"

I arrived in New York and my good friend, Dustin Miles, went with me to CBS for the live shot back to Atlanta.

We arrived at 524 W. 57th Street around four-fifteen p.m. I stepped out of the car and stood before the CBS Broadcast Center. The same building I had stood outside of thirty years before, on the day I had met Dan Rather.

I felt an incredible sense of déjà vu.

"I can't believe this is happening," I said to Dustin as we made our way into the building and through security.

Once more, I was being led into the hallowed halls of CBS News. This time, to report on one of the biggest stories of our lifetime, and certainly the most important day ever for gay Americans.

One of the production coordinators led us through the newsroom and back to the anchor desk. In the distance I could see the giant CBS eye logo. A rush of adrenaline came over me, a high like I had not felt in quite some time.

Around me, crews began to swing into place and the main camera was pushed before the anchor desk.

"Right this way, Mark," another man said. "Let's test the IFB and the shot back to Atlanta."

Like a pro, I settled in behind the anchor desk.

"How are you feeling?" Dustin asked.

"Like I was born for it," I replied.

Another production person slid the lavalier microphone up my suit jacket and attached it just to the left of my tie.

"Two minutes," I heard in my ear.

I looked down at the notes I had scribbled on my note pad in the car.

GREAT DAY FOR GAY AMERICANS
5-4 DECISION
ANTHONY KENNEDY

For a few seconds, I thought about my own personal life–and how this historic day might have changed things. After Paulo, I had two longer-term relationships (thank you Ted and Scott), but marriage was never really a part of the equation. Now, I thought, if luck and love came my way again, it could be.

"This is Atlanta, Mark, can you hear us?"

I nodded my head.

"Okay, you're at the top of the show. Ben and Sharon will toss to you in New York, the show's producer said in my ear."

Again, I nodded.

"Got it."

Then, I heard the thundering news open for the newscast and I could hear the voices of anchors Ben Swann and Sharon Reed as the newscast began.

"…and CBS46 News *Just a Minute* commentator Mark Pettit called it earlier this week when he accurately predicted that the Supreme Court would make the decision it made today, in a stunning 5–4 ruling. Mark, you nailed it."

I smiled from the anchor desk at CBS News and replied.

"Ben and Sharon, it is a great day for gay Americans, who now have the right to marry the person they love and as we predicted it all came down to Justice Anthony Kennedy who cast the deciding vote in this historic ruling…"

It was an incredible moment for me, both professionally and personally, and I honestly couldn't believe it was all happening.

There I was, reporting live from the CBS Broadcast Center in New York. No, it wasn't that famous chair on the set of *60 Minutes*, but it was a triumph wrapped in irony and symbolism. And, as the live shot wrapped, I leaned back in the anchor chair and soaked it all in.

Wow. Just wow. And as Dan Rather might say, the moment "was hotter than a Times Square Rolex."

Back in the Uber, Dustin and I sat in celebratory silence. I think we were both a bit overwhelmed by the events of the day. I'm not sure that either one of us ever expected this moment would come, but it had, and I am so happy we got to celebrate it together.

As often happens with me (when important or traumatic things occur in my life), I had a vivid dream later that night. Dan Rather greeted me as I wrapped the live shot back to Atlanta.

"We want you to anchor the CBS Evening News tonight," he said. "It's a moment in history that needs to be commemorated by someone who understands the significance of this story. You're a real anchorman and you deserve to be sitting in that seat."

In my dream, Dan walked me down a very narrow hallway. It felt like we were in a submarine. He opened what looked like a chamber and in the distance, I saw the anchor desk. It felt like the Holy Grail. The desk was made of glass and in front of the CBS Evening News logoed wall, sat an empty chair.

"You've earned this," Dan told me. "Tonight, that seat belongs to you."

In my dream, the newscast was flawless. I nailed every story–never stuttered or stammered and ended the broadcast like I had always imagined in real life.

"I'm Mark Pettit. For Dan Rather and all of us here at CBS News, goodnight."

I awoke, realizing it was all in my head, but it felt so real.

And yes, while the Supreme Court decision on gay marriage was my first *Just a Minute* commentary on CBS, it would not be the last as it relates to a life-changing event.

The next year, in early August of 2016, I was scrolling through social media when I came across several  posts about a young woman from my hometown of Calhoun. Her name was Grace Key and she had Down Syndrome. Despite that circumstance, Grace loved her hometown Yellow Jackets and dreamed of joining her high school cheer team. However, there had been a backlash against Grace, with some parents saying she shouldn't be allowed to join the team when other girls were more deserving.

I had grown up with Grace's mom, Carrie (Nance) Key, in Calhoun and it really hurt me to see some of the comments people were making about young Grace online. So, I decided to do something about it. Again, I sat down at my computer and started typing out another *Just a Minute* commentary.

On August 14th, this is how it went down.

The news anchor began the coverage like this:

> As we reported earlier in this newscast, the family of a special-needs teenager in Calhoun are fighting to get her back on the cheerleading team at the local high school. Sixteen-year-old Grace Key was kept off the field this past week, after attending summer practices and learning all the cheers. School officials and parents met this morning trying to figure out a compromise.
>
> CBS46 News commentator Mark Pettit is from Calhoun and takes "Just a Minute" to weigh in on his hometown's controversy.

I stepped slightly forward on set and leaned into the camera and delivered my commentary.

> I've never met Grace Key, but I feel like I've known her for years. Her mom and I went to high school together and, through social media, I've watched Grace blossom.

As I spoke, photos of Grace from social media appeared on screen.

> I know she loves cheerleading. Especially for the Calhoun Yellow Jackets, my hometown team, too. So it broke my heart when I heard that

Grace was kept off the field this past week. The coach cited safety reasons.

On social media, at least one parent complained that Grace, who has Down Syndrome, was selected for the cheerleading team when dozens of other girls were cut, because they didn't have the necessary skills.

As I continued to speak, the devastating footage of Grace ran on the screen. It was her, on the outside the fence, of the high school football field. I continued with my commentary.

This is Grace, continuing to cheer for the Yellow Jackets, only from the other side of the fence, where she was cruelly banished.

The footage stopped and the camera returned to me on set and my message was direct.

To the other girls who didn't make the squad, I understand your disappointment. I know what it feels like to be cut from the team. But you and I will never understand what it's like to be a child like Grace. Often excluded and ostracized. Never basking in the glory under Friday night lights.

I hope school officials in Calhoun do the right thing and put this special young lady back on the sidelines.

We should all be cheering for Grace. Not against her.

I'm Mark Pettit.

As the segment ended and we went to break, I walked from the studio and into the newsroom.

"People are furious!" I heard one of the station's social media managers shout from near the assignment desk. "They want Grace back on the team! I think this is going viral!" he said.

In my right pocket, I felt my mobile phone vibrating. I pulled out the device and looked down. Ten missed calls and fifteen text messages. I clicked on the first text.

"Thanks for standing up for Grace, Mark!"

"They should be ashamed of themselves!" another text said.

"Thanks for pointing this out!" read another.

"We're Team Grace!" someone else texted.

I felt a bit overwhelmed and found an empty seat in the news-

room to take it all in. Every message and call I had gotten was in support of Grace.

I realized that despite all that had happened earlier in my news career, something very special had happened. After all this time, I had found my voice just by speaking the truth, and standing up for someone who had no voice to speak for themselves.

The day after my commentary ran, Grace's parents reached a compromise with school officials and Grace was allowed to return to the cheer squad as an honorary member of the team.

As a result of the controversy, Grace made the decision to start her own business and, in March of 2018, she started Candidly Kind to "spread light, love and acceptance through her original art and life." Grace's first design was "Be the Light," which has been followed by dozens of other designs that have been purchased by people in every state and twenty-two countries around the world.

Since starting Candidly Kind, Grace has donated more than $62,000 of her profits and given hundreds of items to charity. All her materials are sourced in the USA from other small businesses. You can follow Grace and Candidly Kind (@candidlykind) on TikTok,

Instagram and Facebook. You can visit her website at www.candid-lykind.com.

I'm so happy I accepted Mark Pimentel's invitation to breakfast and can't thank him enough for bringing me back to TV news like he did in 2015. It began a process of healing for me, to know that I was welcomed back into the profession I loved, and opened the door for a whole new chapter in my life that I had no idea was about to be written.

But first, there was one chapter left to close. The case of Jeremy Jonus. He had gotten his revenge on me, and now it was time to put him out of my misery for good.

It literally took me thirty years to get my hands on the images below (now artistically enhanced from the original black and white drawings) that were provided to me by a prison guard who found the original drawings in Jeremy Jonus' cell back in 1987.

The guard had been working the day shift back in 1987 and was part of the team that conducted an unannounced shakedown of Jonus and his prison cell. As the corrections officers scoured the young killer's room, the guard saw the horrifying drawings on Jonus' work desk. He was shocked at the contents and the level of detail. So much so, that once the contraband had been removed from Jonus' cell, he made copies of the drawings and added them to his collection of confiscated elements found during inmate shakedowns. He kept them in a cardboard box in the closet of his bedroom. The drawings stayed in the box until the prison guard saw on the local news that I had sued the state of Nebraska to release the drawings to the public. and that the state was fighting to keep them private.

"At first, I thought, 'Hey we might be able to make some money.'" the guard told me when I met with him and his wife at their home in Nebraska. "Then, my wife and I decided no, you were doing the right thing, and the public had a right to see the drawings. That's when we called you."

It's people like this man who give journalism a good name. People who provide information that others want kept far from the newsgathering spotlight.

Although I had not seen the drawings until the guard provided them to me--Jonus and I had talked about them in-depth. In fact, Jonus was quite proud of his work and described the renderings in detail to me. Initially, he told me that he made the drawings to "let off steam." He later admitted that his art sessions would also lead to him violently masturbating in

his cell, with his penis in one hand and a drawing in the other.

When I finally saw the drawings—they were just as Jonus had described. In fact, they were much more sophisticated and intricate than I had expected. Down to the belt holding up the killer's pants, to his sleeves rolled up in anticipation of the deadly task at hand and the sunglasses that hid the killer's identity.

"This is not what we would call 'intimate art'—these are detailed manifestations of deviant behavior," said the criminal profiler, Keith Howard, whom I hired to analyze the drawings once I obtained them. "They are depictions of violent sexual fantasies with young males and are not drawings of an actual crime or more specifically an unsolved crime."

Also, note that the killer has his hand draped over the child's back and shoulder. Again, there's a sadistic reason for this, says Howard.

"This is illustrative of control over the victim as the offender inserts the knife into the abdomen of the victim," said Mr. Howard.

The second drawing I obtained from the prison guard is just as disturbing. It depicts what appears to be another teenage boy bound and gagged. He floats in time and space—with no scenery around him. But look closer and again you'll see some ghastly clues behind the fantasy-driven drawing. Specifically, the boy's feet are missing (or cut off) in the illustration. Again, the child's mouth is covered, and his hands bound by rope.

"The detail in the drawings is very significant," said Howard. "Specifically, as it relates to the frayed rope ends used in the bondage. This is in direct relationship to the killer's obsession with details. It was like a movie he could—and would watch over and over."

As in the first drawing, the child's eyes are left uncovered, so he is sure to bear witness to his unimaginable demise.

"The lack of a blindfold is suggestive that Jonus wanted to see the fear in his victim's eyes," Howard told me during a meeting in his office. "It is fear the sexual sadist must elicit from others to achieve sexual excitement."

When we discussed the drawings, and Jonus mentioned the man stabbing the child in the stomach in the first illustration, I asked him pointedly, "Was it you in the drawing?"

In a matter-of-fact manner, he replied, "Yes. Who else would it be?"

I responded candidly, "You realize this is fucked up, right?"

Jonus hung his head and shyly replied, "Yes."

At that moment, I asked Jonus to give me permission to obtain the drawings from prison officials with the offer that I would get them analyzed by a professional and provide him the findings. Again, this was in 1988.

Jonus reached across the table and grabbed my yellow notepad. He tore a page from the pad and wrote a letter to the warden of the prison, instructing him to release the confiscated drawings to me.

The prison system refused, citing inmate confidentiality. I let it go, until I couldn't and decided to sue the state to release the drawings. Initially, we won the case, but it was appealed by the state's attorney general.

The Nebraska Supreme Court took up the case and ruled against us. It didn't matter, as I already had copies of the drawings in my briefcase, as my attorney argued for their release before the court.

Yes, it took thirty years and the courage of the prison guard to provide the drawings to me, but now the case is closed on whether Jonus would have killed again if ever released from prison.

He had already drawn the map and as he said in our first meeting, he just had a need to kill.

And for that, he paid for his crimes with his life.

Jeremy Jonus was executed in Nebraska's electric chair.

CHAPTER 23

A DOG NAMED BOO

*P*romise me you'll get that dog.

Paulo's words rang in my ears as I pulled my car up outside Whole Foods, which many people affectionately refer to as "Whole Paycheck" for the price of its mostly organic and well-lit fare.

It was a gorgeous, late-summer day and the sky was as blue as I ever remembered seeing it.

271

From a distance, I could hear the sharp barks of puppies in their crates outside of the nearby PetSmart. It was adoption day and a thin lady, with graying, long brown hair, was simultaneously tending to and marketing the pups to their prospective parents.

"I think he's part poodle and Jack Russell," she said to a lady looking at a dog through his metal cage. "Shouldn't get to more than thirty pounds," she reassured.

The dog lady seemed overwhelmed, so I made my way to the sidewalk where the dogs were being held in their crates. Along with the puppies, there were older dogs, many of them with sad faces. They had apparently been down this road before, but still left unadopted, they sat in their crates again, hoping today will be the day.

My intentions were pure, just to linger a few minutes with the dogs. A few pats on the head and maybe a belly rub or two. I started at the far right of the line, where most of the older dogs either sat at attention or laid on the concrete below them. I stuck my fingers through the front and sides of the first two cages.

"It's okay to open the door," the dog lady told me. "You can pet them, but just don't let them out. I had one bolt on me last Saturday. Ran all the way down to the Home Depot before we could catch him," she chuckled.

And then he caught my eye. Or my ear.

As I approached the fourth cage, a tiny brown mut with deep brown eyes ran up to the front door and began to bark directly at me. A squeaky shrill of a bark.

"I think he likes you," the dog lady told me. As the tiny dog leapt to the front of his cage, scratching violently at the metal bars, I looked above the top of the crate, where I saw his name scribbled on a two-inch paper panel.

MELVIN, it read.

"It's okay to take that one out and hold him," the dog lady said. "I don't think he's big enough to get away from you."

I did as I was told and opened the metal framed door to the cage. Little Melvin came bounding out and right into my arms. His small body shook excitedly as he licked at my fingers and hands. My heart raced as I pulled him close to my chest.

"Excuse me!" I heard a voice say from behind me. I looked around to see a woman with a harsh Mary Lou Retton bob standing there, her arms planted firmly on her broad hips.

"We were going to get that dog!" she said.

I held Melvin tighter for a moment, then looked at the dog lady just a few feet away. Her eyes darted from mine.

"Okay," I said quietly to the unfriendly lady behind me. "I was just stopping to pet him."

"He's our dog," she said, her eyes turning to her left and a teenage girl, obliviously texting on her smartphone.

I didn't know quite what to do, so I turned to hand her the puppy. Before I let him go, I leaned in and whispered, "Have a good life little guy."

The puppy whimpered and barked sharply again as I handed him over to the rude lady behind me.

And that was that.

I walked away from the dogs and the sidewalk and made my way over to Whole Foods where I bought my groceries for the week.

Later that night, I tossed and turned in my sleep. For some strange reason, I couldn't stop thinking about Melvin. In a way, I felt guilty for handing him over to the rude lady behind me, but it was clear she thought she had dibs on the dog; so at the time I thought I had made the right decision.

I struggled through my Sunday and tried to sleep later that night, but again tossed and turned thinking about the small dog. Without much rest, the next day at work was rough. I made it through each of my meetings, but on my way home from work, I had an idea. I pulled over into the parking lot of a fast-food restaurant and punched PetSmart into the search bar on my cell phone.

The number popped up and I pressed the link to connect.

"PetSmart, this is Josh," the man said, answering the call on the third ring.

"Yes," I told him, slightly unsure of what I was asking. "I was there this weekend during the pet adoption, and I was just wondering if you knew the lady who runs the events?"

"Oh, sure," he said. "That's Liz, from K-9 Rescue. She's here every Saturday."

I grabbed a pen from the console of my car and a napkin from the left door panel.

K-9 Rescue, I wrote on the piece of paper.

"Great, I really appreciate the info," I told him. "Have a good rest of your day."

As soon as I hung up, I typed in the name of the animal shelter and retrieved the phone number. My heart seemed to skip a few beats as I heard the phone line ring.

Four, five, six rings. No answer. And then the recorded voice of whom I assumed to be Liz.

"We're probably out taking care of the dogs now," she said. "Leave a message and we'll be sure to call you back."

After I heard the familiar beep, I fumbled as I left the message.

"Uh, yeah, my name is Mark. I stopped by the PetSmart on Saturday and just wanted to call to check in on one of the dogs I met there," I said. "His name was Melvin, I believe. If you could just call me back to let me know he's okay, that would be great."

I then left my phone number and clicked off the phone.

It was another sleepless night as I tossed and turned once again, unable to shake the image of the tiny dog from my mind.

What the actual fuck? I said to myself as I squeezed my pillow between my legs, hoping sleep would come. Which it did not.

Once again, I pushed my way through work the following day, just trying to make it to the point where I could rush home and fall into my bed. And now, twenty-four hours later, still no return call from the dog lady.

Oh well, I thought. At least I tried to make sure he had been adopted.

And then, I had another idea. I reached for the paper napkin on the kitchen counter and dialed the number again.

This time, a lady answered on the second ring.

"K-9 Rescue, this is Liz," the woman said politely.

"Hi Liz, uh, my name is Mark," I said, again, starting to stumble. "Sorry, I left a message last night, and I'm sorry to bother you again. I just had to check in on that little dog named Melvin."

There was a slight pause on the line and then, "Wait. Were you the guy in the blue T-shirt and jeans on Saturday?" she asked.

"Yes. I wear blue a lot," I told her, trying to apologize if she had seen me several Saturdays in a row in the same T-shirt. It's kind of a thing with me.

"Oh, yeah, I remember you," she said, bringing a bit of hope to my spirit.

"It's a funny thing. As soon as you handed him to that lady behind you and walked away, Melvin threw up on the woman," she said, now in a full laugh. "She put him right back in the cage."

Right back in the cage?

"Wait a minute," I said. "You said she put him right back in the cage. That means she didn't adopt him, right?"

"Nope. Said she didn't want him after he puked on her," Liz said.

"Okay," I responded. "Where is Melvin now?"

"Oh, he's right here at my feet," Liz said. "All five pounds of him."

"And where are you located?"

"We're out in Lawrenceville," she said, which is about forty-five minutes northeast of Atlanta.

"I'm on my way to get him," I blurted out, without really thinking things through. "Can you please just wait for me to get there?"

"Uh, okay. Do you have a dog bed, or something to transport him in?" she asked like a protective mother.

"No, I don't. But I can stop at PetSmart and then head to you. Please. Just wait for me to get there."

"Sure thing, honey. I'll give the little guy a bath, so he'll smell good when you get here," she said with a sweet laugh.

And the rest is history.

275

I ran to the PetSmart, grabbed a bed, a small crate and some dog food and headed to Lawrenceville.

"He was my constant companion for thirteen years," I said, as I looked out from the stage into the crowd before me. I scanned the audience, seeing the faces of many of my friends and former colleagues from TV news.

Behind me, Emmy statues decorated the screen that read: LIFETIME ACHIEVEMENT AWARD.

I held the plaque that read "Silver Circle," one of the highest honors bestowed on those in and around TV news for more than twenty-five years. I was being inducted into the Emmy Hall of Fame, courtesy of my dear friend, Evelyn Mims, the president of the southeastern chapter of the National Academy of Television Arts and Sciences.

Evelyn and I had worked together at the TV station in Atlanta many years before and had remained friends for all the years that followed. She was a tireless activist and, as it turned out, one of the strongest allies for the gay community in Atlanta.

"Thank you, Evelyn, for bringing me back into the Emmy fold," I said, looking at my friend as she beamed her trillion-dollar

smile.

"I thank you for this award," I said to the crowd. And I dedicate it to my sweet dog, Boo, who passed away this summer. And now, you know where he got his name," I said, trying to hold back the tears as my voice cracked.

"In honor of Paulo and because of the movie, *Ghost*," I told them, my full story now told.

I almost buckled before regaining my composure.

"I've spent my entire life being obsessed with the truth, and finally found it," I said. "The truth is if you're out there struggling with your own identity or feeling like there is no hope, stay strong and stay true to yourself. Love yourself, even when it seems those around you don't love you."

I looked down from the stage to see a young waiter softly crying. He, or she, I couldn't quite tell which, had been deeply moved by my words. Our eyes met and the sad expression on their face changed to a smile.

I finished my acceptance speech by saying, "Someday, like me, you will find your voice. And when you do, I hope you will use it for good."

The crowd erupted in applause and rose to its feet. I paused for a few seconds to soak in the moment and then walked from the stage, down the stairs and into Evelyn's embrace.

"I'm so proud of you," she whispered. "And I thank you for having the courage to tell your story," she said. "Welcome home."

It was an amazing night. A full-circle, life event that I will never forget.

Later on, I slipped into my bed and into a wonderful deep sleep.

The next day was a beautiful fall day in Atlanta. The trees were brushed in vibrant reds, yellows and oranges as I made my way down my favorite path in Piedmont Park, Atlanta's equivalent to Central Park in New York.

As I turned the corner of the path, not far from Lake Clara Meer, I saw a small group of musicians set up along the side of the pavement. One held a cello, one a viola and another an electric violin.

The lead singer stepped up to the microphone with the violin and our eyes met. I recognized the person as the waiter from the Silver Circle event. They recognized me as well and stepped back from the microphone to huddle with the other members of the group.

There was slight shuffling as the band regrouped.

The lead singer then stepped back up to the microphone, placed the electric violin beneath their chin and the beautiful instrumental began. To my left, I spotted a small bench where I took a seat to enjoy the view and the music, which I recognized immediately.

The opening notes of "Unchained Melody" rang through the park as the younger waiter, turned singer, began to sing the haunting lyrics.

Oh, my love, my darling,
I've hungered for your touch,
A long, lonely time.

Completely mesmerized, I sat on the bench and listened.

And time goes by, so slowly,
And time can do so much.
Are you still mine?

In a wistful, *Ghost*-like moment, Boo appeared at my feet. He jumped into my lap and I held his head gently to my chest. Then, I felt a hand lightly land on my shoulder. I looked over to see that it was the hand of a man, wrinkled, but familiar.

I turned to see who it was. And it was Paulo standing next to me. He was much older than when I last saw him, his dark hair now streaked with gray. But he was as handsome as he ever was before his diagnosis.

We shared a tender loving look. A magical moment in time that I had longed for–forever it seemed.

As the melancholy music continued, I looked back to the musicians, enjoying every second of the song as I sat on the bench with the loves of my life.

My boys.

I need your love. I need your love. Godspeed your love, to me.

CHAPTER

24

YOU CAN GO HOME AGAIN

Feb. 1, 2021 (8:18 a.m.)

was startled from my deep sleep by the familiar, piercing *ding* of Facebook Messenger. I had forgotten to silence my phone before going to bed the night before and now regretted it.

I realized that my beautiful visions of Paulo and Boo in the park was just a vivid dream. A dream that I had experienced several times before, each just as clear as the one before it.

Groggily, I reached for my phone on the nightstand. I rolled back on my pillow and pressed the Facebook Messenger icon on the home screen.

"Good morning, Mark," the message began. "I'm not sure if Leigh reached out to you or if the social media info hit your page, but mother passed away last Wednesday while being attended to at the hospital. Daddy has been adamant about notifying you of her passing."

The message was from Bruce Potts, who had helped me move to Omaha. The man I considered a brother for so many years. His mother was Lorene Potts, the woman I also mentioned earlier. The woman I considered my second mother and whom I loved dearly.

My heart sank.

Yes, I had read about his mom's passing on Facebook and had been frozen into inaction. Paralyzing inaction.

Lorene's personality was simply over the top and there was a reason they called her "Big Mama." She wasn't a petite woman and everything she did was big. She had

been an athlete in high school and, I'm told, was an excellent softball and basketball player. When she drank, which she did regularly when I was in high school, she got even louder. I can still hear her laugh ringing through her home as we opened Christmas presents and her cursing as we watched our hapless Atlanta Falcons.

Solid and stout, with a mop of blonde hair, Lorene could knock the shit out of a golf ball. We must have played a hundred rounds together once I reached the age where I could swing a club. She even came to visit me in Omaha, and I took her to play several of my favorite courses out there.

Lorene had given me my nickname as a teenager, "Pokey." Let's just say I wasn't the fastest guy on the little league team and ate a little too much of my mother's country cooking (fried chicken, biscuits and gravy) and carried a little extra weight from time to time, as I mentioned.

Not to be deterred, I ironed a lightning bolt onto the front of my baseball shirt to promote my speed running the bases. Or lack thereof. Lorene thought it was so funny she named her sporting goods story after me, "Pokey's Sporting Goods." I worked at the store part-time as it was right across the street from the S&H Grocery Store, where I also worked part-time as a bag boy during high school. Next to Pokey's was the Family Restaurant, owned by Harold and Margie Crump, two of my favorite people in the world. As I mentioned earlier, it was Harold and Margie who loaned me their truck when I moved to Chattanooga. On countless occasions, I would gather with friends and family at Harold and Margie's restaurant. I consider them some of the best days of my life—and a reason I carried a little extra weight from time to time.

Yes, I adored Lorene Potts and that's why I was shocked when she called me to her home once *the word* got out about me in 1991. Of course, I drove up from Atlanta to see her. She met me at the front door and didn't commence with small talk.

"If you're going to pursue *that lifestyle,*" she said from the doorway, not even allowing me inside the house where we had spent so many good times together, "then, you're not welcome here anymore. We don't believe in that. And don't even think about bringing *a boyfriend here.*"

She paused and looked at me and summed everything she was thinking in two sentences. "You're a different person now," she said. "It's like the person I knew has died." After a couple of seconds of awkward silence between us, she politely closed the door.

I'm a writer and still can't find the words to convey how horrible and worthless I felt in the moment. It was crushing.

I had not spoken to Lorene, or her husband Ronald, whom we all called "Pee Wee," in thirty years. Not since the day I stood on their porch and the door closed on our relationship.

For my part, there was no decision to make. I was what I was and that was a gay man. I could either go back into the closet and never speak about my sexuality and be welcomed back into their home, or I could try to build a new home where I was loved unconditionally.

I chose the latter. To start my life over. With new friends and a chosen family.

While we never spoke about what happened in the doorway, oh so long ago, I accepted Facebook friendship requests from both Bruce and his sister Leigh years later. I had no beef with them, and perhaps they had no idea of the callous words their mother spoke to me that day. Or maybe they did know but still loved me anyway.

Slowly, more former friends and casual acquaintances from my hometown also began to request my online friendship via Facebook. It was as if they wanted to finally peek into my world. Perhaps to see if I was okay? Or perhaps to see if I had fallen off the cliff of life?

Or maybe, just maybe, the world was changing, and they wanted to connect. To at least extend an olive branch across the superficial landscape of Facebook. Maybe they had a niece or nephew who was gay? Perhaps a co-worker? For whatever reason, they were reaching out to me, and I accepted pretty much every request.

The way I looked at it was it was my life now, and my silly Facebook page and I would say and post whatever I wanted. They could unfriend me if they didn't like what they saw. I did unfriend some of them after they made racist or homophobic remarks online.

That *fuck it all* mentality feels great sometimes.

I looked back to my phone and the message from Bruce.

"I know we have not visited together but mother and daddy consider you one of their own," the text continued. "You are listed in her obituary as part of the family because that is what Daddy wants. I will attach her obituary in case you have not read this through social media. If you wish to talk, please call."

As if a P.S., Bruce wrote, "Additionally, you being listed was what Leigh and myself wanted as well. Time rolls fast but memories are for life." He left his mobile phone number for me to call if I so desired.

I sat in silence for the next six minutes. I could hear Kody, my French Bulldog, snoring as he had now crawled up from beside my chest onto the pillow next to my head. I leaned over and gave him a kiss on his tiny head.

He was my closest family member now.

I then looked back at my phone and typed my response to Bruce.

> *Hi Bruce. Thank you for reaching out to me as I have been thinking of you, Leigh and Pee Wee all weekend and was planning to contact you. Honestly, I could not bring myself to read your mom's obituary yet as it all seems surreal. I loved Lorene very much and even though our relationship changed— my feelings for you and your family did not. You and Leigh are like my brother and sister and your Mom and Dad were always so good to me—and I considered them a second set of parents. I will go read the obituary now and come back to you. I am so sorry this happened and regret that I didn't get to see Lorene again after all these years and before she passed.*

I then clicked on the obituary included in Bruce's message.

It was a beautiful tribute to Lorene's life.

And then I got to the line.

"Survivors include… *and Mark Pettit.*"

As I read the inclusion, I began sobbing. I'm crying now as I type these words. We had let thirty years go by without making amends.

But, there at least, it was in writing.

We were family after all.

Lorene's celebration of life service was scheduled for Saturday, March 20, 2021. After much deliberation, I told Bruce and Leigh that I would be honored to sit with the family at the funeral.

This is the part about *healing wounds.*

My mind raced as I made the one-hour drive from Atlanta to Calhoun. I didn't know what to expect. I knew a lot of Lorene's family and friends would be at the service. I hadn't seen them since the last day I saw Lorene.

Bruce had told me to meet the family at a side door at the church. As I pulled into the parking lot, I saw Bruce's face among them. It was as if he was looking for me as well. He saw me parking the car and waved me over to the small group.

I shut the driver's side door and opened the left side passenger door and retrieved my suit jacket from the hanger above the window. I quickly put the jacket on, fearing I was now sweating through my shirt like Will Ferrel in *Anchorman*.

Bruce stepped away from the crowd, approached and hugged me.

"Daddy really wants to see you," he said.

I pulled my face mask from my pocket and placed it over my nose and mouth and hooked the elastic bands around my ears. We were still in the middle of COVID.

"I'm ready to see him," I replied.

We paused briefly so I could hug Bruce's sister, Leigh. The years that had flown by saw her turn into a beautiful woman, almost the spitting image of her mom.

"I'm so glad you're here," she whispered in my ear. "Mama loved you very much."

Choking back tears, I said, "I loved her too."

I continued walking into the church with Bruce. It was a modern-day cathedral that pop-up in places like old shopping center stores, and where music, lights and sound are just as important as the sermon. These days, people must be entertained if they're going to church.

Back in my day, hearing an old lady sing way out of tune and key in the choir kept me coming back for more. I can't tell you how many times the preacher gave my friend Lynn and me the evil eye as we cackled as she belted out "I'll Fly Away."

As we continued down the sloping floor, Bruce brought me back to the present day.

"We're live streaming the service on Facebook as well," he said. "You know, COVID and all."

Yes, I knew. I had watched the bitter debates over the pandemic and vaccines play out on social media in my hometown with a mix of sadness and contempt, even as people were dropping like flies.

We made our way down to the front of the church. There were flowers and arrangements on the stage in tribute to Lorene. I then spotted Pee Wee in the front row, near the stage. He looked terrible, still reeling with his own bout with COVID. He was wearing shorts and one of his lower legs was wrapped in bandages.

Bruce touched my shoulder and led me closer to his father.

"Daddy, look who's here," he said, brimming with excitement. Pee Wee turned his head and, as soon as he saw me, he burst into tears. Full on sobbing, like me when I read Lorene's obituary. Gently, he reached his hand behind my neck and pulled my face close to his.

"I am so, so, sorry," he said through his tears. "We wasted so much time," he continued. Then he said the words that sent me into tears.

"You are our son, too."

As I bawled, I told him, "I love you, Pee Wee. Thank you for being so good to me when we were growing up."

Oh, God. How was I going to get through this? All these terrible feelings coming back in this horrible time of celebration.

We held our heads together for another moment and then Bruce tapped me on the shoulder.

"We have a seat right there for you," he said, pointing to a chair two rows behind his father. I composed myself and made my way to the metal framed chair with a cushion seat.

The service then began with a series of photos appearing on the screen, showing memories from Lorene's life. Bruce, Leigh, Pee Wee, Bruce's wife and children, close friends and family members' faces flashed on the screen in front of me.

As the slide show changed from image to image, I realized how much of our lives we had lived, separately. Because of the way things ended, I didn't get to watch Bruce's children grow up as Lorene and Pee Wee spoiled them. I didn't get to celebrate birthdays and holidays together like we once had done.

I realized there was a huge hole in my heart and I wished I had just picked up the phone. Called her and said, "I know you didn't really mean what you said. Let me come see you, let's make this right."

But I was either too stubborn, too immature or too hurt. Whatever the reason, it never happened, and here I sat saying good-bye, as the song says, to someone that I used to know.

The moment came for the pastor to speak at the service. He rose from his chair and walked feebly to the podium. It was the same pastor who had shunned my aunt, my brother and me as my stepfather was being wheeled into surgery years before.

DEAR GOD, WHAT ARE YOU DOING TO ME? WHY IS THIS HAPPENING?

He began with verses of Scripture and finally ended with personal reflections.

"You did not *know* Lorene Potts," he said. "You *experienced* her." He was right. Lorene was one of a kind and it hurt me deeply that I didn't try harder to repair our relationship.

He went on to mention all the grandchildren, and the children of children. He then said, "We also have a number of Lorene's special friends here today including Dave and Deca Ellis and Mark Pettit."

At first, I wanted to shrink into the floor, not to be called out in this time of grief. Then, I simply sat up straight in my chair. To show my respect for Lorene and this moment. Tears poured from my eyes, down onto my face mask. I felt a sense of relief in the audience, or maybe it was just me, feeling the weight of thirty years falling from my shoulders.

It was awful and awesome at the same time. And, what I took away from the service was simple. Sometimes God does in death what we humans can't do in life. He brings families back together.

When the service ended, several people, including old friends that I had not seen or spoken to in years, came up to me. Many of them hugged me. And I hugged them back, trying to forget about the time, the distance, the misunderstandings between us.

And then, I turned and the preacher stood before me. I didn't know what to do and before I had time to react, he reached out, and pulled me to him.

"I'm so sorry for what all happened," he said. "We are all very proud of the man that you have become."

Again, tears poured down my face as I tried to remember the lessons from Sunday school. The parts about forgiveness and second chances.

"Thank you. This has been a lot, but I'm glad I'm here and I appreciate what you just said."

Later, in the parking lot, I walked over to Leigh's car, where Pee Wee sat in the passenger's seat. He had a distant look in his eyes and I knew what it meant. He missed his wife, his life partner and all the good times they had together. And maybe, he was reflecting on our reunion as I was.

I walked up to the window and placed my arm on his.

"Thank you for including me today," I told him. "I only wish I had come home sooner."

He lowered his head and said, "Me, too, son. Me, too."

I had hoped to see him more, to have another Sunday lunch or dinner together, but COVID continued to rage, and time slipped by. We never got to have that Sunday dinner.

Ronald "Pee Wee" Potts died on April 4, 2022. Again, I went home to Calhoun to be at his funeral. Again, I sat with the family. Again, photos and memories played on the big screen on stage. And in my mind, memories flashed too.

Specifically, one from our days playing little league baseball. A team photo, with Pee Wee on the right back corner, proudly standing as one of our coaches.

And me, kneeling, smiling, front and center. Next to Bruce, with the lightning bolt ironed boldly on my shirt.

What a team. What a memory, from lives lived and lost.

Before finishing this book, I wrote to Bruce and Leigh letting them know I planned to include mentions of some not so pleasant things, including my relationship with their mother. I asked for their permission to use their real names, and those of Lorene and Pee Wee in the book. To tell the truth about what happened that caused us to drift apart. I explained that I could change their names to protect their privacy. But I wanted this chapter to be different. To be authentic, as much as it hurts.

I then asked a favor. If we could be closer again. Have lunch or dinner occasionally. I just wanted a reason to be near them. To be around them so I could also be close to their mom and dad again.

"I'm good with it," Leigh wrote back. "I would love for us to be closer. I know we all get busy with life. Love you and can't wait to read it," she said of the book.

"All is good with me," Bruce replied. "I will help out all I can."

I want to thank Bruce and Leigh, my brother and my sister from another mother and father. For their courage in letting me discuss this difficult part of our lives. I mean no disrespect to Lorene, nor Pee Wee by mentioning them in this book.

I write these words, as I said at the start, to heal wounds.

That healing has begun.

Bruce, Leigh and I plan to spend more time together. Catching up and getting to know each other better.

To be a family again.

THE THIRD ACT

A ccording to Wikipedia: "The third act features the resolution of the story and its subplots. The climax is the scene or sequence in which the main tensions of the story are brought to their most intense point and the dramatic question answered, leaving the protagonist and other characters with a new sense of who they really are."

Larry Samuel, author and founder of Age Friendly Consulting told *The Christian Science Monitor,* "If the first act of life is mostly about education and youthful exuberance, and the second act mostly about career and family, the third act of life is about the pursuit of wisdom, self-actualization, and leaving some kind of legacy."

I have entered my third act of life and it started with a simple question at a dinner party.

Are you serious about becoming an actor?

The question came from one of my best friends, Caleb J. Spivak, who three years before the dinner party had started acting.

I remember when he told us he was going to do it. And, you know how it is when a friend tells you they're going to do something dramatic (so to speak), you nod your head politely and say something smart, like "Cool" or "Good for you!" When someone tells me, "Good for you," I hear it as "Thank god, I'm *not you!*"

But Caleb wasn't joking.

He started taking acting classes religiously, got signed by an agent and then started landing parts. Small ones at first and then big ones. This past year, Caleb starred in a feature film called *Witnesses*. His face was plastered on movie posters across the United States, and he did an excellent job of portraying Oliver Cowdery, one of the Three Witnesses of the Book of Mormon plates. Cowdery also helped supervise the publication of the Book of Mormon and was a founding member of the Church on April 6, 1930. Caleb recently co-starred in the movie *Wait with Me* and has a lot of other great things in the works.

Caleb's question to me at the dinner party came after I asked him a question.

"Do you think I could play the part of a reporter or an anchorman in a movie or TV show," I asked him innocently.

Those of us who know Caleb, know he doesn't do things half-assed. If he's in, he's all in and he does it with passion and conviction. He started a restaurant and retail blog called *What Now Atlanta* in 2010, and today *What Now Media Group* has web properties in thirty-one markets across the country.

"Because, if you're serious, I'll help you," he told me. "I had a friend help me get started," Caleb said. "It'll be like paying it forward."

That Saturday he showed up at my condo in Atlanta with a red folder in his right hand. He handed me the folder and I opened it cautiously.

Inside, there was a typewritten index page. At the top, Caleb had typed *From Emmy to Oscar, The Mark Pettit Story.*

On the paper beneath the headline, he had typed out ten steps to help me become an actor.

1. Email Dustin about Drama Inc. classes
2. Format resume/resume example, materials, discussion
3. Select headshots
4. Craft reel/performance clips
5. Actor's Access
6. Backstage
7. Casting Networks
8. IMDb
9. Discuss breakdowns/go through the process.
10. Discuss meeting with Jacob

In the left pocket of the folder, Caleb had enclosed examples of his resume and headshots. We spent the next couple of hours going down the list of discussion points.

It was a life altering exercise and a gift from Caleb that I will always cherish. I thanked him profusely after our meeting and offered to buy him lunch or dinner for the assistance.

"Don't worry about it," he said. "Brad Thomason did the same thing for me. Like I told you at dinner, this is just me paying it forward."

Brad was a sweet guy, always the first to greet you at a dinner party or gathering. He had movie star teeth and a full head of dark brown hair.

"Damn, Benjamin Button!" he said to me the last time I saw him. "What's *your* secret to aging backwards?"

We both shared a good laugh, and it was the last time I ever saw him.

Not long after that, Brad passed away in his sleep. The gift he passed on to Caleb had now been passed on to me.

On March 2018, I announced on social media that I was going to become an actor.

And, as promised, I started my acting classes at Drama Inc. on Wednesday, April 11, 2018. Drama Inc. is a local acting school and community in Atlanta. It was founded and is run by four working actors: Catherine Dyer, Jason MacDonald, Claire Bronson and Scott Poythress.

My first course was *On Camera 1*, the most basic of classes taught at Drama Inc. There were maybe fifteen people in the class. Early on, I remember Catherine and Jason calling each of us up in front of the camera in the classroom.

"Tell us your name and how much acting experience you have," Catherine instructed.

When it was my turn, I stepped up to the camera.

"My name is Mark Pettit and

I have no acting experience," I said looking directly into the camera. "Oh, wait. I take that back. I was Buffalo Bill in *Annie Get Your Gun* in our high school musical."

As the next couple of weeks of classes continued, I became increasingly uncomfortable. I didn't feel like I belonged in the group. I felt like I was a fake, something I would later learn was referred to as "Imposter Syndrome."

One night in class, Catherine cut to the core of my problem.

"We have to break you from that newscaster thing. Newscasters *project*, actors *react*. I need you to be smaller, to show more stillness in the moment," she said.

Now I understood actors like Matthew McConaughey. If you watch him, he speaks softly, in some cases not much more than a whisper. The way he speaks draws you in. The way he acts keeps you coming back for more.

And then it happened. Another night in class, I was assigned an emotional scene to audition in front of the group with another classmate.

I found a stillness within me that I hadn't experienced before. I focused on my scene partner. What she was saying, what she was feeling. I delivered my lines in a hushed tone. At that very moment, *everything clicked.*

"That's it! That's it!" Catherine said. "That's acting."

From that moment on, almost anything I posted about acting included the hashtag #RealActor. That wasn't to say I was exactly ready for my close-up.

"Just stop! Stop right there!" Alex Collins said sternly to me in the next level of acting class at Drama Inc. He stepped toward me and flipped the baseball cap he was wearing around on his head, bill now to the back. He stepped even closer to me and leveled his assessment of my performance.

"I don't believe a fucking word you're saying right now."

Alrighty then.

In the audition scene, I was playing a detective falsely accused in the shooting of a teenage suspect. My character was being interrogated in a heated internal affairs investigation. Alex wasn't buying what I was trying to sell.

"Okay, okay," he said, his face turning bright red. "You have a new puppy, right? Kody? I've seen him on Facebook. Is that right?"

"Yes," I replied, not sure where he was headed.

"Let's pretend that the internal affairs officer has just taken Kody out of your hands, and he rips his head off."

There was an audible gasp in the room.

"How would you feel?" Alex asked.

"I'd be upset," I said quietly.

"No!" Alex shouted, "You'd be fucking furious. "That guy just took everything that mattered to you away. Tell me how you really feel."

"I'd be fucking furious!" I shouted back.

"That's what I want to see in this scene!" Alex said. "I want to see a slow burn that boils over into a rage. Got it?"

"Yes," I said.

"Back to one!" Alex said, flipping his baseball cap back around on his head. "Back to one" is what a director says when he or she wants you to start over, to take it from the top.

"Action!"

We did the audition again and I actually started crying as my scene partner questioned me. All I could think about was him ripping Kody's head off. I wanted to come across the table and rip his head off.

"Cut! "That's more like it!" Alex shouted from the back of the room. "That's the intensity you need to bring to this type of scene."

That's part of the beauty of training at a place like Drama Inc. Coaches like Catherine and Jason are more low-key, almost loving in the way they train their actors. Then, there are guys like Alex who are all business, but in a tough love way. They all care deeply about their craft and training the next wave of actors.

One thing they also teach you in acting school is that you must have a "technique." It's one thing to memorize lines, it's another to bring emotions to a scene, especially if you're shooting it for the tenth time on set. Or you're a day player and you've been waiting eight hours to deliver your lines and the production is about to head into "Golden Time," the penalty for violating the sixteen-hour rule of production.

There are various techniques, Method, Strasberg, Meisner. One night at Drama Inc., I joined what is known as an "audit" of a Meisner technique class. Meisner famously said, "Acting is living truthfully under imaginary circumstances." His technique was about being in the moment and not "think[ing] too much." The repetition required to perfect the technique was driving me crazy in the class and I couldn't take it anymore.

I left the room at the mid-point break and wasn't coming back.

As I walked dejectedly down the hall, I ran into Jason MacDonald.

"How's it going in there?" he asked.

"I hate it. I can't stand the Meisner technique," I confessed.

"Come with me," Jason said, leading me back into his office. He walked over and picked up a book and handed it to me.

The book's title was *The Power of The Actor: The Chubbuck Technique.*

"You're a more *mature actor*," Jason said, a nice way of saying "old." "Chubbuck is the technique for you. Take the book. It's my gift to you."

Chubbuk's technique comprised twelve objectives, or "pieces of advice," to help the actor attain their goal. You use your personality to *be* a character as opposed to *playing* one. One uses their personality, past, the scene and set to create the moment. She emphasized taking risks.

Again, something changed inside of my brain. I started using the Chubbuck Technique in my auditions and they started getting better and better, more authentic and realistic. The simple fact in acting is that there are a lot of tools and techniques. You must decide which arrows go in your quiver.

On a whim, I took another workshop at Drama Inc. called "Get Ready for Set." As the name of the class suggests, it's all about teaching the basics behind what to expect once you do book the gig. Simple things like reading a Call Sheet, terminology used on set, etc.

The most important thing Jason taught us is to *act like you belong there. You've earned the right to be there.*

"*And* it's always breakfast on set," he said. "You're going to get there, and an assistant AD is going to meet you at your trailer and they're going to say, 'Welcome. Your script is in your trailer. Would you like some breakfast?' Come with your order already in your mind."

Two weeks later, I booked my first significant role on the hit HBO series, *True Detective.* They flew me to Arkansas first-class. A car was waiting for me at the airport. And, just as Jason predicted, I arrived to set and a young AD met me as I checked in.

"Would you like some breakfast?" she asked.

"As a matter of fact, I would. How about turkey sausage and egg whites on an English muffin? And unsweet iced tea if you have it," I said with a smile.

"Coming right up!" she said cheerfully.

They had also taught us in class how important eye contact was when in a dramatic scene with another actor. In my scene in *True Detective*, I played a reporter grilling Attorney General Gerald Kindt, played by the veteran actor Brett Cullen, whom you might recognize from shows like *Falcon Crest*, *Desperate Housewives*, *The West Wing*, *NCIS* and *Friday Night Lights*. Also on set, and flanking Cullen on stage at the make-believe press conference, were Mahershala Ali, Stephen Dorff and Scoot McNair.

McNair played the part of a grieving father, pleading for the release of his missing daughter. His main scene was about a three-minute monologue where he comes close to tears near the end of the speech. Director Nick Pizzolatto had McNair do the scene maybe five times and each time, McNair nailed it. It was very impressive.

And then, as McNair's character was led from the podium, I'm on.

"Mr. Attorney General!" I said in a calm but firm voice. As Cullen leaned into the podium, I looked him dead in the eyes and suddenly, I felt the intensity of the scene rise. Cullen looked back at me with the stare of a copperhead snake.

The shit got real.

"What do you make of this petition to have the original conviction overturned?" I asked him.

His tone became serious and sullen.

"The possibility of the Purcell girl being alive doesn't change our conclusion. That Bret Woodard murdered Will Purcell and kidnapped his sister. Now, what he did with her from there, we can't know."

Boom! TV magic!

Backstage, cast members high-fived me and I thanked them, telling them it was my first real gig as an actor. Bret Cullen reached for my sides (lines from the script) and pulled a pen from his jacket pocket.

"Congrats, Mark!" he wrote, before signing the sides. He then passed the pen and the small sheets of paper down the line which all the main actors signed.

"You killed it!" Jon Tenney wrote along with his name. "Peace!" Mahershala Ali wrote on the paper along with his signature. And finally, Nick Pizolatto wrote, "Thank You!" along with his signature.

It was an incredible moment that I thought would be hard to top.

And then, a few weeks later, I got an audition for the hit TV series *Mindhunter*. Again, it was for an anchorman role. What I didn't know at the time of the audition, was that Season 2 of the show was about.

I nailed the audition and booked the part.

It took several months for things to shake out around when the show would be shot and then, on November 2nd, I received access to the scripts for my episodes and couldn't believe my eyes.

Season 2 of *Mindhunter* would focus on Atlanta's "Missing and Murdered Children's Case."

Yes. *Wayne Williams.*

The very reason I had wanted to get into TV news and here I would be playing the part of an anchorman covering the case. As my friend Caleb said, it was an unbelievable case of art imitating life imitating art.

I was flown to Pittsburgh for the taping and arrived at the costume department as instructed.

"Hi Mark, it's great to have you," the costume designer said. "Let's get you back to your dressing room and take a look at the outfits *David* has selected for you. And by David, she meant David Fincher who had famously directed *Se7en*, *Fight Club*, *Zodiac* and *The Social Network*.

We walked back through a hallway and up to a door. On the door was a sign that read NEWS ANCHOR #2 (Mark).

The costume designer opened the door and pointed me inside. I entered the room, and my eyes were drawn to what looked like vision boards in the corner. Or maybe a classroom project. On the oversized boards were images of many of the Atlanta newscasters I had grown up watching in the early-to-mid 1980s and photos of several news anchors, including Tom Brokaw. There were pictures of the news sets and closeups of the fabrics the anchormen wore in their suits, shirts and ties.

It was like stepping back in time.

"Wow. You guys are taking this really seriously," I said to the costume designer.

"David is a perfectionist," she said. "He wants everything to look like it did at the time it happened. Including you."

She pointed to what looked like a dozen combinations of suits, shirts, ties, belts and two pairs of shoes on a rack on the other side of the room. I'm going to have you try on all these and we'll text the photos to David and he'll decide which ones make the show," the woman said.

I almost had to pinch myself to make sure this was happening. But the fun was just beginning. The next morning, I arrived on set, had my breakfast and waited patiently to be called to the set.

Then, an AD popped her head into the room.

"They're ready for you Mark!" she said.

She led me through a winding area, which felt like backstage at a maze and, in the distance, I could make out the light through an

opening of a curtain. We continued walking and as I passed through them, I was shocked.

The production and design team had created exact replicas of the set from the TV station where I had worked, but from the early eighties. Of course, I recognized it, because I had grown up idolizing the anchors that sat at the desk.

To the right, there was a second set.

"Good morning, Mark!" I heard a voice say to my right. I looked in that direction and realized the voice belonged to David Fincher himself. "It's great to have you on the show," he said, reaching to shake my hand.

"You've got the script, but I want this to feel authentic," he said," as he led me to the anchor desk. "If any of this feels like something that you would never say on TV tell me and we'll change it."

I nodded in bridled astonishment.

The cameras and crew scurred about and into place as I took my seat at the anchor desk. Again, a surreal moment that words on paper can't quite convey.

We shot the scene four times, and I was on point for each take. Not one word flubbed. It was clear David was pleased.

"Okay, that was excellent. For the second episode," he said, "you're getting a promotion. Frank Reynolds. ABC News."

What the actual fuck?

Yes. He wanted me to play Frank Reynolds, anchorman of ABC's *World News Tonight* from 1975 till his death in 1983. I walked back to my dressing room and made a quick change into the second costume David had selected for me.

I hustled back to the set and saw David at the desk feverishly typing on a laptop.

"He's writing more lines for you," the AD said. "He thinks you're good."

Again, WTAF?

I made my way to the anchor desk of ABC News. As I sat down in the chair, it slowly sunk to the floor.

"Get him another chair," David shouted to no one as he finished his thoughts on the computer.

"Print it and hand it to him," he said to an assistant.

"I said get him a fucking chair!" he yelled, again to no one specific. The crew scattered and a new chair was brought to the desk and swapped for the one that had sunken to the floor.

"Okay, you're Frank," he said. "Breaking news from Atlanta in the Williams case he said," as a production assistant handed me the new lines.

Thank God I was trained as both an anchorman and now an actor as the pressure was at about a 9 on the Tightened Sphincter Scale of 1 to 10.

I read the lines twice and closed my eyes and repeated them to myself twice.

"Okay, here we go," the assistant director yelled. David took it from there.

"You've got this Mark. I mean, Frank!"

I smiled at him.

"Speed… camera… ACTION!"

I looked into the camera and delivered the lines just like Frank would have.

"In Atlanta today, the public safety commissioner and the district attorney held a press conference to announce developments in the case of the city's missing and murdered children."

I landed with emphasis on *-dren*, just like Frank used to do it when I watched him from the couch in Calhoun.

"Cut! Got it. Moving on!" David shouted from behind the camera.

He then walked over and shook my hand.

"Just like the real fucking deal," he said.

"That's why you hired me," I said with a smile.

In the actual episode of the show, Jonathan Groff, who plays FBI Agent Holden Ford, is in his apartment watching me on the news. He walks to the kitchen sink and removes his shirt, ostensibly to try and wash a stain from it.

As my line ends, the camera pans down to a tight shot of Groff's ass. My voice. His ass. Ten seconds of great television.

Since then, I've gone on to book twenty-six gigs including roles on *Mr. Mercedes, Reprisal, The First Lady, The Game, Sweet Magnolias, Reptile, They Cloned Tyrone* and most recently a recurring role on the new Peacock series *Hysteria!*

And a few other things that I'm not at liberty to talk about. As I used to say on the news: *stay tuned.*

One evening during a break in writing this book, I had a long conversation with my good friend, Bill Wallace. Bill is one of the key investors in our horror movie, *The Curse of La Patasola* and he and I were working on a global distribution strategy. Then, the conversation turned to my book

"Walk me through what *ANKRBOY* is all about," he said.

I spent the next twenty minutes or so giving him the background, including very personal details from my private life that he was not aware of before the discussion.

"I know it sounds corny," I said to Bill. "But when I touch the keyboard it's like my heart and soul spill onto the screen in front of me. There have been nights where I was doubled over crying in front of my computer. The pain was often unbearable. But I just kept writing. Fifteen thousand words became 25,000, then 60,000 and then 80,000. The more I just kept writing, the easier it became to finish the book."

There was a slight pause in the conversation and then Bill asked me a simple question.

"Have you prayed about this book?" he asked.

"I'm not sure what you're asking. I'm not an overly religious person. I'm more of a spiritualist."

"But you believe in God, right?" Bill replied.

"Yes."

Like a good lawyer, Bill continued his line of questioning.

"And do you believe God puts people through tests, to make them stronger, to find their purpose in life?" he asked.

"Actually, I do," I said.

"And do you think he sometimes uses people to reach other people with a message? To keep going, to not give up?"

"Yes," I said.

"Maybe the reason this book is so easy for you to write is that God is speaking through you," Bill said. "Maybe God said, 'You know what, I'm going to put Mark through Holy Hell. Break him down, beat him up and then help him back up on his knees and then to his feet. He's going to find happiness in his life and I'm going to bless him with this book—and his message will be my message to others: To not give up, to keep going. To put down that bottle, push away those pills or not pick up that gun.'"

It then clicked in my head. Everyone I had asked for permission to include them (or family members) in this book had said *yes*. Gio, James, Steve, Catherine, Jason, Alex, Carrie M., Judy, Carrie K., Grace, Glenn, Evelyn, Jane, Gail, Bruce, Leigh, Mark, Sabrina, Dan and Kay.

Some of them, like Bruce and Leigh, knew the words I wrote would be painful but, still, they said *yes*.

I repeated their names to Bill.

"Maybe God spoke to them, too," he said. "Or through them. None of this is a coincidence."

I was struck by the words and sat with them in silence after we ended our conversation. A few days later, I called Bill to ask if I could repeat our conversation in the book.

"Of course," he said. "This is an amazing vehicle. You may never know who you touch or help by writing this book. Put it out there, and if you make a little money, do a little good with some of the profits," he advised.

Looking back on everything, I now understand there was a reason I had to smash that frame holding my TV news publicity photo. I had to shatter the glass to free the man inside so that he could live his authentic existence.

No frame. No shame.

"I think the shattered frame on the cover is symbolic," my great friend Tracy Green told me over drinks two days before I finished this book. "We all have cracks in our lives–and that's what lets in the light that allows us to shine," she said.

Tracy and I worked together years ago at Fearless4 before she went on to help start *Extra* and launch *The Roseanne Show* and *Deadliest Catch*. Some of her other credits include *Big Brother*, *The Littlest Groom*, and *New Day*.

Tracy recently moved back home to help lead the news division at Atlanta News First—the flagship station for Gray Television. Through everything—good and bad—in our lives, Tracy and I have remained great friends—and true friends want each other to win.

"Get out there and shine!" she told me. "I'll do anything I can to help you."

I then joked with Tracy that the most ironic part of it all is that more people have now watched me *play* the role of an anchorman in movies and TV shows than ever watched me as a real one. I worried all those years about people finding me out, afraid to remove my mask. When it took me becoming my authentic self to be able to put on the mask of the characters I play as an actor.

Speaking of acting, my favorite part of being on set is that magical moment when the director yells, "Sound, speed..." and then there is a pause.

I am addicted to that brief second of silence—between nothing—and then, "ACTION!" It is a moment of sheer terror and exhilaration where there is no net and I understand clearly that I will soar or fall flat on my face. And if I have properly prepared for the role, there is no question that I will fly.

And, when the scene is done, and you know you've nailed it, you hear the three most magical words an actor can hear from a director.

"Cut! Got it. Moving on."

That's it, the take on my life. I should have been my true-self from the start—because that's all you have at the end.

I've now realized that God wrote the script and I am the director of my life story. I call the shots. And the happy ending has been ensured because I finally learned to deal with my own truth. To live my life openly and honestly, no matter the cost.

I am an example of what is won when all is seemingly lost. When the truth, indeed, sets you free.

Cut!

Got it.

Moving on.

PHOTO CREDITS

Introduction:

Pg. ix: Courtesy of Gio Benitez and Tommy DiDario. Photo credit: Pierre Torset.

Pg. ix: Courtesy of Gio Benitez and Tom DiDario.

Pg. x: Courtesy of What Now Media Group and Steve Osunsami.

Pg. x: Courtesy of James Longman and Alex Brannan.

Pg. xi: Courtesy of Mark Edge.

Pg. xi: Courtesy of Mark Edge.

Pg. xii: From the author's collection.

Chapter 5:

Pg. 39: FBI photo.

Pg. 39: FBI photo.

Chapter 6:

Pg. 64: From the author's collection.

Chapter 10:

Pg. 97: Courtesy of the Mulkey family.

Chapter 12:

Pg. 125: Courtesy of Sabrina Bell Poole.

Pg. 126: Courtesy of Sabrina Bell Poole.

Chapter 15:
Pg. 166: From the author's collection.

Chapter 17:
Pg. 198: From the author's collection.
Pg. 199: From the author's collection.

Chapter 19:
Pg. 212: From the author's collection.

Chapter 20:
Pg. 220: From the author's collection.
Pg. 221: "Hartsfield Airport Security Men caught with their pants down attack the messenger–the T.V. man who records the story," *Atlanta Journal and Constitution*, 1990, Gene Basset Editorial Cartoons, Richard B. Russell Library for Political Research and Studies, The University of Georgia Libraries.

Chapter 22:
Pg. 250: From the author's collection.
Pg. 256: From the author's collection.
Pg. 257: From the author's collection.
Pg. 258: From the author's collection.
Pg. 261: From the author's collection.
Pg. 263: Courtesy of Carrie and Grace Key.
Pg. 266: Courtesy of Candidly Kind.
Pg. 268: Illustration by Marcelo Galvão.
Pg. 268: Illustration by Marcelo Galvão.

Chapter 23:
Pg. 271: From the author's collection.
Pg. 276: Courtesy of Evelyn Mims.
Pg. 276: From the author's collection.

Pg. 277: From the author's collection.

Chapter 24:
Pg. 280: Courtesy of the Potts Family. Photo credit: JR Greeson.
Pg. 288: From the author's collection.

Chapter 25:
Pg. 290: Courtesy of Caleb J. Spivak. Photo credit: Bjoern Kommerell.
Pg. 293: From the author's collection.
Pg. 298: From the author's collection.
Pg. 299: From the author's collection.
Pg. 299: From the author's collection.
Pg. 300: From the author's collection.
Pg. 302: From the author's collection.

About the Author:
Pg. 304: From the author's collection.

ABOUT THE AUTHOR

Mark Pettit first achieved success as a television news anchorman, for which he has won three Emmy® awards. His reporting spawned a best-selling book, *A Need to Kill*. Over 125,000 copies sold worldwide, and it went to No. 1 on three Amazon charts.

In 1998, Mark founded the Atlanta-based marketing firm Creaxion®. Creaxion has worked for some of the world's best-known brands, excelling at entertainment, business-to-business, and cause-related marketing.

Mark's creative energy also turned to acting in 2018. Since then, he has appeared in many successful hit movies and TV shows including *True Detective, Mr. Mercedes, Mindhunter, Reprisal, Women of The Movement, Sweet Magnolias, The Game,* and *They Cloned Tyrone and Reptile*. He is executive producer of and acted in *The Curse of La Patasola*. According to *Screen Rant*, it "offers a thrilling option for creature feature enthusiasts" and was listed at the top spot of their "10 Best Horror Movies Based on Latin American Folklore."

Mark enjoys working out, world travel and quality time with his French Bulldog, Kody.

Made in the USA
Columbia, SC
07 May 2024

c9d09936-a81c-43cb-a0f4-efab471bb3eaR03